W9-CQI-550

Collector's Encyclopedia of

COMPACTS

VOLUME II

CARRYALLS & FACE POWDER BOXES

LAURA M. MUELLER

COLLECTOR BOOKS

A Division of Schroeder Publishing Co., Inc.

The current values in this book should be used only as a guide. They are not intended to set prices, which vary from one section of the country to another. Auction prices as well as dealer prices vary greatly and are affected by condition as well as demand. Neither the Author nor the Publisher assumes responsibility for any losses that might be incurred as a result of consulting this guide.

On the cover:
Top left: *Queen Mary*, 4" x 2¾" x ¼ ", $250.00 – 275.00.
Bottom left: Femme profile, 1¾" dia. x ½", $225.00 – 250.00.
Center: Powder Box, 3½" dia. x 1⅝", $65.00 – 80.00.
Top right: Padlock, 2⅜" heart x ½", $150.00 – 175.00.
Bottom right: Flag, 3½" sq. x ⅜", $125.00 – 150.00.

SEARCHING FOR A PUBLISHER?

We are always looking for knowledgeable people considered to be experts within their fields. If you feel that there is a real need for a book on your collectible subject and have a large comprehensive collection, contact Collector Books.

Cover design by Beth Summers

Additional copies of this book may be ordered from:

Collector Books
P.O. Box 3009
Paducah, Kentucky 42002-3009

@ $24.95. Add $2.00 for postage and handling.

Copyright: Laura M. Mueller, 1997

This book or any part thereof may not be reproduced without the written consent of the Author and Publisher.

Dedication

To Ann Mueller Zdeb
Loving cousin, kind critic
exacting editor

◆◆◆◆◆◆◆◆

LAURA M. MUELLER
P.O. BOX 151445 • COLUMBUS, OHIO 43215

◆◆◆◆◆◆◆◆

<u>Photography</u>
Brent Turner

◆◆◆◆◆◆◆◆

British Compact Collectors' Society
P.O. Box 131
Woking
Surrey, GU24 9YR
UK

Acknowledgments

It's about time to give thanks to the Paducah crew at Collector Books: Billy Schroeder for faith and patience; Beth Summers for the fabulous book covers; Holly Long for piecing the interior puzzle together; Paula Bunting for accepting my sometimes scratchy phone calls; and very large thanks to my unflappable editor, Lisa Stroup, who, with her exquisite Southern manners and professionalism, always managed to soothe my pre- and post-publication nerves.

Again gratitude to my silent partners, who did without choice items from their collections for what must have seemed an age: Melinda Churchfield, Rita Eldridge, Helen E. Farnsworth, Ruth A. Forsythe, Ellen Foster, Donna G. Sims, and Ann Mueller Zdeb.

To the late Cedric Gray for keeping my ship ideas afloat and bringing me into the U.K. Compact Collectors Club, a true English gentleman.

Helen Farnsworth receives special thanks, not only for her spectacular loan and good humor, but also for the roles she assumed: archivist, historian, and researcher. Whenever a large question loomed, she always had a quick, accurate answer.

And more than appreciation for the most important hand holding from Harry Addison Mowery and my caring brothers, Vincent Edward and Donald Joseph Mueller.

Contents

Preface

Reflections on the Fair Vanity© —
An Overview on Collecting

Cosmopolitan, 1944

Artist signed

"..Richard Le Gallienne says: 'It is not necessarily vanity that brings out the powder puff, but a courteous regard for the aesthetic sensibilities of others.'"

The Theatre Magazine, 1914

This second volume takes a larger view than Volume I and timidly enters the international scene where many familiar case names originated. Also several new fields of collecting are presented: ocean liner souvenir cases with a ship appendix, broader World War II item coverage, artist signed cosmetic advertisements, and an expanded powder box chapter.

The glossary and bibliography have been updated and work has been done to solve the riddle of some of those alphabet signed cases. A few are still stubbornly unknown. Ongoing research of some of the unmarked cases has had results with a few surprises. The carryall does a bit of chapter roaming as military and non-metal versions have surfaced and become crossovers within this book. A few pendant vanities also joined the action; otherwise the chapter headings stand.

That's the good news. The bad news is the brick walls and blind alleys which made pursuing further research on the history of this collectible futile; although some very good attempts were made by some very knowledgeable researchers.

The major trouble was the constant consolidation and discarding of records as companies merged and remerged ever fighting for a niche in the marketplace, i.e., Shields of Attleboro, Mass., was founded as the Fillkwick Co. in 1920 and purchased in 1937 under the present name... purchased by Rex Co. of N.Y. in 1939 — production W.W. II insignia and medals — purchased by Volupte´ of N.J. in 1957.

One tragedy was the abrupt departure of Elgin American. After a long history beginning with the parent company, Illinois Watch Co., in the 1880s in Elgin, Ill., a decision was made in 1963 after a long acrimonious labor dispute to close the plant and move to Japan. (Elgin cases signed "Made in Japan" are the genuine Elgin item.) To date, no trace of the company's records has been found, although visits were made and queries and ads attempted.

Evans has also vanished in a surge of changes. Listed in the 1920s in North Attleboro, Mass., as the D. Evans Case Co., at an unknown date it became a division of Hilsingor Corp. of Plainville, Mass., then disappears after 1965.

Some case companies are still in business, but again, a search for history and information was either politely ignored or curtly dismissed. Several were cooperative, but second and third generation memories are a fragile basis for hard facts. The cosmetic houses never made their own cases; always buying from wholesale manufacturers such as W.C. Ritchie and Co. (made powder boxes for Coty), Bridgeport Metal Goods Mfg. Co. (Max Factor), E.N. Rowell Co. (Pond's boxes), Sagamor (who had the patents on the sliding powder dispenser) & Scovill of Waterbury, Conn. (Helena Rubinstein). Julius Schmid made "Superior Compacts and Vanity Powder Puffs."

Majestic Metal Specialties' ads depict every form of case for the trade, and they also had a retail division. Pallas Mfg. Co. in 1928 introduces fold-out vanity cases with the hinged mirrors.

This volume offers some new thoughts — don't be deterred by the wide range of values. These pricey pretties are in the commercial case category and deserve a picture or two to display their workmanship.

There are still ample opportunities to compile relatively inexpensive collections by choosing a case or two and using them as building blocks. If space is a problem, minis are great buys now in powder boxes, rouge compacts, sample tins, or the range of puffs and beauty ephemera. Lipsticks and the ephemera novelties are still a good bargain now. The Elgin hearts, book, and snuff box cases, the big Rexes or Dorsets, and early pendant vanities — gathered astutely as a family, could be a joyful union.

One of the biggest surges has been in the W.W. II military cases which began with the 1995 50th anniversary. This is a cross-over collectible and prices are already climbing. Special events or places are good places to pick up cases.

The artist signed ads are making their way into compact collections. Paper dealers at shows have now given these ads a separate category. These ads, if you find a case match-up, bestows pedigree. However, remember their fragility. Do not frame or expose them to light or dampness for any length of time. Store them in the proper plastic sleeving (mylar or polyester) and acid-free boards. No forms of kitchen plastics or self-mounting photo album sleeves should be used; the less exposure the better.

It is a pleasure to go to shows and see compacts displayed in cases formerly reserved for jewelry. The collectible has risen from obscurity from shoe boxes, sale tables, and other forms of dealer storage. However, the use of strong lighting and outdoor weather conditions can destroy in a day an exquisite case which has survived half of a century: melting lipsticks, delicate enamels with disastrous price stickers, and the newest threat — remodeling cases into personal mementos. This action totally negates any value and seems to be mainly directed at those cases which were made for only a short time and could be considered endangered species. There are enough damaged cases that, although almost worthless, may be utilized nicely as craft items.

The overview is exciting as new compacts with imaginative designs are entering the cosmetic market and younger collectors are seen at the shows. They are curious and hopefully they will force the media to move the compact case out of the Miscellaneous heading in the trade publications and give this esteemed collectible its proper due.

Chapter One

COMPACTS

The Illustrated London News, 1929

"...THE LITTLE BROWN COMPACT WHICH IS ESPECIALLY SUITED TO COUNTRY CLOTHES IS NOW MADE WITH A CLIP TO BE FASTENED TO THE BELT OF THE GOLFER, HORSE BACK RIDER OR OTHER SPORTSWOMEN WHO LOSE THINGS."
WOMAN'S HOME COMPANION, 1932

In a 1928 trade ad for a wholesale case manufacturer the copy reads: "...I know I have a dozen, but this one is such a beauty." The speaker is an elegantly dressed woman addressing a saleswoman in an obviously "better store" with an equally stylish man standing over her shoulder, a concurring smile on his face. The ad says further: "...Let our artists work with you in creating designs that will catch the feminine eye...and produce articles of rare beauty."

Another quote: "... Each time the clock ticks a Reich-Ash compact is sold somewhere in the United States." It is hard to grasp that such an aggressive industry has all but disappeared. The earliest compact in this book is a tiny "tin can" case which has no hinges, no clasp, no ornamentation other than a lithographic pattern, a tin powder screen with five punched-out holes (for loose powder,) a handmade felt puff, and a mirror on the outside of the lid. The name "Blue Danube" is on the inside, with a patent date of April 15, 1902. It is called "Toilet Powder Box" and has a "Plurality of Apertures." (I love this jargon for holes.) The designer, Ella Lichenstein, is named in the patent information.

E. Lichenstein's idea eventually changed a whole set of rigid mores that prevailed. Bigotry and sexism were reenforced not only from church pulpits in sermons about painted women but also by warnings of dire health danger given by medical professionals. The best epithet raised was the cry of "Vanity." This kept household egg money safe from such sinful excesses. The cosmetic industry didn't help by harping on the unproven curative powers of its products.

The little tin case did what the alchemists could not, change tin to gold, and change the local general store and Sears catalogs to New York's Fifth Avenue and the rue de la Paix in Paris.

This primal case also brings down the myth that pressed or compacted powder was the semantic basis for adjusting the verb "compacted" to the now accepted noun "compact." Loose and pressed powder have dueled without a touché for years; neither strong enough to gain the genre title in several languages. A compact, is a compact, is a ... in various reference sources; no mention of type or manner of face powder — only puff, powder, and mirror.

The international market which is being introduced here may have a different time span, because of the catastrophic events in Europe during two world conflicts. Records may be hard to trace for different reasons than the U.S. habit of casually disposing of its past. Two periods of patriotic metal recycling during both wars eliminated many an early case; most of the European documented case dating begins in the fifties. Pre-W.W. I cases were more likely made of precious materials and sold to the carriage trade for spe-cific occasions by noted jewelers. Requesting information today from those houses still in business is like asking for a Swiss bank account number.

Volume II will continue to follow a chronological order. Some case names will look like spelling errors, but remember the U.K. and the U.S. are two countries divided by a common language. Also note that international cases are identified by country-of-origin initials; no initials indicates U.S. companies. There will be odd combinations as familiar U.S. names shared some patents and designs.

A word on the use of patent information to date cases. The only sure way to date a case is to see it in a dated ad or in that rare instance, a documented case with provenance — such as the little tin can. The ad proves production and maybe a saleable design. Patents are ideas; concepts that look good as a model but may be unable to make the manufacturing transition. Granted some patents are great matches to existing cases but remember a patent date may be in effect for years.

The history of cases gets more tangled when two or more companies decided to battle it out in ads with similar case models. Coty and Marie Earle squared off and Coty won. The Henriette and Wadsworth puzzle of identical models — such as the fans and novelty balls was solved. The parent company was Wadsworth Watch Case Co. and Henriette was their compact division. Then Wadsworth at some point decided to go retail and have two markets. The missing Elgin American records might have explained all the E.A.M. names. One puzzle has been solved: Clarice Jane was the daughter of one of the Illinois Watch Co. owners. No such luck on Elginite or the time switch from E.A.M. to Elgin American and the continued use of the Illinois Watch Co. signature. The ultimate in cosmetic house in-fighting has to be over the Sagamor Metal Goods Co. of N.Y. sliding powder well dispenser. Five different houses tried to tout the uniqueness of their case features. Aristocratic status prevailed with Comtesse D'Orsay bowing out to Prince Matchabelli, et al.

Presentation boxes are making a belated bow. The definitive classification of MIB (Mint In Box) must be redefined to specify what box or which box? A presentation box with enhancing design or color raises the case to higher elegance. Some of these boxes are works of art by themselves and should be collected with or without the interior case. This is where th ads prove their worth; values may double with a perfect marriage. A sincere collection should always reach for the best within its price range restrictions. To paraphrase Robert Browning: "...Or what's a collection for?"

```
1       3       6
2       4       7
        5
```

1. Dubarry (U.K.) – Goldtone, Loose Powder Can Compact. Domed lid with script logo, convex metallic mirror, 1¾" x ¾", $75.00 – 90.00.

2. Richard Hudnut – Goldtone, Pressed Powder Can Compact. Engine-turned case with monogram cartouche, "Gardenia," case signed, framed mirror, 2½" dia. x ⅝", $50.00 – 65.00.

3. Lady Esther – Goldtone, Pressed Powder Can Compact. Embossed lid logo with skirted femme and votaries, faint orange tinted border of hearts, framed mirror, 2½" dia. x ½", $45.00 – 60.00.

4. Imperial Cincinnati – Goldtone, Pressed Powder Can Compact. Embossed lid logo with niello effect on rose garland circlet, framed mirror, 2½" dia. x ⅝", $75.00 – 90.00.

5. W.T. Rawleigh Co. – Goldtone, Pressed Powder Can Compact. Embossed lid motif: "TreVere," with laurel wreath framing, reverse signed, framed mirror, 1½" dia. x ⅝", $35.00 –50.00.

6. Deere – Goldtone, Pressed Powder Can Compact. Embossed lid logo of seated femme nude in frame with rosettes, script logo, glass powder paten, framed mirror, 2⅜" dia. x ½", $50.00 – 65.00.

7. Armand – Goldtone, Pressed Powder Can Compact. Chased lid motif of eighteenth century femme in profile, Greek key frame, script logo, framed mirror, 2½" dia. x ½", $45.00 – 60.00

```
1    3    5
2    4    6
```

1. Majestic – Goldtone, Loose Powder Can Compact. Domed lid with petal motif, no case I.D., puff with logo, case glued mirror, 2" dia. x ¾", $30.00 – 45.00.

2. Morris, Mann & Reilly – Goldtone, Pressed Powder Can Compact. Pierced filigree lid wreathing, affixed leaves, collet mounted faceted faux topaz and smaller rhinestones, no case I.D., papers and puff with logo; "M.M.R.'S," framed mirror, 2½" dia. x ¾", $75.00 – 90.00.

3. R. Robert (Fr.) – Goldtone, Loose Powder Compact. Aqua carved glass high relief Art Nouveau egret lid motif, engine-turned sloped case shoulders, glass lid inset has molded signature, framed mirror, 2¾" dia. x ⅝", Rare.
This might be René Robert who worked with René Lalique in Paris. The case has been altered and does not have its original aqua silk tassel and ring chain with a perfume flacon, but as an objet d'art it deserves a showing even in this mutilated state.

4. Unknown – Goldtone, Loose Powder Compact. Decagonal case with rococo repoussé design and niello accents, lid collet mounted faux gem stones, foil backed carved faux diamond center rosette, knife-edge, "Made in Czechoslovakia," no case I.D., framed mirror, 3¼" x ⅜", $90.00 – 125.00.

5. Langlois – Bimetal, Pressed Powder Compact. Chinoiserie lid motif in bas-relief, silvertone case signed: "Shari," framed mirror, notation: "XMAS, 1928," 2¼" dia. x ⅜" $35.00 – 50.00.

6. Unmarked – Goldtone, Pressed Powder Compact. Art Nouveau rococo lid filigree, collet mounted faux gem stones and mounted pearl, framed mirror, 2½" dia. x ⅝", $45.00 – 60.00.

1	5	8
2	6	9
3	7	10
4		

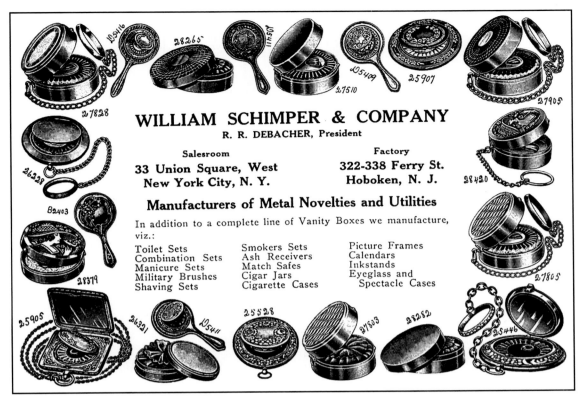

American Perfumer, 1921

1. Colgate & Co. – Black Enamel and Goldtone, Pressed Powder Can Compact. "Black Box" (reference. Volume I – P16 #4) hand painted femme with fan, artist signed: "KC," acanthus border, framed mirror, 2½" dia. x ⅝", Ref.: 1924 Ad., $75.00 – 90.00.

2. Plough, Inc. – Red Enamel and Goldtone, Pressed Powder Compact. Domed case with white/black narcissus lid motif, no case I.D. (Ref.: Vol. I – P260 #2), framed mirror, 2" dia. x ⅝", $50.00 – 65.00.

3. Divine – Goldtone, Pressed Powder Compact. Domed case, faux crackled eggshell lid enamel, basket of rose blooms, no case I.D., powder paper logo, framed mirror, Ref.: Pat. 7/1/24, 1⅞" dia. x ½", $50.00 – 65.00.

4. Florian and Armand – White Metal, Pressed Powder Compact. Domed case, trademark box, eighteenth century femme head silhouette logo, case signed, framed mirror, Ref.: Pat. 7/1/24, 1⅞" dia. x ⅜", $50.00 – 65.00.

Although all information points to U.S. manufacturing, this case was made for U.K. distribution, i.e. name difference, smaller case, variation in lid design, and American version does not fit this box.

5. Devine – Goldtone, Pressed Powder Glove Compact. Enameled lid with hand-painted dancing couple, case signed, framed mirror, 1¾" x 1" x ⅜", $100.00 – 125.00.

6. Devine – Goldtone, Pressed Powder Glove Compact. Enameled lid with Art Deco hand-painted multi-flora, case signed, affixed metallic mirror, 1⅛" sq x ⅜", $125.00 – 140.00.

7. Tre-Jur – White Metal, Pressed Powder Compact. "The Little One," engine-turned lid motif, logo cartouche, reverse information: "Charvai," case signed, powder puff and papers with logo, framed mirror, Ref.: 1926 Ad., 2" dia. x ¼", $45.00 – 60.00.

8. Roger & Gallet – Goldtone, Pressed Powder Compact. Dome lidded case, bird-in-flight, green tinted incised motif, small initial lid logo, box: "Le Jade," puff with logo, no other case I.D., framed mirror, Ref.: 1926 Ad., 2" dia x ½", $65.00 – 80.00.

9. Guerlain – Enamel and Goldtone, Pressed Powder Compact. Incised rosette motif through to goldtone casing, reverse logo cartouche, puff with logo, framed mirror, 2" dia. x ⅜", $50.00 – 65.00.

10. Woodworth – White Metal, Pressed Powder Compact. Engine-turned rococo lid motif with orange tint, case signed: "Fiancée" (Coty refill), framed mirror, 1⅞" dia. x ½," $35.00 – 50.00.

```
        3   6
    1   4   7
    2       5
```

1. Norida – White Metal, Pressed Powder Compact. Domed case, engine-turned lid motif, circle monogram cartouche, case signed, reverse information, puff with logo, framed mirror, 2" dia. x ⅜", $45.00 – 60.00.

2. Unknown – White Metal, Loose Powder Compact. Stamped stylized peacock tail lid design, pierced celluloid powder screen, "Sole Mfgrs Abonita & Co, Chicago" Pat. Pending "Tap-it-Pac" Trademark, framed metallic mirror, 2" dia. x ¼", $30.00 – 45.00.

Ref.: Volume I – P75 #6, good guess this is an early Nylotis. Abonita was a wholesale manufacturer and held the patents on the powder screen.

3. Melba – Silver-plated, Loose Powder Compact. Box with logo and extra powder refill in lid, hammered case lid, arrow framing, niello effect, shield lid cartouche, no case I.D., framed metallic mirror, Ref.: Pat. (on refill) 6/15/26, 2⅛" dia. x ½", $75.00 – 90.00.

4. Speed (Fr.) – White Metal, Loose Powder Compact. Matchbook case with engine-turned bands, mechanical powder control, case and puff with an "arrow" logo, framed metallic mirror, 2⅜" x 1¾" x ⅝" (tapers to knife edge), $75.00 – 90.00.

5. Dennison Watch Case Co. (U.K.) – Sterling, Loose Powder Compact. "The DQ Powder Box," City of Birmingham 1927 silver hallmarks, yellow guilloché lid band, reverse logo, framed wide beveled mirror, Art Deco box with logo, 2" dia. x ⅝", $135.00 – 150.00.

6. Veolay (Fr.) – White Metal, Loose Powder Compact. Mechanical powder control, hammered, glossy, and engine-turned lid finishes with sugar loaf collet mounted jade stone, Art Moderne reverse motif, case affixed metallic mirror, case signed, 2⅛" dia. x ½", $75.00 – 100.00.

7. Dhaussy (Fr.) – White Metal, Loose Powder Compact. Exterior powder loading access, engine-turned case, lid with monogram cartouche, logo on reverse, framed mirror, Ref.: Eur. Pat. 1923 – 1925, 2⅛" dia. x ⅝", $75.00 – 90.00.

The reverse is shown here, see #1 Norida for an almost identical lid design (Norida is domed and has internal mechanism).

```
            3    6
     1      4    7
     2      5    8
```

1. Jaciel – White Metal, Pressed Powder Compact. Domed case, faux hammered finish, embossed butterfly and flora lid motif, reverse logo, framed mirror, 2" dia. x ⅜", $50.00 – 65.00.

2. Unknown – White Metal, Pressed Powder Compact. Cameo lid effect, torso nude in round frame, script: "Muguet de Mai" (Lily of the Valley of May), affixed metallic mirror, 1⅞" sq. x ⅜", $75.00 – 100.00.

3. Langlois – Bimetal, Pressed Powder Compact. Domed lid, goldtone overlay of chinoiserie motif, script "Shari" on lid, reverse logo, framed mirror, Ref.: Ad. 1931, 1⅞" oct. x ⅜", box: $125.00 – 150.00, case only: $60.00 – 65.00.
> *The silk covered box is very fragile and so is the brushed silver finish on the case lid. The case must be the octagon shape to fit the box base as the ad depicts.*

4. Vinolia (U.K.) – White Metal, Pressed Powder Compact. Sylvan deity embossed lid motif, reverse signed "Aralys," mirror with black enameled frame 2" dia. x ⅜", $125.00 – 150.00.

5. Belcano – Goldtone, Pressed Powder Compact. Patch box, domed case, standing femme nude lid motif, lid signed, engine-turned reverse, framed mirror, 1⅛ dia. x ½", $65.00 – 90.00.

6. Celma Co., – White Metal, Loose Powder Compact. Engine-turned domed lid, shield monogram cartouche, reverse logo, framed mirror, pierced celluloid powder screen, Pat. Ref.: 1928, as Loospact, 2" dia. x ⅜", $35.00 – 50.00.

7. Witcherie – Goldtone, Pressed Powder Compact. Flying witch on a broomstick in repoussé lid motif, full moon framing, reverse logo, puff with logo, framed mirror, powder paten, Ref.: 1917 Pat., 2" dia. x ½", $75.00 – 90.00.

8. Lady Gay (U.K.) – White Metal, Pressed Powder Compact (Vanipact). Art Nouveau femme nudes embossed lid design, signed, "De Fleury," paper label on niello reverse, framed mirror, 1⅞" sq. x ⅜", $75.00 – 90.00.

Postcard – N.D.

1. Unmarked Stratnoid – White Metal, Loose Powder Compact. Art Deco plastic reverse transfer lid inset of dancing couple, patterned blue foil ground, no case I.D. (see Vol. 1 – P40 #1 Pat. Design No. #767198), case framed mirror, 2" dia. x ⅜", $75.00 – 90.00.

2. Dubarry (U.K.) – White Metal, Loose Powder Compact. "Baby Jack(?)" domed case, plastic reverse transfer lid inset, ballerina silhouette and logo, enameled sun rays, gold foil ground, black enameled reverse, polished metallic mirrored interior lid, 2¼" dia. x ⅜", $50.00 – 65.00.

3. Woodworth – White Metal, Pressed Powder Compact. Art Deco plastic reverse transfer lid inset, stylized scene: moon, dhow, and water against black ground, case overlay of metallic bands, signed "Fiancée," framed mirror, 1¾" dia. x ½", $100.00 – 125.00.

4. Sweet Petals (U.K.) – Goldtone, Pressed Powder Compact. Plastic reverse transfer lid inset of Dutch children and windmill, gold foil ground, case signed, framed mirror, 2" dia. x ⅜", $45.00 – 60.00.

5. Gwenda (U.K.) – White Metal, Loose Powder Compact. Plastic reverse transfer lid river/village scene inset, patterned blue foil ground, coved signed case, green enameled reverse, polished metallic mirrored interior lid, 2¼" sq. x ⅜", $45.00 – 60.00.

6. Darnée – Goldtone, Pressed Powder Compact. Plastic reverse transfer lid temple and sylvan scene inset, logo "Lola Montez," beveled chased sides tinted blue, case signed, framed mirror, 2" x 1¾", x ½", $75.00 – 90.00.

Lola Montez was the stage name of a legendary Spanish dancer and mistress of Louis I of Bavaria. Exiled after the 1848 revolution, she toured the U.S. in 1851, married an American, and died in the U.S. in 1861.

7. Atkinsons (U.K.) – White Metal, Pressed Powder Compact. Coated paper lithograph lid inset, Art Deco femme head, silver overlay, case signed, framed mirror, 2" dia. x ⅜", $45.00 – 60.00.

8. Unmarked – White Metal, Loose Powder Compact. Yellow faux guilloché lid enamel with overlay of femme and dog in black silhouette, polished metallic mirrored interior lid, 1⅝" dia. x ¼", $75.00 – 90.00.

"Silver dollar" slim – see collection lockets and clips for other case examples of this unknown manufacturer.

```
            4
     1            6
  2        5      7
     3        8
```

```
        3
1       4       6
2       5       7
```

1. Marie and Dorette – Goldtone, Loose Powder Compact. Enameled case, broad bar opener, case signed, framed beveled mirror, 3½" (with opener) x 2⅜" x ⅜", $50.00 – 65.00.

2. Unmarked – Goldtone, Loose Powder Glove Compact. Art Moderne enameled lid, coved top and bottom, glued metallic mirror, 2¼" x 1¾" x ½", $45.00 – 60.00.

3. Embassy – White Metal, Pressed Powder Glove Compact. Enameled case, crest logo on lid, embossed powder with logo, glued metallic mirror, 1¾" sq. x ⅜", $45.00 – 60.00.
   Powder box (see P276 #3) has Ltd. – U.S.A. agent A.A. Vantine, N.Y.

4. Unknown – Goldtone, Loose Powder Compact. Mock tortoise-shell case enameling, beveled case sides, signed mirror frame "Paris, Made in France" (very heavy), 3½" x 2¾" x ⅜", $100.00 – 125.00.

5. Garay Bags – Goldtone, Loose Powder Compact. Cushion case, chevron lid motif, puff with logo, no case I.D., case glued mirror, 2¼" sq. x ½", $50.00 – 65.00.
   Might have been part of a fitted purse set.

6. Evans (Aus.) – White Metal, Loose Powder Compact. "Flapjack," enameled case with guilloché enameled oval disk affixed to lid, beveled mirror frame signed "Premier by Evans Made in Austria," 3" x 2¼" x ⅜", $75.00 – 90.00.
   Research does not answer to this Evans anomaly. The block signature is typical of the U.S. company, but the spring action lid is a European flapjack.

7. Ann Barton – Goldtone, Loose Powder Compact. Cushion enameled case, no case I.D., puff with logo, framed mirror, 2¼" sq. x ½", $75.00 – 90.00.

```
        1              6
        2      4       7
          3     5     8
```

1. Marly – Goldtone, Loose Powder Glove Compact. Enameled lid panels, beveled sides, case signed, framed mirror, 2" x 1½" x 1", $35.00 – 50.00.

2. Harriet Hubbard Ayer – White Metal, Pressed Powder Glove Compact. Enameled lid bands, beveled sides, case signed, framed mirror, 2" x 1½" x ½", $45.00 – 60.00.

3. Woodworth – Goldtone, Pressed Powder Glove Compact. Art Moderne engine-turned lightning lid design, coved sides, case signed "Karess," framed mirror, 2" x 1⅝" x ⅜", $45.00 – 60.00.

4. Marie Earle – Goldtone, Pressed Powder Glove Compact. Faux carved ivory side panels, lid quatrefoil motif, vase signed, framed mirror, 2¼" x 1½" x ⅜", Ref.: 1933 Ad., $35.00 – 50.00.

This case has a Coty powder refill and puff. A good example of the interaction on refills between the cosmetic houses who used the same case manufacturer.

5. Mary Dunhill – Goldtone, Loose Powder Compact. Enameled case, affixed "Perlbud" lid bijou and faux pearl, no case I.D., puff with logo, framed mirror, 2½" x 2" x ⅜" (with bijou: ⅝"), Ref.: 1938 Ad., $35.00 – 50.00.

6. Volupté – Goldtone, Pressed Powder Glove Compact. Diagonal enameled lid with logo, beveled sides, case signed twice, framed mirror, 2" x 1⅝" x ⅜", $50.00 – 65.00.

7. Harriet Hubbard Ayer – White Metal, Loose Powder Glove Compact. Enameled lid, diamond monogram cartouche, case signed, puff with logo initials, framed mirror, 2" x 1½" x ½", $35.00 – 50.00.

8. Volupté – White Metal, Pressed Powder Glove Compact. Engine-turned and enameled lid bands, monogram cartouche, coved sides, case signed, framed mirror, 2" x 1⅝" x ¼", $50.00 – 65.00.

This case and #3 are identical with different lid motifs. Volupté was a case manufacturer, Woodworth was not.

```
1        3        6
2        4        7
         5
```

1. Ciner – Goldtone, Loose Powder Compact. Wood paneled lid with trunk-like handcrafted hinges and false lock or opener, case signed, framed mirror (2¼" with lid ornamentation), 2" sq. x ⅜", $50.00 – 65.00.

2. Unmarked Pilcher – White Metal, Loose Powder Compact. Pigskin clad coved with affixed molded plastic Scottie dogs, framed mirror, 3⅛" dia. x ⅝", $65.00 – 80.00.

3. Unmarked Pilcher – White Metal, Loose Powder Compact. Maple wood lid panel, affixed molded plastic horse's head, case glued mirror, 2⅞" sq. x ½", $45.00 – 60.00.

4. Unmarked (For.) – White Metal, Loose Powder Compact. Kid leather padded case, tube flange hinged leather clad closure clip, attached paper framed mirror, 3½" sq. x ⅜" (w/clip 3⅝" and ¾"), $75.00 – 90.00.

5. Zell – Gun-metal, Loose Powder Compact. Leather clad case, lid palm trees and sea view, broad beveled glued mirror with silver foil sticker "Hand Painted in Florida," no case I.D., puff with logo, 3" sq. x ⅜", $125.00 – 150.00.

6. Koket – White Metal, Loose Powder Compact. Beige leather pouch case, interior metallic frame, enameled femme silhouette lid motif, no case I.D., puff with logo, case glued mirror, 2½" dia. x ½", $50.00 – 65.00.

7. Unmarked – White Metal, Loose Powder Compact. Brown pigskin clad case, lid affixed running Scottie dog, case glued mirror, 3¼" dia. x ⅜", $65.00 – 80.00.

1	3	6
2	4	7
	5	

1. Unknown (Ger.) – Goldtone, Loose Powder Compact. Domed case to knife edge, Art Moderne enameled lid accents, framed wide beveled mirror, "Made in Germany," 2½" dia. x ⅜", $125.00 – 150.00.

2. Deerie – White Metal, Loose Powder Compact. Domed enameled case, champlevé enameled signed lid, goldtone interior, framed mirror, 2" dia. x ½", $45.00 – 60.00.

3. Unknown (For.) – White Metal, Pressed Powder Compact. Champlevé enameled Art Moderne lid design, framed mirror, 2½" dia. x ⅜", $150.00 – 175.00.

4. Evans – White Metal, Loose Powder Pouch Compact. Mail mesh case, owl face domed enameled lid motif, embossed flora, no case I. D., puff with logo, affixed framed mirror, 2½" dia. x ½", Ref.: 1941 catalog, $50.00 – 65.00.

5. Unmarked – Goldtone, Loose Powder Patch Box Compact. Enameled case, eggshell lid keyhole motif, framed mirror, 1¾" dia. x ¼", $125.00 – 150.00.

6. Unmarked – White Metal, Loose Powder Compact. Domed case, champlevé enameled Art Moderne comet lid motif, framed mirror, 2" dia. x ½", $65.00 – 80.00.

7. Montral (U.K.) – White Metal, Loose Powder Compact. Watch Case powder dispenser with exterior winder and reverse powder filler access, various country patents, blue champlevé enameled lid motif of Art Deco male jazz dancers, case glued metallic mirror, 2" oct. x ⅜", Ref.: 1930 Ad., $175.00 – 200.00.

The ultimate in Art Deco compact case design, so cross-collecting is affecting the price as is condition; enamel is extremely fragile — flakes and chips are a major — and common problem.

3
1   4   6
2   7
5

1. Unmarked – Molded Bakelite, Loose Powder Compact. Black cushion with domed goldtone lid inset, gilt rococo inlay, dimpled reverse, framed mirror, 2¼" sq. x ⅜", $65.00 – 80.00.

2. Unmarked – Molded Bakelite, Loose Powder Compact. Red case with lid affixed marcasite butterfly, framed mirror, knife-edge beveled sides, 3" dia. x ⅜", $90.00 – 115.00.

3. Unknown (Fr.) – Molded Bakelite, Loose Powder Compact. Black cushion, domed goldtone lid inset, mountain scenery display, case signed "Made in France," dimpled reverse, framed mirror, 3" sq. x ⅜", $65.00 – 80.00.

4. Unmarked – Molded Bakelite, Loose Powder Compact. Ivory domed case, goldtone lid bucolic scene under celluloid, knife edges, framed mirror, 3¼" dia. x ½", $75.00 – 90.00.

5. Terri – Molded Bakelite, Loose Powder Compact. Black domed case, faux guilloché lid enamel, sterling inlay of Spanish figures, case signed, framed mirror, 2" dia. x ½", $75.00 – 100.00.

6. Riga – Molded Bakelite, Loose Powder Compact. Ivory shield beveled case with white metal lid inset, signature lid logo, puff with logo, framed mirror, 2¾" x 2¾" x ½", $65.00 – 80.00.

7. Unmarked – Ebonite, Loose Powder Compact. Domed case white metal and faceted rhinestone lid display, knife edges, framed mirror, 2¾" dia. x ½", $50.00 – 65.00.

1
2

4
5

3

1. Kigu (U.K.) – Goldtone, Loose Powder Compact. Domed case, cut-out Ivorene lid inset of sylvan duo, broad lid engine-turned border, case signed, puff with logo, framed mirror, 3½" dia. x ½", $75.00 – 90.00.

2. Kigu (U.K.) – Goldtone, Loose Powder Convertible Compact. Faux cameo femme profile, lid inset, case signed, papers, framed mirror, 3⅛" sq. x ⅝", $65.00 – 80.00.

3. Framus (Aus.) – Goldtone, Loose Powder Compact. Hand-carved chinoiserie iridescent butterscotch Bakelite case, coved lid and flange side spring-action openers, black enamel reverse, case signed "Made in Austria," beveled framed mirror, 3½" x 2½" x ½", $125.00 – 150.00.

The photo cannot capture the light moods of this case. It literally glows. Interior and exterior lids flip open by squeezing the sides.

4. Unmarked – Yellow Bakelite, Loose Powder Compact. Hand-carved case, opaque base with goldtone domed chinoiserie translucent lid inset, smooth base, case glued with lunette beveling, 3⅛" dia. x ⅝", $150.00 – 175.00.

The carving on this case is almost identical to #3, but may have been a less expensive model; this one lacks the interior quality of #3, but the yellow color is much rarer, hence the value range.

5. Dexter – Goldtone, Loose Powder Compact. Cut-out Ivorene lid inset of sylvan duo, black enamel lid border, case signed "Compact by Dexter," puff with logo, framed mirror, 3¼" dia. x ½", $90.00 – 110.00.

No hint on how #1 and this case have the same lid inset; the cases are totally dissimilar. The Kigu case with its domed lid is showing some slight fracturing in the Ivorene, the flat lid has none.

Helena Rubinstein brochure, 1931

1. Unknown – Goldtone, Loose Powder Compact.
Handworked petit point lid inset with engine-turned scroll border (no protective cover), puff with "Original Wien" logo, framed mirror, 3" dia. x ¼", $50.00 – 65.00.

The dichotomy of this case is puzzling with its pairing of German and English. The case has a continental style. Maybe it was bought in Vienna, Austria, as a souvenir, so no signed country of origin was needed.

2. Unmarked – Bakelite, Loose Powder Compact.
Handworked silk petit point case, goldtone lid inset, celluloid protective cover, interior goldtone framed mirror, reverse framed metallic mirror, Ref.: 1935 Pat., 2½" oct. x ½", $65.00 – 80.00.

3. Pilcher – Rosetone, Loose Powder Compact.
Dark blue leather case panels, lid with enameled flora sprays and oval cabochon collet mounted faux turquoise, no case I.D., puff with logo, framed beveled mirror, 3¼" x 3⅛" x ½", $65.00 – 80.00.

4. Nash, Inc. – Goldtone, Loose Powder Compact.
Gold stamped dark green leather lid panel, plastic domed novelty femme, costumed in silk and lace, signed "Daniél," with papers, lid display horizontal to hinge and opener, puff with logo, framed mirror, 3¾" oval x ½" (with dome ¾"), $100.00 – 125.00.

5. Nash, Inc. – Goldtone, Loose Powder Compact.
Handworked beaded silk lid inset, leather padded panels, interior goldtone backed and framed mirror slides out beneath the lid (does not flip up), no case I.D., puff with logo, 2⅞" sq. x ¾", $75.00 – 90.00.

Tiny pin-like handles for mirror extraction are very weak and bend. Missing pins seriously lower the price. See #4 for papers, signed "Daniél."

6. "Paris WW" (Fr.) – Goldtone, Loose Powder Compact. Handworked beaded and embroidered case motif, case signed "Fabrique en France, Paris WW," framed mirror, 2¾" sq. x ⅝", $65.00 – 80.00.

7. Schildkraut – Goldtone, Loose Powder Case.
Handworked beads, buttons, and sequins, gold threading, case with logo "Fleurs de Paris by Schildkraut," gold foil label on mirror, case glued mirror, 2¾" dia. x ⅜", $75.00 – 90.00.

Fragility rules the market place with all this handwork.

```
                    3
        1           4           6
        2           5           7
```

1	4
2	5
3	6

1. Elgin American – Goldtone, Loose Powder Compact and Black Satin Carrier. M.O.P. top in one piece, case and carrier signed, snap closure, puff with logo, framed mirror, 2¾" x 2¼" x ⅜", Ref.: 1951 Ad., $65.00 – 80.00; with carrier $75.00 – 100.00.

Condition of fabric carrier causes the price variation.

2. Schildkraut – Goldtone, Loose Powder Compact. Domed lid with affixed plate of marbled plastic, cluster of green jade chips, no case I.D., case glued mirror, beveled and signed sticker, 2¾" dia. x ½", $75.00 – 90.00.

3. S.F. Co. Fifth Avenue – Goldtone, Loose Powder Compact. Multicolored shells and faux seed pearls, no case I.D., puff with logo, case glued mirror, 2¾" x 2⅜" x ⅝", $100.00 – 125.00.

4. Marian Bialac – Goldtone, Convertible Compact. Jade chips, no case I.D., gold foil sticker on reverse, case glued mirror with blue script signature, fleece puff with logo, "Genuine Stones" sticker, 3⅛" dia. x ⅝", $75.00 – 90.00.

What kind of "Genuine Stones?" Neither this case or #2 mentions jade, but they look like jade, feel like....

5. Melissa (U.K.) – Goldtone, Loose Powder Compact. Domed carved M.O.P. lid plate, case signed, puff with logo, framed mirror, 3" dia. x ½", $65.00 – 80.00.

6. Unknown (Ger.) – Goldtone, Loose Powder Compact. Lid plate of brown agate, brown enameled faux agate reverse, "Germany" on beveled mirror frame, 2¾" sq. x ½", $125.00 – 150.00.

The two jades, the Elgin M.O.P., and this case are heavy enough to be lethal weapons.

1	4
2	5
3	6
	7

1. Whiting & Davis – Goldtone, Loose Powder Compact and Pearlized Mesh Carrier. M.O.P. lid plate with multi-square design, no carrier or case I.D., puff with logo "Whiting and Davis," case glued mirror, snap closure on carrier, 2¾" x 2⅜" x ⅜", $75.00 – 90.00.

2. Elgin American – Goldtone and Silver Wash, Loose Powder Compact. Chased rococo tinted lid motif, domed M.O.P. lid plate, case signed, puff with logo, case glued mirror, 3" dia. x ⅜", $100.00 – 125.00.

3. Unmarked – Goldtone, Loose Powder Compact. M.O.P. cross-banded lid plate, case glued mirror, 2¾" x 2⅜" x ⅜", $65.00 – 80.00.

4. Volupté – Goldtone, Loose Powder Compact. Multi-shell scenic lid display, abalone border, flanged, fluted sides, case signed, puff with logo, framed beveled mirror, 3" x 2⅜" x ½", Ref.: Ad.

(var.) 1945, $90.00 – 110.00.

The case featured in the Ad. is 14K gold, hence the jump into the post-war market with a metal case — brass was still restricted at this Ad. date (May).

5. Schick Mfg. Co. – Goldtone, Loose Powder Compact. Star pattern M.O.P. lid plate, no case I.D., gold foil sticker, case glued beveled mirror, 2¾" x 2⅜" x ⅜", $50.00 – 65.00.

6. Unmarked – Goldtone, Loose Powder Compact. Chased niello sterling rococo lid, M.O.P. border, case glued beveled mirror, 2½" sq. x ½", $100.00 – 125.00.

7. Kaycraft – Goldtone, Loose Powder Compact. M.O.P. lid panel and affixed heart, abalone heart insets, no case I.D., puff with logo, case glued beveled mirror, 2¾" x 2⅜" x ½", $75.00 – 90.00.

1   4
2   5
3   6

1. Pilcher – Brushed Silvertone, Loose Powder Compact. Painted lid display, case signed, fleece puff with logo, framed mirror, 3¼" sq. x ⅜", $35.00 – 50.00.

2. Dorset Fifth Avenue – Goldtone, Loose Powder Compact. Painted lid flora display, domed signed case, puff with Dorset-Rex logo, framed mirror, 3¼" dia. x ⅝", $30.00 – 45.00.

3. Kigu (U.K.) – Goldtone, Loose Powder Compact. Decal flora lid motif, exterior powder door release, beveled sides, case signed "Kigu of London," foam rubber puff with same logo, framed metallic mirror, 2½" sq. x ¼", $25.00 – 40.00.

4. Margaret Rose (U.K.) – Goldtone, Convertible Compact. Disk hole and loose powder screen, decal flora lid motif, case signed, framed mirror, 2¾" dia. x ½", $25.00 – 40.00.

5. Dorset Fifth Avenue – Goldtone, Loose Powder Compact. Enameled dome lid with engine-turned scrolling, see #2 for information.

6. Van-Ace Fifth Avenue – Goldtone, Loose Powder Compact. Baroque case, painted lid flora, case signed, box with logo (see Vol. I – P215 #5 for variation), 3⅝" x 2¼" x ½", $45.00 – 60.00.

1   4
2   5
3   6

1. Pilcher – Bimetal, Loose Powder Compact. Silvertone case with goldtone interior, bells and ribbon lid motif, no case I.D., papers, case glued beveled mirror, 2⅞" sq. x ⅜", $30.00 – 45.00.

2. Margaret Rose (U.K.) – Bimetal, Convertible Compact. Silvertone case, chased star lid motif, goldtone interior, case signed "Made in England," papers, framed mirror, 3" dia. x ½", $25.00 – 40.00.

3. Pegi Paris – Goldtone, Loose Powder Compact. Art Moderne chameleon lid motif, no case I.D., puff with logo, case glued mirror, 2¾" x 2⅜" x ½", $45.00 – 60.00.

4. Roger & Gallet – Spun Aluminum, Pressed Powder Compact. "Fleurs d'Amour" Cupid lid logo, case signed, suede/fleece puff with logo, framed mirror, 3¼" dia. x ⅝", $65.00 – 90.00.

5. Dermetics – Goldtone, Pressed Powder Compact. Lid logo motif of sunrays and post Deco gazelle, piano keyboard box design and logo, reverse signed sticker, puff with logo, case glued mirror, 2¾" dia. x ½", Ref.: 1949 Ad., $35.00 – 50.00.
Ad does not explain any connection between the case design and the piano box design.

6. Hampden – Spun Aluminum, Loose Powder Compact. Art Deco flora lid motif, case signed, puff with logo, case glued beveled mirror, 3" dia. x ⅜", $50.00 – 65.00.
See Vol. I – P35 #5 for Tre-Jur look-alike.

1	4
2	5
3	6

1. Stratton (U.K.) – Goldtone, Loose Powder Compact. Domed case, artist signed (Cecil Golding), lid portrait of ballet duo, "hand logo" case signature, framed mirror, 3¼" dia. x ⅜", $75.00 – 90.00.

2. Patrys (Fr.) – Goldtone, Loose Powder Compact. Domed Limoges signed plaque lid inset, case signed "Made in France," foam rubber puff with logo, framed beveled mirror, 2¾" x 2" x ⅜" (plaque to 2"), $75.00 – 90.00.

3. Volupté – Goldtone, Loose Powder Compact. Carved femme cameo lid bijou in faux pearl and diamond border, case signed, puff with logo, framed mirror, 2⅞" sq. x ⅜" (to cameo ¾"), $100.00 – 125.00.

4. Unknown (For.) – Goldtone, Loose Powder Compact. Domed lid eighteenth century duo porcelain inset, beveled glass reverse, case glued beveled mirror, 2¾" dia. x ¾", $50.00 – 65.00.

5. Vashé – Goldtone, Loose Powder Compact. Domed lid, femme head silhouette decal, "Great Lakes Exposition, Cleveland" (1936 – 37), reverse decal, no case I.D., puff with logo, framed mirror, 2¾" dia. x ⅜", $45.00 – 60.00.

6. Volupté – Goldtone, Loose Powder Compact. Faux Wedgwood lid motif of eighteenth century duo, case signed, puff with logo, framed mirror, 2⅞" sq. x ⅜", Ref.: Ad. 1955, $40.00 – 55.00.

1	4
2	5
3	6

1. Richard Hudnut – Goldtone, Loose Powder Compact. Embossed golden weave lid, faux emerald and rhinestone affixed bijou, case signed, fleece puff and moire pouch with logo, framed mirror, 2¾" sq. x ½", $50.00 – 65.00.

2. Jules Richard – Goldtone, Loose Powder Compact. Hand-painted lid scene, rhinestone and square carved faux amber pagoda insets, no case I.D., puff with logo, case glued beveled mirror, 2" x 1½" x ⅜", $75.00 – 90.00.

3. Foster – Goldtone, Loose Powder Compact. "Lucky Charms," each (17) with suitable enamel and rhinestones, no case I.D. (#5 has case logo), puff with logo, framed mirror, 2¾" x 2⅜" x ½", $150.00 – 175.00.

The hand workmanship on this case is amazing because of the small scale of the pieces.

4. Unmarked – Goldtone, Loose Powder Compact. Striding femme toting faux gemstone suitcases, pavé rhinestone jacket and enamel accents, framed beveled mirror, 3" x 2⅜" x ⅜", $65.00 – 90.00.

5. Foster – Goldtone, Loose Powder Compact. Faux gemstone set filigree bijou, case signed (on powder door), puff with logo, framed mirror, 2¾" x 2⅜" x ½", $100.00 – 125.00.

6. Columbia Fifth Avenue – Goldtone, Loose Powder Compact. Filigree lid plate, faux gemstone bijou, no case I.D., damask puff with logo, case glued beveled mirror, 2⅝" sq. x ½", $65.00 – 80.00.

1   3   5
       4
2   6

1. Zenette (U.K.) – Goldtone, Loose Powder Compact. Parrot pair on wisteria branch, faux crushed eggshell effect, signed coved case "Made in England," puff with logo, framed mirror, 3⅛" x 2⅜" x ⅜", $75.00 – 90.00.

2. Erica (For.) – White Metal, Loose Powder Compact. Faux shagreen enamel, lid hunting scene, case signed, framed mirror, 3¼" x 2⅝" x ¼", $75.00 – 90.00.

3. Lucretia Vanderbilt – Goldtone, Pressed Powder Compact. Enameled case, butterfly logo, case signed on side, framed mirror, 2" dia. x ⅜", $50.00 – 65.00.

4. Kigu (U.K.) – Goldtone, Loose Powder Compact. Domed, scalloped case, stylized enameled lid scene, case signed "Made in England," puff with logo, framed mirror, 3½" x 2½" x ⅜", $65.00 – 80.00.

5. Flapjack 1000 (Aus.) – Goldtone, Loose Powder Compact. Spring action lid, decal Persian court scene on chameleon ground, yellow enameled reverse, case signed "Made in Austria," framed mirror, 3" x 2¼" x ¼", $75.00 – 90.00.

6. Stratton (U.K.) – Goldtone, Loose Powder Compact. Hand painted flamingos in iridescent enamel, slight doming, case signed ("hand"), puff with logo, framed mirror, 2⅞" dia. x ⅜", $100.00 – 125.00.
Part of the 1950s "Waterbirds" artist series.

1
2 3 5
4 6

1. Schildkraut – Goldtone, Loose Powder Compact. Cloisonné lid disk, opposing peacocks on branches, case signed, puff with logo, case glued mirror, 2¾" dia. x ⅜", $65.00 – 90.00.

2. Cohn & Rosenberger – Goldtone, Loose Powder Compact. Rose faux guilloché spring action inset, knife-edge domed case, script logo "Wafer," framed mirror, 2⅝" dia. x ½", $75.00 – 90.00.

3. Coro – Goldtone, Loose Powder Compact. Yellow faux guilloché lid inset, no case I.D., puff with logo, collet mounted mirror, 4" oval x 3" x ⅜", $50.00 – 65.00.

4. Rex Fifth Avenue – Goldtone, Loose Powder Compact. Aqua faux guilloché inset panels, champlevé enameled borders (identical reverse), case signed, puff with logo, framed mirror, 3" x 2⅛" x ½", $45.00 – 60.00.

5. Unmarked Evans – Goldtone, Loose Powder Compact. Ivory faux guilloché lid with enameled border, no case I.D., case glued mirror, 3" dia. x ⅜", $45.00 – 60.00.

6. Annette – White Metal, Pressed Powder Compact. Red faux guilloché celluloid lid inset, case signed, framed mirror, 2" dia. x ⅜", $35.00 – 50.00.

1
2
5
6
3
4

1. Schildkraut – Goldtone, Loose Powder Compact. Plastic lid plate of chrysanthemums, case signed, case glued mirror, 2¾" dia. x ⅜", $25.00 – 40.00.

2. Elgin American – Goldtone, Loose Powder Compact. Black enameled case, raised ivory enameled "string of pearls" lid motif, case signed, puff with logo, case glued mirror, 3" dia. x ¼", $45.00 – 60.00.

3. Volupté – Goldtone, Loose Powder Compact. Encased transfer design of flora faux petit point, case signed, puff with logo, framed mirror, 2⅞" sq. x ⅜", $50.00 – 65.00.

4. Unmarked – Goldtone, Loose Powder Compact. Six-sided case, red, white, and blue enameled lid flora circle and scalloped border, case glued beveled mirror, 3" x ⅜", $35.00 – 50.00.

5. Richard Hudnut – Goldtone, Pressed Powder Compact. Blue enameled faux pouch case, red, white, and blue champlevé enameled lid motif of ribbons and bows, case signed, puff with logo, framed mirror, 2¾" dia. x ½", $40.00 – 55.00.

6. Unmarked – Goldtone, Loose Powder Compact. Embossed flora lid spray in cerise, blue, and white, case glued beveled mirror, 3" dia. x ½", $45.00 – 60.00.

The BEAU BRUMMEL

Snuff-Box Compact

Your servant, madame! As wasp-waists and curves return to favor, Volupté presents a compact original inspired by the dandy's snuff-box...to be used with a graceful flourish! Scalloped oval of fine enamel and golden finish metal...with wistful pastel floral motif on black or white. Or chaste monotones. Deep loose powder well, sumptuous oval puff.

VOLUPTÉ

Compacts and Cigarette Cases · 347 Fifth Avenue, N.Y.

Vogue, 1939

3
1   4
2   5
             6

1. Evans – Goldtone, Loose Powder Compact.
Snuff box, sunray etched lid, enameled white and pink flora motif, faux rubies and marcasite inlay lid rings, no case I.D., puff with logo, case glued mirror, 2¾" x 2⅛" x ½", $65.00 – 80.00.

2. Majestic – Goldtone, Loose Powder Compact.
Snuff box, ribbed sunray lid, inlay with graduated rhinestones, case signed, puff with logo, case framed mirror, 2⅞" x 2¼" x ⅝" Ref.: 1946 Ad., $75.00 – 90.00.

3. Wadsworth – Goldtone, Loose Powder Compact. Snuff box, black and red satin presentation box with logo, snap closure, rhinestone enhanced linked heart duo, case signed, fleece puff with logo, metallic mesh screen, case glued beveled mirror, 2⅝" x 2¼" x ¾", Ref.: 1951 Ad., $65.00 – 80.00 (with box, $100.00 – 125.00.)

4. Volupté – Goldtone, Loose Powder Compact.
Boudoir snuff box, black enameled case, flat bottom, sloped sides, goldtone ornamental lid with swags, urns, and sunrays, case signed, puff with logo, case framed mirror, 3" x 2½" x ¾", $75.00 – 100.00.

5. Evans – Goldtone, Loose Powder Compact.
Snuff box, "Russian" blue, white, and green encrusted lid enamel, no case I.D., puff with logo, case glued beveled mirror, 2¾" x 2¼" x ⅝", $50.00 – 65.00.

6. Elgin American – Goldtone, Loose Powder Compact. Snuff box, pearl and leaf lid bijou, cased signed, puff with logo, papers, case glued beveled mirror, 3" x 2⅛" x ⅝" (with bijou 1"), $50.00 – 65.00.

3

1   4
2   5

1. Wadsworth – Goldtone, Loose Powder Compact. Snuff box, sunray lid design, mirror sticker "hand engine turned," case signed, fleece puff with logo, metallic powder screen, case glued beveled mirror, 2⅝" x 2¼" x ⅝", $35.00 – 50.00.

2. Evans – Sterling, Loose Powder Compact. Snuff box, encased basketweave, rose, silver, and gold wash, case signed, "Sterling" sticker on mirror, case glued mirror, 2¾" x 2¼" x ½", Ref.: Pat. 1940, $90.00 – 125.00.

3. Langlois – Goldtone, Loose Powder Compact. Snuff box, presentation box, sunray lid, center

flower basket logo, case signed "Cara Nome, Boston," pocket puff with logo, no box I.D., framed mirror, 3" x 2⅛" x ½", $65.00 – 80.00.

4. Volupté – Goldtone, Loose Powder Compact. Snuff box, scalloped case, flora decals in petal lid motif, case signed, puff with logo, framed mirror, 3⅛" x 2¼" x ⅝", Ref.: 1939 Ad., $45.00 – 60.00.

5. K & K – Goldtone, Loose Powder Compact. Snuff box, copper Indian head coin on lid, coin signed "Okoboji Indians," no case I.D., puff with logo, 3" x 2⅜" x ½", $65.00 – 80.00.
South Dakota Sioux tribe, no other reference.

VOLUPTÉ

*reflects
the prettiest faces
on Christmas
morning...*

Top: HIGH TIDE...Compact about $5; Powder Baby (miniature compact), about $3; Pillbox about $2.
Center: CARRIAGE SET...Compact about $7.50; Cigarette Case about $7.50. Bottom: GOLDEN LOOM...
Sumptuous fitted carry-alls, Portmanteau about $15 (plus Fed. Tax)—Sophisticase about $25 (plus Fed. Tax);
Compact about $7.50; Cigarette Case about $10.   AT ALL FINE STORES.
Hostess gown by Tina Leser.

Vogue, 1947

```
1    4
2    5
3    6
```

1. Volupté – Goldtone, Loose Powder Compact.
Horizontal ribbed lid band, faceted faux emerald, coin purse closure, case signed, puff with logo, case glued beveled mirror 3" sq. x ⅜", $35.00 – 50.00.

2. Volupté – Goldtone, Loose Powder Compact.
"Bamboo" encased vertical cross woven motif, case signed, puff with logo, case glued beveled mirror 3" sq. x ½", Ref.: 1948 Ad., $50.00 – 65.00.

3. Volupté – Goldtone, Loose Powder Compact.
Encased embossed chevron design, rope "Swing–Lok" closure, mirror sticker, "Genuine Collector's Item by Volupté," Ref.: 1948 Ad., see #1 for case information.

4. Majestic – Bimetal, Loose Powder Compact.
White metal mechanical "cheese grater" powder dispenser, reverse powder loader, chevron lid motif, "Majesty" case signed, fleece puff with logo, framed mirror, 2⅞" sq. x ½", Ref.: 1948 Ad., $75.00 – 90.00.

5. Luzier's of Kansas City, MO – Goldtone, Loose Powder Compact. Domed lid, center logo crest, blue tints, puff with logo, framed mirror, 3" dia. x ½", $25.00 – 40.00.

6. Volupté – Goldtone, Loose Powder Compact.
Encased wave design, "High Tide," case signed, puff with logo, framed mirror, 3" sq. x ½", Ref.: 1947 Ad., $50.00 – 65.00.

1   4
2   5
3   6

1. Tussy – Goldtone, Loose Powder Compact.
Ribbed, banded, and circle lid motif, flanged case, signed on reverse, puff with logo, framed mirror, 3¼" dia. x ¼", $50.00 – 65.00.

2. Blatt & Ludwig – Goldtone, Loose Powder Compact. Chameleon horseshoe case, woven band lid effect, case signed, framed mirror, 3¼" x 2⅞" x ⅜", $65.00 – 80.00.

3. Gourielli – Goldtone, Loose Powder Compact.
"Bow Tie" lid effect, case signed, fleece puff with logo, framed mirror, 2⅞" sq. x ½", $75.00 – 90.00.
Helena Rubinstein married Prince Gourielli, and in 1938, opened the New York House of Gourielli. May have been a presentation item when the perfume "Bow Tie" was introduced early in 1942.

4. Faberge – Goldtone, Pressed Powder Compact.
Inverted flanged triangular case, rajah, elephants, and palm trees motif, refill kit and papers (1962), box with logo, gold foil I.D. sticker on reverse, disintegrating foam rubber puffs, case glued mirror, 2⅞" tri. x ⅜", complete, $75.00 – 90.00.

5. Beauty Counselor – Goldtone, Loose Powder Compact. Vertical lid ribs, case signed, puff with logo, framed mirror, 2¾" sq. x ⅜", $30.00 – 45.00.

6. Volupté – Goldtone, Loose Powder Compact.
Vertical banded lid, enameled flora cartouche, case signed, puff with logo, framed mirror, 2⅜" sq. x ⅜", $50.00 – 65.00.

3

1
2

4
5

1. Zell Fifth Avenue – Goldtone, Loose Powder Compact. Center rococo framed oval mirror cartouche, no case I.D., but acanthus powder door and pearlized paper well, puff with logo, framed mirror (see P205 #3) for case lid variation, 3⅛" sq. x ¼", $35.00 – 50.00.

2. Evans – Sterling, Loose Powder Compact. Post Deco, "leaping" gazelle motif, rose and goldtone finish, case signed, puff with logo, case glued mirror, Ref.: Pat. 1940, 3⅛" x 2¼" x ⅝", $125.00 – 150.00.

Evans certainly got mileage out of this design (see other collection examples). Most are in sterling or a lucite pairing, with various case shapes and highlight finishes, which got them through the war years with the brass and copper restrictions.

3. Charles of the Ritz – Goldtone, Pressed Powder Compact. Sliding doors presentation box with logo, lid with six-sided faceted white metal initialed disk, case signed, brown pouch and fleece puff with logo, case glued beveled mirror, 1⅞" sq. x ⅜" (box 3⅝" x 3½" x ¾"), complete $75.00 – 100.00.

4. Unmarked – Rosetone, Loose Powder Compact. Impressed rococo lid flora motif, framed mirror, 2¾" sq. x ½", $50.00 – 65.00.

5. Stratton – Goldtone, Convertible Compact. Domed lid, black enamel and diagonal gold overlay bands, French and English papers, case signed, foam rubber puff with logo, framed mirror, 3¼" dia. x ⅜", $35.00 – 50.00.

Fabulous Replicas

Two amazingly faithful reproductions in design
and workmanship of Volupte's most fabulous $500
14K gold compacts. In gleaming metal . . .
$5 . . . (no Federal tax)

VOLUPTÉ

reflects the prettiest faces

FURS BY ESTHER DOROTHY • DRESS—PATTULLO ORIGINAL BY JO COPELAND

Vogue, 1947

1	4
2	5
3	6

1. Volupté – Goldtone, Loose Powder Compact. Encased "spider web with trapped butterfly" motif, cased signed, puff with logo, framed mirror, 3" sq. x ½", Ref.: 1947 Ad., $100.00 – 125.00.

2. Unmarked – Goldtone, Loose Powder Compact. Chameleon, race track pavilion, jockey and race horse lid ornament, nine etched track names Churchill Downs, Hialeah etc., case glued beveled mirror, 2⅞" sq. x ⅜", $50.00 – 65.00.

3. Jeanne Bernard (Fr.) – Gold-plated, Loose Powder Compact. Cut-out lid motif backed by damask and M.O.P., gowned femme against stylized Paris monuments, red and green tints, case signed, gold foil initialed stickers and Eiffel Tower, framed mirror, 3¼" dia. x ⅝", $125.00 – 150.00.

4. Henriette – Goldtone, Loose Powder Compact. Federal-styled lid affixed mirror, eagle, green enamel and rhinestone wreathing, case signed, framed mirror, 3¼" dia. x ⅜", Ref.: 1941 Ad., $50.00 – 65.00.

5. Elgin American – Goldtone, Loose Powder Compact. Chameleon lighthouse and ocean lid effect, affixed sailing ship with faux sapphires and blue enameled accents, beveled sides, case signed, puff with logo, framed mirror, 3½" x 3" x ½", $75.00 – 90.00.

Very heavy case; designer goof: ship's wind pennant blowing in reverse to sails.

6. Volupté – Goldtone, Loose Powder Compact. Black enameled lid matte finish, affixed entwined rope circles, case signed, puff with logo, framed mirror, 2⅞" sq. x ⅜", $100.00 – 125.00.

How this matte finish survived fingernail scratches or other mishandling is a miracle. Matte finishes are a rarity, hence the price — mint please.

```
        3
1       4       5
2               6
```

1. Kigu (U.K.) – Goldtone, Loose Powder Compact. Heart, domed case, Post Deco leaping gazelles, monogram cartouche, coved sides, sunray interior, case signed "Made In England," framed mirror, 3" x 3" x ⅜", $45.00 – 60.00.

2. Elgin American – Bimetal, Loose Powder Compact. Heart "Heart's Desire," domed silvertone case, etched design through to goldtone base, green tinted flora, goldtone interior, case signed, puff with logo, framed mirror, 3½" x 3¼" x ⅜", Ref.: 1947 Ad., $50.00 – 65.00.

The brushed silvertone finishes on these cases are extremely fragile — but since rarity is not a problem, mint condition is a must.

3. Superb – Goldtone, Loose Powder Compact. Heart, hand-painted horse's head on lid, case signed, framed mirror, 2⅞" x 2⅞" x ½", $35.00 – 50.00.

4. Melissa (U.K.) – Goldtone, Loose Powder Compact. Oval domed "soapbar" case, incised rococo lid, circle monogram cartouche, case signed "Made In England," framed mirror, 3¾" x 2⅜" x ½", $45.00 – 50.00.

5. Kigu (U.K.) – Goldtone, Loose Powder Compact. Heart, pierced filigree lid bijou, see #1 for similar case.

6. Elgin American – Goldtone, Loose Powder Compact. Heart, lid display of wheat sheaves and butterfly, rose and green tinting, see #2 for similar case.

The numerous variations Elgin marketed with these heart cases is as yet uncounted. A wise start in collecting at this time while scarcity is not a problem, would result in an extremely attractive collection — as the designs are well made and imaginative.

1   4
2   5
3   6

1. Elizabeth Arden – Goldtone, Loose Powder Compact. "Swiss Twist," exterior wind shaft for powder release, reverse powder door entry, rococo incised lid, shield lid cartouche, case signed "Made In Switzerland," instruction papers, fleece puff with logo, framed mirror (see Vol.I – P236 #6 for var.), 2¾" dia. x ⅜", $35.00 – 50.00.

2. Volupté – Goldtone, Loose Powder Compact. Palette, clam shell (?) lid closure, sunray effect, case signed, puff with logo, framed mirror, 3¼" x 3" x ½", Ref.: 1940 Ad. (var.), $50.00 – 65.00.

3. Yardley – Goldtone, Pressed Powder Compact. Bee and honeycomb motif, tinted white circles, case signed, embossed feathers on powder, foam rubber puff/no logo, framed mirror, 3½" x 3¼" x ½" (elliptical), Ref.: 1952 U.S. Ad., $35.00 – 50.00.

The use of foam rubber for washable powder puffs had a short life in the post W.W.II era. Good idea, but too delicate for the job requirements.

4. Volupté – Goldtone, Loose Powder Compact. Triptych case with spring action lids, interior metallic side panels reflect as mirrors, case signed, framed mirror, 2½" sq. x ⅜", $75.00 – 100.00.

5. Lucien LeLong – Goldtone, Loose Powder Compact. Lid with stylized turtle dove pair and tree, eight rings attached to sides, lid release logo tag coin, case signed, framed mirror, 2½" dia. x ½", $175.00 – 200.00.

In 1948 Lucien LeLong packaged a limited Christmas presentation set called Ting-A-Ling which included "Indiscret" perfume and this case. For design symmetry three more rings were added to the "five golden rings." The two turtle doves and pear tree had some liberties taken, but are recognizable.

6. Elgin American – Goldtone, Loose Powder Compact. Saddle bag, seated gowned femme, curtain swags, red tinted crown, scrolled legend "Queen for a Day," case signed, papers, puff with logo, framed mirror, 2½" x 2⅞" x ½", Ref.: 1950 Ad., $50.00 – 65.00.

Featured in a Mother's Day ad (P329). Research does not show any connection to the then popular radio show "Queen For A Day."

1   4
2   5
3   6

1. Volupté – Goldtone, Pressed Powder Compact.
Flatter Face by Dubarry round powder paten, case signed with both names, "Swing–Lock" closure bar, rhinestone pavé white metal lid ornament, vertical ribbing, framed mirror, 3" sq. x ⅜", $65.00 – 80.00.

2. S.F. CO. Fifth Avenue – Goldtone, Loose Powder Compact. Pierced filigree lid plate, faux jade and emeralds amid random florets, no case I.D., puff with logo, case glued mirror, 2¾" x 2⅜" x ½", $75.00 – 90.00.

3. Volupté – Bimetal, Loose Powder Compact.
Brushed silvertone case finish, faux calibri cut emeralds, mesh belt buckle, goldtone interior, case signed, framed beveled mirror, 3" sq. x ⅜", $100.00 – 125.00.

4. Volupté – Goldtone, Loose Powder Compact.
Butterfly, rhinestone bijou lid clip on stylized wings, case signed, puff with logo, framed mirror, 3¼" x 2½" x ½", Ref.: 1951 Ad., $75.00 – 90.00.

5. Volupté – Spun Aluminum, Loose Powder Compact. Art Moderne rhinestone and faux ruby jeweler's clip, glossy interior, case signed, fleece puff with logo, framed mirror, 3" sq. x ⅜", $65.00 – 90.00.

6. Elgin American – Goldtone, Loose Powder Compact. Lid bijou of fiery sun and rays inlaid with various faceted rhinestones, case signed, puff with logo, framed mirror, 3" dia. x ⅜", $100.00 – 125.00.

1
2   3   5
4   6

1. Dorset Fifth Avenue – Goldtone, Loose Powder Compact. Lid spray of pink and blue porcelain flora and green enameled leaves, puff with Dorset*Rex logo, coved signed case, framed mirror, 3⅛" sq. x ½", $75.00 – 90.00.
The porcelain must be unchipped.

2. Evans – Goldtone, Loose Powder Compact. White metal filigree lid plate, goldtone and faux pearl insets, case signed, box #461–396/3, puff with logo, framed mirror, 2½" sq. x ½", $50.00 – 65.00.

3. Dorset Fifth Avenue – White Metal, Loose Powder Compact. Pierced lid plate, mounted Italian glass cabochons, faux pearl insets, no case I.D., puff with logo, case glued mirror, 3½" oval x ¾", $75.00 – 90.00.

4. Wadsworth – Goldtone, Loose Powder Compact. Pierced lid inset, pear tree and dangling "pear" faux pearls, black lucite ground, coved signed case, puff with logo, framed mirror, 3⅛" sq. x ½", Rare.
To find all eight "pears" hanging in situ with their pearlized coating intact directs the rarity. Almost wins the award for most impractical case.

5. Robért – Goldtone, Loose Powder Compact. Hand worked blue and orange lid enamel, scattered goldtone beads and faux gray and white pearls, no case I.D., case glued mirror with sticker, "Original by Robért," 2¾" x 2⅜" x ½", Ref.: 1952 (var.) Ad., Rare.

6. Melissa (U.K.) – Goldtone, Loose Powder Compact. Pierced lid plate, prong mounted faux turquoises, citrines, amethysts sides inverted, case signed "Made in England," puff with logo, framed mirror, 2¾" dia. x ⅝", $65.00 – 80.00.

```
1   3
    4
2   5
```

1. Christian Dior – Goldtone, Loose Powder Compact. Horizontal ribbed case, lid bijou with baguette rhinestones, case signed "Made in Switzerland," logo on powder door, pouch, and box, framed beveled mirror, 3⅜" x 2⅞" x ½", $150.00 – 175.00.

See Vol. I, P52 #1 for AGME logo, although both are identical, this case has no AGME signature.

2. Evans – Goldtone, Loose Powder Compact. Black enameled case, shooting star lid motif, prong mounted baguette rhinestones, no case I.D., puff with logo, case glued beveled mirror, 2½" dia. x ¾", $150.00 – 175.00.

3. Allwyn Case Co. – Goldtone, Loose Powder Compact. "Mystery Case," ivory enameled lid and reverse, hidden lid release, domed oval case filigree, rhinestone accents, no case I.D., 2½" x 1¾" x ¾", Ref.: 1940 Ad., $125.00 – 150.00.

Nearly impossible to open without a screwdriver! Might not be too many intact cases, so price is a good guess.

4. Eisenberg/Henriette – Goldtone, Loose Powder Compact. Case signed with both names, interior Henriette, Eisenberg on reverse, faux topaz Eisenberg Original modified clip on lid, framed mirror, broad bar opener, 3" sq. x ⅜", Ref.: 1942 Ad., $200.00 – 250.00.

This was the first venture of Eisenberg in the compact business. They used a contemporary case and applied a stock piece to lid. Several clues here: the pre-war Henriette bar opener (Feb. 1942 advance ad was placed before W.W.II began); 1947 ad has button opener (Vol. I P43 #3). Unsigned Dorset? Dorset did not sign their cases — Henriette, if possible, did.

5. K & K – Goldtone, Loose Powder Compact. Lunette case, scalloped sides, rhinestones in etched star lid motif, no case I.D., puff with logo, scalloped mirror frame, 3½" x 2⅛" x ½", Ref.: 1947 Ad. (var.), $65.00 – 80.00.

1 4
2 5
3 6

1. Unmarked (For.) – Goldtone, Loose Powder Compact. Domed lid to knife-edge, marcasite and carved faux jade coin purse closure, framed mirror, signed "#31," 3" dia. x ¼", $65.00 – 80.00.

2. Napier – Sterling, Loose Powder Compact. Clover leaf flanged case, lid monogram, case signed, round framed mirror, 2¾" sq. x ⅜", $150.00 – 165.00.

3. Evans – Goldtone, Loose Powder Compact. Enameled lid bijou, rhinestone enhanced flower bowl, no case I.D., puff with logo, case glued beveled mirror, 2½" dia. x ⅝", $75.00 – 90.00.

4. Georg Jensen (N.Y.) – Sterling, Loose Powder Compact. Acorn lid motif, no case I.D., pouch and presentation box with logo, framed mirror, 2¾" x 2¼" x ¼", Ref.: 1946 Ad., $150.00 – 175.00.

5. Birks (Can.) – Gold Filled, Loose Powder Compact. Rococo flora lid display, coved case signed, framed mirror, 2½" dia. x ¼", $100.00 – 125.00.

6. Elizabeth Arden – Goldtone, Pressed Powder Compact. Art Moderne case effect, baguette faux sapphires and marcasites, case signed, "Made in Germany," puff with logo, framed mirror, 3¼" x 2¼" x ⅜", $85.00 – 100.00.
    Superb workmanship, spring action lid.

1

3

2

1. Evans – Bimetal, Loose Powder Compact. Flapjack, white metal domed case to knife-edge, rococo goldtone overlay etched to sunray base metal, case signed, framed mirror, 3⅞" dia. x ⅜", $75.00 – 100.00.

2. Elgin American – Goldtone, Loose Powder Compact. Flapjack, domed case, "Whirl," chameleon lid effect, engraved rococo flora and scrolls, case signed, puff with logo, framed mirror, 4½" dia. x ⅝", Ref.: 1947 Ad., $100.00 – 125.00.

3. American Beauty/Elgin American – Bimetal, Loose Powder Compact. Flapjack, white metal case, lid motif of "Iris," banding chased to base metal, goldtone interior, case signed, presentation box and pouch with logo, 3⅞" dia. x ⅜", Ref.: 1950 Ad., $75.00 – 100.00.

1

2
3

1. Rex Fifth Avenue – Silver-plated, Loose Powder Compact. Flapjack, domed center, etched flora and wavy circlet, no case I.D., puff with logo, case glued beveled mirror, "Silverplated" sticker, 4" dia. x ½", $150.00 – 175.00.

2. Evans – Sterling, Loose Powder Compact. Flapjack, post Deco leaping gazelles lid, rose vermeil

accent, case signed, case glued beveled mirror, "Sterling" sticker, 3⅞" dia. x ⅝", $225.00 – 250.00.

3. Volupté – Sterling, Loose Powder Compact. Flapjack, "Couturier" compact, center embossed lid rosette and border, case signed, case glued beveled mirror, 4" dia. x ½", Ref.: 1944 Ad., $175.00 – 200.00.

1   2   4
3

1. Volupté – Goldtone, Loose Powder Compact. Flapjack, domed case, embossed and chased rococo lid design, case signed, papers, puff with logo, framed mirror, 3½" dia. x ⅜", $50.00 – 65.00.

2. Unmarked – Damascene, Loose Powder Compact. Flapjack, domed case, niello effect lid and black plastic reverse, rolled flanged edges, genuine rabbit fur puff, maroon silk damask carrier, framed mirror, 3½" dia. x ½", $75.00 – 90.00.
    Value with or without carrier.

3. Madame Pompadour – Goldtone, Loose Powder Compact. Flapjack, twined ribbons and woven lid effect, case signed, puff with logo, case glued mirror, 4" dia. x ⅜" $65.00 – 80.00.

4. American Maid – Goldtone, Loose Powder Compact. Flapjack, eight convex disks and center lid dome, no case I.D., puff with logo, case glued mirror, 3½" dia. x ½", $50.00 – 65.00.

2

1   3

1. Majestic – Goldtone, Loose Powder Compact. Flapjack, chameleon, horizontal ripple lid effect, case signed, puff with logo, framed mirror, 4" dia. x ½", $75.00 – 100.00.

2. Elizabeth Arden – Goldtone, Loose Powder Compact. Flapjack, domed case to knife edge, pierced lid ornament of faux sapphires and rhinestones, case signed, framed mirror, 3⅞" dia. x ⅜" (with ornament ½"), Ref.: 1949 Ad., $150.00 – 175.00.

This is definitely an Evans case in Arden clothing; not unusual for cosmetic houses to use cases from case manufacturers, i.e. Evans.

3. Zenette (U.K.) – Goldtone, Loose Powder Compact. Flapjack, Art Moderne sunray lid motif, flanged sides, case signed "Made in England," puff with logo, framed mirror, 3¾" dia. x ⅜", $100.00 – 125.00.

1
2

3
4

1. Evans – Sterling, Loose Powder Compact. Flap-jack, encased mock tortoise shell over sterling frame, case signed, puff with logo, case framed mirror, 3⅞" dia. x ½" Ref.: 1944 Ad., $75.00 – 100.00.
A rare example by Evans to sidestep the W.W.II metal restrictions in this marriage of plastic and sterling; not successful as both materials are prone to warping.

2. Rex Fifth Avenue – Pigskin, Loose Powder Compact. Flapjack, encased goldtone frame, stamped gilt scrolled lid border, no case I.D., pink vinyl pierced powder screen, puff with logo, 4½" dia. x ½", Ref.: 1945 Ad., $65.00 – 80.00.

3. Varsity/Zell – Naugahyde, Loose Powder Compact. Encased faux tan kidskin over oval copper frame, no case I.D., puff with "Varsity," box with Zell logo, case glued beveled mirror, 4½" x 3½" x ½, $50.00 – 65.00.

4. Rex Fifth Avenue – Vinyl, Loose Powder Compact. Flapjack, encased yellow vinyl over white metal frame, vinyl lid inset, no case I.D., puff with logo, 4" dia. x ½", $125.00 – 150.00.
Yellow is an unusual color in cases. It is difficult to coordinate for day and evening use and was not as popular as the standard colors which were more clothes compatible.

1   2
3

1. Henriette – Bimetal, Loose Powder Compact. Flapjack, etched brushed silver over goldtone, flora and ribbons lid design, exterior square case hinge, no case I.D., puff with logo, case glued mirror, 4" dia. x ⅜", $65.00 – 80.00.

2. Rex Fifth Avenue – Silver-plated, Loose Powder Compact. Flapjack, chased lid flora wreathing to goldtone ground, no case I.D., pouch and char-

treuse velvet puff with logo, case glued mirror, "silverplated" sticker, and logo, 4" dia. x ⅝", $100.00 – 125.00.

3. Pilcher – Bimetal, Loose Powder Compact. Flapjack, "Gold Plate on Silver Finish," etched abstract flora lid motif, no case I.D., blue fleece puff with logo, framed beveled mirror, information sticker with logo, 3¾" dia. x ½", $100.00 – 125.00.

1
2
3

1. Vanstyle – White Metal, Loose Powder Compact. Flapjack, black enameled domed case to knife edge, embossed water bird and reeds on lid, case signed, framed beveled mirror, 3⅞" dia. x ½", Ref.: 1934 Ad., $75.00 – 100.00.

2. Dorset Fifth Avenue – Goldtone, Loose Powder Compact. Flapjack, black enameled domed case, glossy goldtone winged cupids with etched outline, case signed, puff with logo, framed mirror, 3⅞" dia. x ⅝", $65.00 – 80.00.

3. Zell – Goldtone, Loose Powder Compact. Flapjack, black enameled lid, robed femme with lute, arched tree and border, no case I.D., puff with logo, case glued mirror, 4" dia. x ⅜", $65.00 – 80.00.

1
2   3

1. Unmarked – Goldtone, Loose Powder Compact.
Flapjack, chameleon, "Southern Belle" silhouette,
faint incising, case framed mirror, 3⅞" x ⅜", $50.00
– 65.00.

   *Refer to Volume I, P57 #2 for similar case by
Dorset.*

**2. Elgin American – Goldtone, Loose Powder
Compact.** Flapjack, chameleon, eight phases of
women's styles in stylized oval frames, etched outline, case signed, framed mirror, 3¾" dia. x ⅜",
$65.00 – 90.00.

*Fashions begin with Egyptian, Middle Ages,
Tudor, French eighteenth century, colonial,
Edwardian, twenties, and pre Dior (slim skirt).*

**3. Elgin American – Goldtone, Loose Powder
Compact.** Flapjack, chameleon, Art Deco femme
profile, etched outline, case signed, puff with logo,
framed mirror, 3¾" dia. x ½", $75.00 – 100.00.

*Finding this case in unscuffed condition is very
rare, so values are subject to buyer's tolerance of
defects.*

1   3
2   4

1. Rex Fifth Avenue – Goldtone, Loose Powder Compact. Flapjack, white enameled lid, embossed goldtone flora, no case I.D., puff with logo, pink vinyl powder screen, 4" dia. x ⅜", $65.00 – 90.00.

2. Vogue Vanities (U.K.) – Goldtone, Loose Powder Compact. Flapjack, Persian armed horseman enameled lid scene, case signed "Made in England," framed mirror, 3¾" dia. x ⅜", $100.00 – 125.00.

3. Dorset Fifth Avenue – Goldtone, Loose Powder Compact. Flapjack, white enameled dome case, plastic lid and reverse inset of multi-flora panels, no case I.D., puff with logo, framed mirror, 3½" dia. x ⅜", $50.00 – 65.00.

4. Rex Fifth Avenue – Goldtone, Loose Powder Compact. Flapjack, pink flamingo pair on white enameled lid aquatic scene, "A Nor-Blu Miami Original Hand Painted" information sticker on mirror, no case I.D., puff with logo, framed beveled mirror, 4" dia. x ⅜", $150.00 – 175.00.

1
　　2
　　3

1. Henriette – Bimetal, Loose Powder Compact. Flapjack, glossy goldtone case, silvertone finish, post Deco swans on water, no case I.D., puff with logo, broad exterior hinge, case glued mirror, 4" dia. x ⅜", $125.00 – 150.00.

2. Belle Fifth Avenue – Bimetal, Loose Powder Compact. Flapjack, goldtone case, silvertone lid overlay, engraved concentric circles, no case I.D., puff with logo, case glued mirror, 4" dia. x ⅜", $65.00 – 90.00.

3. Metalfield – Bimetal, Loose Powder Compact. Super, goldtone lid, hand-engraved roses on alternate grids, center monogram cartouche, case signed, case glued mirror, 3¾" sq. x ½", $65.00 – 90.00.

1
2   3

1. Rex Fifth Avenue – Gold-plated and Lucite, Loose Powder Compact. Flapjack, open — showing mock tortoise-shell case, see #3.

2. Evans – Goldtone and Lucite, Loose Powder Compact. Flapjack, chased sunray and center sun motif, black Lucite case framing, no case I.D., puff with logo, case glued mirror, 3⅞" dia. x ⅜", $100.00 – 125.00.

3. Rex Fifth Avenue – Silver-plated and Lucite, Loose Powder Compact. Flapjack, see #1 open, engraved silverplated lid, mock tortoise-shell case, case glued mirror, sticker "Silverplated by Rex," case signed, puff with logo, 4" dia. x ½", Ref.: 1945 Ad. (var.), $125.00 – 150.00.

Another example of case manufacturers trying to combine non-essential materials during W.W.II restrictions.

"*Instantly Recognized*"

Like a meteor flashing on the fashion scene, this new Rex Compact . . . of craftsman-engraved silver or gold plate, that tops a mock tortoise shell powder case. So huge . . . so competent . . . so featherlight. At better stores. About $5. Demoiselle size, about $3. (Patent Pending)

REX PRODUCTS CORPORATION • 302 FIFTH AVENUE • NEW YORK

Charm, 1945

1   3
2   4

1. Rex Fifth Avenue – Goldtone, Loose Powder Compact. Super, blue plastic domed lid plate, affixed to lid with four corner rivets, hand-painted "Gold Banded Lily," no case or artist I.D., puff with logo, case glued mirror, 3¾" sq. x ⅝", $75.00 – 100.00.

    Watch for missing rivets or stress cracks; case is almost valueless with these flaws.

2. Gloria Vanderbilt – Goldtone, Loose Powder Compact. Super, lid decals of homme and femme empire figures and umbrellas with raindrops, French weather comments, case signed, puff with logo, case glued beveled mirror, 3¾" sq. x ½", $150.00 – 175.00.

Mrs. Reginald Vanderbilt nee: Gloria Morgan, opened a N.Y. salon from July 1946 to October 1947. It was mainly a parfumerie.

3. Vogue Vanities (U.K.) – Goldtone, Loose Powder Compact. Flapjack, medieval character lid scene, case signed "Made in England," framed mirror, 3¾" dia. x ⅜", $75.00 – 100.00.

4. Zell – Silver-plated, Loose Powder Compact. Flapjack, blue enameled lid, embossed silver swathes, no case I.D., papers, puff with logo, case glued mirror, 4" dia. x ⅜", $100.00 – 125.00.

1
3
2

1. Rhojan – Goldtone, Loose Powder Compact. Super, Art Deco intaglio flower basket motif, no case I.D., puff with logo, case glued mirror, 3½" sq. x ⅜", $125.00 – 150.00.

2. Heyco Fifth Avenue – Bimetal, Loose Powder Compact. Super, goldtone domed case, silver plated lid, embossed aquatic lid scene with ducks in flight, no case I.D., puff with logo, framed mirror, 3½" sq. x ⅜", $75.00 – 90.00.

3. Rhojan – Goldtone, Loose Powder Compact. Super, Art Deco gazelle, see #1 for information.

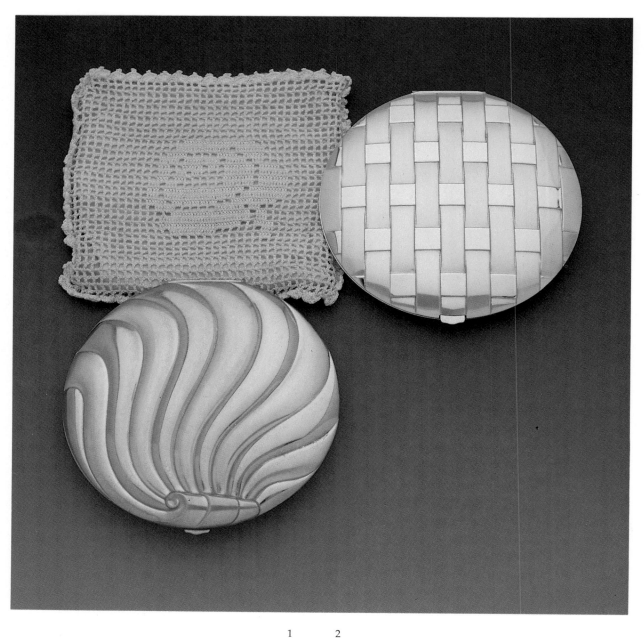

1   2

1. Evans – Goldtone, Loose Powder Compact.
Flapjack, domed case to knife-edge, rose goldtone
scrolls, case signed, puff with logo, case glued
beveled mirror, 4¾" dia. x ½", Ref.: 1946 Ad. (var.),
$125.00 – 150.00.

2. Evans – Goldtone, Loose Powder Compact.
Flapjack, domed case to knife-edge, basket weave
motif, rose goldtone contrasts, no case I.D. (interior
identical to #1), puff with logo, case glued mirror,
crochet pink silk lined string pouch, center rose
motif, 4¾" dia. x ½", $125.00 – 150.00.

1

2

1. Volupté – Goldtone, Loose Powder Compact.
Super flapjack, "Baby Grand," encased segmented
design, domed center, case signed, puff with heat
pressed logo, framed mirror, 5" dia. x ⅝", Ref.: 1947
Ad., $125.00 – 150.00.

   *Ad touts this case as "...For the whole face," how-
ever lid only opens at a right angle precluding a
"whole" view. A grand big baby.*

**2. Columbia Fifth Avenue – Goldtone, Loose Pow-
der Compact.** Super flapjack, chameleon, domed
lid, alternating segments of performing musicians,
no case I.D., puff with logo, case glued beveled mirror, 5" dia. x ½", $100.00 – 125.00.

   *The "Bill Clinton" case — musicians are saxo-
phone players and maraca shakers.*

Chapter Two

VANITY CASES

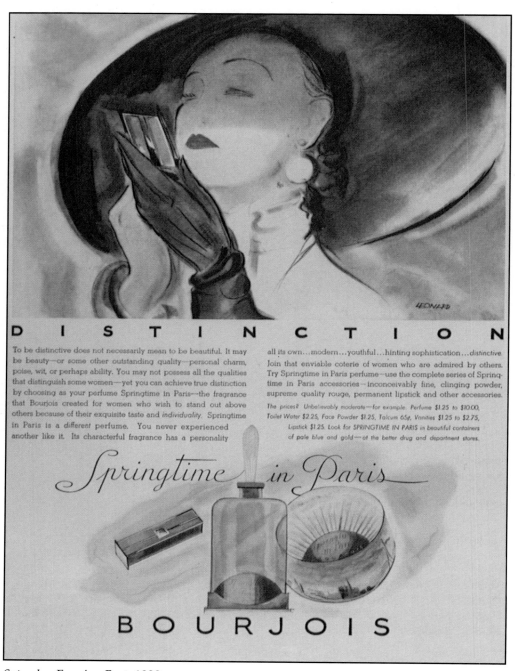

DISTINCTION

To be distinctive does not necessarily mean to be beautiful. It may be beauty—or some other outstanding quality—personal charm, poise, wit, or perhaps ability. You may not possess all the qualities that distinguish some women—yet you can achieve true distinction by choosing as your perfume Springtime in Paris—the fragrance that Bourjois created for women who wish to stand out above others because of their exquisite taste and individuality. Springtime in Paris is a different perfume. You never experienced another like it. Its characterful fragrance has a personality all its own...modern...youthful...hinting sophistication...distinctive. Join that enviable coterie of women who are admired by others. Try Springtime in Paris perfume—use the complete series of Springtime in Paris accessories—inconceivably fine, clinging powder, supreme quality rouge, permanent lipstick and other accessories.

The prices? Unbelievably moderate—for example, Perfume $1.25 to $10.00, Toilet Water $2.25, Face Powder $1.25, Talcum 65¢, Vanities $1.25 to $2.75, Lipstick $1.25. Look for SPRINGTIME IN PARIS in beautiful containers of pale blue and gold—at the better drug and department stores.

Springtime in Paris

BOURJOIS

Saturday Evening Post, 1933

Artist signed

"..SUSPENDED FROM HER WRIST BY A CHAIN AND CONTAINING SEPARATE COMPARTMENTS FOR POWDER-PUFF, BEAUTY PLASTERS, MIRROR, VISITING CARDS AND SMALL CHANGE, THE SOCIETY BELLE CARRIES HER VANITY CASE ALL DAY LONG."

DESIGNER MAGAZINE, *1905*

International cases take a rest in this chapter. These vanity and pendant vanity cases shown seem to be particularly American. Yardley, Stratton, Gwenda, etc. have more time in other chapters.

Kigu — aka *Gustav Kiashek Co.*, 1947 – 1960, had over 500 styles after W.W.II, including the valise and flower basket cases — rarely powder/rouge cases. This popular company is U.K.'s version of the merger game. Bought out by *A.S. Brown*, in turn absorbed by Stratton. Another prominent U.K. company, who emphasized the large pancake or flapjack case, Vogue Vanities, was taken by Dennison Quality Products in 1945, and later it too became a part of Stratton.

The U.S. vanities begin early in the twenties with the double access and oval duo snuff box cases featured by Luxor and Rigaud's Mary Garden line. The introduction of the glove vanity and the book cases was an attempt to create the smallest possible vanity. The triple book with its 1¼" x ¼" lipstick case pushes the limit in miniaturization. The lipstick probably had to be replaced after only one or two social encounters; if the case hadn't disappeared first in a purse or pocket. The limit was reached in the pendant vanities with some lipsticks not exceeding an inch.

In retrospect the vanity case industry seemed highly structured. Nowhere else is the difference between the cosmetic houses and the case makers so apparent. The big case names such as Girey with the Kamra case as its workhorse for souvenirs and military cases don't come to mind as an explorer of other styles. Zell also had a variation on the Kamra, but during its lifetime borrowed designs rather than instigating them. Mondaine coasted on its few designs.

Elgin as a case maker took care of its clientele by offering refills (Elgina) for powder, rouge, and creme rouge, ignoring the retail cosmetic houses. The Elgina creme rouge trays rather than lipstick tubes, simplified the design problems that tubes posed. For a short time the early E.A.M. pendants did have small oval tubes and offered tandem lip coloring and either eyebrow crayons or solid perfume sticks. These tubes did not prevail into the later Elgin American cases.

Evans supplied nothing in their classic carryalls; the lipstick tubes and powder wells were empty. This too was a major digression from their early days as the premier maker of pendant vanity cases which contained pressed powder and rouge and had a large "M" embossed on the pressed rouge and powder in the Mayfair cases. This indicates that refills were probably available from the company.

The pendant vanity was the logical spin-off of the big watch case makers such as Evans and Illinois Watch Co. (parent company of Elgin), as wrist watches almost buried the pocket watch. In an amazing turn around the pendant vanity was born, but it was short lived. While in their glory they were the epitome of U.S. case artistry. Smaller watch case companies lured by the trend presented their personal artistry and the market place again became a place of widely diverse offerings.

The majority of these smaller makers were centered in Attleboro or North Attleboro, Mass., and Providence, R.I., flourishing in the twenties and early thirties. They were true artisans in enameling, hand chasing, engine-turning, and engraving. These are the alphabet manufacturers that signed as jewelers do with only initials or hallmarks. Slowly these marks are being decoded so they will receive the respect they deserve.

Although impractical, the pendant vanity with such pedigree, became an ornamental jewel complimenting dress and occasion. When the cachet filtered down to affordable cases, the catalogs show a wide range of workmanship and cost, nevertheless they had skillful artisans as finishers. The enameling alone speaks for talent and design flair.

In 1928 and 1929 two companies, one a 50-year-old case manufacturer and the other an innovator in the design and presentation of cosmetics, broke into the pendant design field with a crash. Influenced by the 1925 Paris Exposition Des Arts Decoratifs, J.M. Fisher Co. of Attleboro, Mass., and Richard Hudnut, Parfumeur, of New York and Paris, both had occasions that warranted a new direction. Fisher had an anniversary and Hudnut, an American, was opening his beauty salon on 20 rue de la Paix in Paris.

The Fishers stand alone in Art Deco and Art Moderne case design. The enamel lid's cubist images and vivid palette beg for the name of the designer. To add another frisson to the cases, the images have names. Sadly the cases are not of the best quality and the enamel requires careful handling. Their rarity may increase as the enamels deteriorate.

The Hudnut le Début collection is better news for case collectors: sturdy enamel (excepting the Art Deco face cases in Vol. I), excellent case work, and outstanding presentation boxes. Introduced at the Paris Salon opening in 1928, this line of cases were very popular on both sides of the Atlantic. They might be the apogee, in retrospect, of U.S. case making.

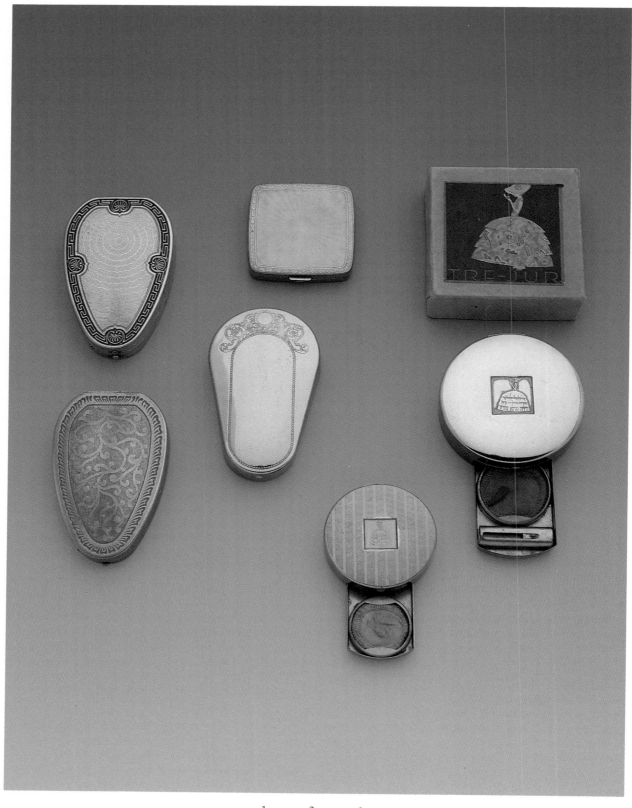

1
2
3
4
5
6

Cosmopolitan, 1924

1. Woodworth – Goldtone, Loose Powder Vanity.
Arrowhead, sunray lid motif, stylized flora, case signed "Vanipat," fleece puffs, framed mirror, 3¼" x 2" x ⅝", $100.00 – 125.00.

2. Woodworth – Goldtone, Pressed Powder Vanity.
Arrowhead, rococo lid motif, orange accents, case signed "Fiancée," orange damask backed fleece puffs, framed mirror, 3¼" x 2" x ½", $85.00 – 110.00.
The goldtone Woodworth cases are scarce; the Vanipat (#1) loose powder in particular, also the Fiancee orange cases.

3. Unmarked – Goldtone, Loose Powder Vanity. Sunray lid motif, acanthus border, hinged metallic double mirrors, papers, 2½" sq. x ⅜", $50.00 – 65.00.
The papers declare the case a Christmas gift to the fans of "Mary Noble, Backstage Wife," an NBC radio soap opera from 1936 to 1959; Larry Noble concurs.

4. Plaza – Goldtone, Pressed Powder Vanity. Arrowhead domed lid, chased scolling and chain border, case signed, framed mirror, 3¼" x 2" x ⅝", $100.00 – 125.00.

5. Tre-Jur – Goldtone, Pressed Powder Vanity Can. Center lid recessed square logo "The Little One," slide-out rouge tray, case signed "The United Toilet Goods Co. N.Y.," framed mirror, 2" dia. x ½", Ref.: 1925 Ad., $75.00 – 90.00.

6. Tre-Jur – Goldtone, Pressed Powder Vanity Can. Domed lid, recessed square center logo "The Little One," box with reverse information "The United Toilet Goods Co. N.Y." and portrait logo, slide-out rouge and lipstick tube tray, framed mirror, 2½" dia. x ¾", Ref.: 1924 Ad., $125.00 – 150.00.

3
1   4   6
2   5   7

1. Langlois – White Metal, Pressed Powder Vanity Can. Flower basket logo in lid cartouche, case signed "Cara Nome," framed mirror, 2½" dia. x ⅞", $50.00 – 65.00.

2. Unmarked – Goldtone, Pressed Powder Vanity Can. Center monogram cartouche, interior swivel powder paten, framed mirror, 2" dia. x ½", $65.00 – 80.00.

3. Richard Hudnut – Gold Filled, Pressed Powder Vanity Can. Double access, lid center monogram cartouche, case signed "DuBarry," presentation box with logo, double framed mirrors, 2½" dia. x 1¼", Ref.: Pat. 1922, $175.00 – 200.00.

4. Rigaud, Paris – Goldtone, Pressed Powder Vanity. Snuff box, lid cartouche "Mary Garden," paper labels on reverse, N.Y. manufacture, framed mirror, 2¾" oval x 1½" x ¾", Ref.: Pat. 1916, $75.00 – 90.00.

No dents please, and complete interior.

5. Unmarked – Bimetal, Pressed Powder Vanity. Cushion, crown tiara lid motif, goldtone interior, top hinged framed double mirrors, powder paten signed "Houbigant," 1¾" x 1¾" x ½", Ref.: 1928 Ad., $65.00 – 80.00.

The Ad. is for Pallas Mfg. Co. N.Y., a wholesale case maker and sold without cosmetics, hence the Houbigant refill. See pages 82 – 83 for identical cases with different cosmetic house brands and appearance.

6. Djer-Kiss – Goldtone, Pressed Powder Vanity Can. Green accented laurel wreath border, triangular monogram cartouche, case signed, hinged framed double mirrors (one convex), 2½" dia. x ¾", Ref.: 1924 Ad., $75.00 – 100.00.

7. Jergen's – Goldtone, Pressed Powder Vanity. No case I.D., embossed powder and papers: "Ben Hur," framed mirror, Ref.: 1927 film, $50.00 – 65.00.

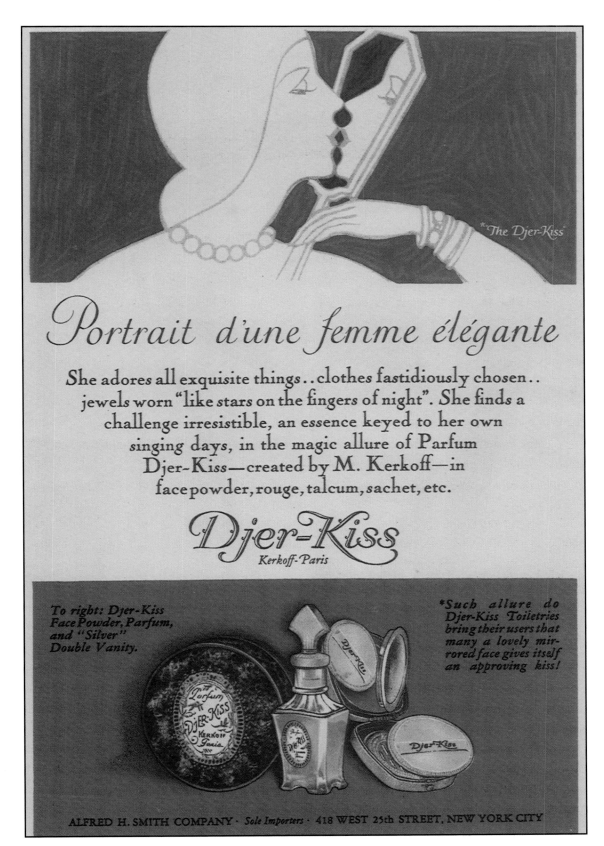

New York Theatre program, 1927

```
1       3       6
2       4       7
        5
```

1. Woodworth – Silver-plated, Pressed Powder Vanity. Art Nouveau flora and tendril case chasing, niello accents, case signed "Karess," bottom hinged framed mirror (see #3) with identical case motif, puffs with design but no logo, presentation box with logo, 2⅛" x 1¾" x ½", Ref.: 1928 Ad., $125.00 – 150.00 (with box add $25.00).

2. Denney's of Philadelphia – White Metal, Pressed Powder Vanity. Domed octagon case, center lid monogram cartouche, flora accents, case signed, bottom hinged framed mirror with "Bizaar (sic) Royale" in red accents, presentation box signed, 2" oct. x ½", $125.00 – 150.00 (with box add $25.00).

3. Bourjois – Silver-plated, Pressed Powder Vanity. Case signed "Karess," see #1 for information.

4. Unmarked – Goldtone, Pressed Powder Vanity. Art Moderne sunray motif and monogram cartouche on domed lid, side hinged metallic mirrors, 2" dia. x ⅝", $45.00 – 60.00.

5. Unmarked – White Metal, Pressed Powder Vanity. Domed case rolled flanged sides, sunray lid motif, side hinged metallic mirrors, 1⅝" dia. x ⅜" (tiny!), $35.00 – 50.00.

6. Salm – White Metal, Loose Powder Vanity Can. Abalone shell lid inset, double access, no case I.D., box with logo, papers, framed mirror and side hinged metallic mirror, 2" dia. x ⅝" (w/shell ¾"), $100.00 – 125.00 (with box).

7. Amami – White Metal, Loose Powder Vanity. Art Moderne domed case, geometric lid patterns, pop-up hinged framed mirror as internal divider, case signed with Pat. 1926, 2" dia. x ½", $65.00 – 80.00.

1   3
2   4
5

1. Unmarked – White Metal, Pressed Powder Vanity. Domed case with rivet attached celluloid lid plate, Spanish fan dancing femme in rose and goldtone accents, no case I.D., top hinged framed mirror, 2" dia. x ⅝", $50.00 – 65.00.

2. Adolph Klar Co. – Gun-metal, Pressed Powder Vanity Can. Lid inset of hand-painted Spanish dancer on nacre ground, case signed "Akl'ar," paper label on reverse, embossed powder logo, puffs with logo, bottom hinged framed mirror, 2½" dia. x ¾", $75.00 – 100.00.

3. Morris, Mann and Reilly – Goldtone, Pressed Powder Vanity Can. Double access, domed porcelain lid inset, bucolic scene, pierced filigree border, no case or box I.D., papers and puffs with logo "M.M.R'S,"

framed powder mirror, metallic rouge mirror, 2½" dia. x 1⅛", Ref.: 1926 Ad., $175.00 – 200.00.

4. Unmarked – Goldtone, Pressed Powder Vanity. Domed case, lid encased silk embroidery and metallic clasp border, fan and ball closure, bottom hinged framed mirror, 2" oct. x ¾", Rare.
The silk fragment is a piece of a Chinese Imperial court robe, research identifies the pattern as one used on robes of the Dowager Empress. There is no protective cover over the silk — how did it survive all these years? May be a one-of-a-kind treasure.

5. Norida – Goldtone, Loose Powder Vanity. Domed case, femme logo, flanged sides, box and case signed, reverse powder load, swivel framed mirror, papers and puffs with logo, 2" dia. x ¾", $125.00 – 150.00.

```
        1   4       7
    2       5
    3       6       8
```

1. Lenthéric – White Metal, Pressed Powder Vanity.
Black enameled beveled case, lid logo of opposing L's
and gold foil seal on box, papers "Miracle," case
hinged metallic mirrors, puffs with script logo, 1¾" x
1½" x ⅝", Ref.: 1930 Ad., $100.00 – 125.00.

**2. Unmarked – White Metal, Loose Powder Glove
Vanity.** Coved case, Spanish fan dancer on brown
enameled lid, framed mirror, 2½" x 1½" x ½", $50.00 –
65.00.

**3. E.B.M. Co. – White Metal, Pressed Powder Glove
Vanity.** Coved case, Art Moderne lid motif, case
signed, framed mirror, 2½" x 1½" x ⅜", $65.00 – 80.00.

**4. Unmarked – White Metal, Loose Powder Glove
Vanity.** Cushion, brown enameled case, Art Nouveau
lid tendrils, top hinged metallic mirrors, 1½" sq. x ½",
$45.00 – 60.00.

**5. Comtesse D'Orsay – White Metal, Loose Powder
Vanity.** Green enameled lid, center crest logo, case
signed, mechanical sliding powder dispenser, papers,

puffs with logo, top hinged metallic mirrors, 2¼" x
1¾" x ½", $75.00 – 100.00.
*See Prince Matchabelli, Max Factor, and Markoff
for the identical powder dispenser feature under this
1931 Pat. number. These cosmetic houses bought
from wholesale case makers and changed the lids to
their logo.*

**6. Bourjois – White Metal, Pressed Powder Glove
Vanity.** Beveled case, pink and blue enameled lid
panels with logo, case signed, puffs with "Springtime
in Paris," top hinged metallic mirrors, powder
embossed "Bourjois," 2" x 1⅝" x ½", Ref.: 1933 Ad.,
$75.00 – 90.00.

7. Bourjois – White Metal, Loose Glove Vanity.
Beveled case, blue and white lid enamel, monogram
cartouche, case signed, puffs with script logo (no
"Evening in Paris" I.D.), top hinged metallic mirrors,
2" x 1⅝" x ½", Ref.: 1933 Ad., $50.00 – 65.00.

**8. Charles of the Ritz – White Metal, Pressed Powder
Glove Triple Vanity.** See P75 #8 closed.

```
1    4    7
2    5    8
3    6    9
```

1. Primrose House – White Metal, Pressed Powder Glove Triple Vanity. Black enameled case, lid logo initials, no other case I.D., puffs with script logo, bottom hinged metallic mirrors, 2¼" x 1⅝" x ½", Ref.: 1928 Ad., $60.00 – 75.00.

2. Unmarked – White Metal, Loose Powder Glove Vanity. White enameled lid, swan and bridge motif, framed mirror, 2½" x 1½" x ⅜", $65.00 – 80.00.

3. Unmarked – White Metal, Loose Powder Glove Vanity. Black enameled case, Art Deco walking femme silhouette, mechanical sliding powder dispenser, framed mirror, 2½" x 1½" x ⅜", $125.00 – 150.00.
These beach pajamas became popular among the "rich young things" during the Roaring Twenties.

4. Comtesse D'Orsay – White Metal, Loose Powder Vanity. See P74 #5 for information.

5. Cara Mia – White Metal, Loose Powder Vanity. Black enameled lid, faux pearl in rhinestone circlet, no case I.D., puffs with Art Moderne logo, bottom hinged metallic mirrors, 1⅞" x 1⅝" x ½", $60.00 – 75.00.

6. Charmant – Goldtone, Pressed Powder Glove Vanity. Ink sketch on balsa wood, case signed, flange opening, framed mirror, 2⅝" x 1⅝" x ⅜", $75.00 – 90.00.

7. Sosy – White Metal, Loose Powder Glove Vanity. Blue lid enamel, embossed narcissi, case signed, bottom hinged metallic mirrors, 2⅛" x 1½" x ⅜", $75.00 – 90.00.
Several of these cases have Art Moderne engine-turned geometric designs on the reverse.

8. Charles of the Ritz – White Metal, Pressed Powder Glove Triple Vanity. Domed case, Art Deco stylized femme lid logo, puffs with logo, bottom hinged metallic mirrors, 2" x 1½" x ⅜", $100.00 – 125.00.

9. Unmarked – White Metal, Loose Powder Glove Vanity. Wood encased with bands of walnut and maple, burned lid initials, framed mirror, 2½" x 1¾" x ½", $35.00 – 50.00.
This looks like a high school shop item; very crude and lots of glue residue. A Mother's Day gift?

Praise Be for this So-Nice Replenisher of Beauty

In Colors to Match the Costume

SUCH a joy to behold—this newest and nicest of de luxe beauty books for the convenient replenishment of one's good looks. Such gorgeous colors—to harmonize or contrast with the costume, or to match the purse.

Such a joy to hold in the hand, such a delight to use, that the fortunate possessor almost wishes her lips or cheeks might more often need renewal.

And such a joy to uphold before the admiring and covetous eyes of envious others.

All because this so-smart Vanity Book by Raquel is bound in luxuri-

ous *leather*—leather of regal richness and softness; as befits a book for the tending of one's beauty.

Choice of three choicest leathers, each in the smartest of colors: De Luxe—in Red, Green, Black, Blue, Snake-Skin or Lizard—for all-purpose-wear; Ecrasé—in pastel shades to match gay afternoon and party frocks; and Gold, to go with evening gowns.

Each tiny book contains both Rouge and Powder Compacts (Re-fill) with separate puff for each. Plus an unbreakable mirror. As swanky and pleasing inside as out.

Re-fills, with puff, 50 cents each.

If not yet at your favorite counter, order direct from Raquel, Inc. Simply state leather and color desired, and enclose price.

Three choice leathers and eleven smart colors to choose from, as listed in the column at the right.

Raquel Vanity Book

De Luxe Leather $2.50   *Ecrasé Leather* $3.50   *Gold Leather* $5.00

RAQUEL, INC.

475 FIFTH AVENUE   NEW YORK CITY

*Creators of those Three Fascinating and Unforgetable Perfumes - Orange Blossom Fragrancia - L'Endeley - Olor de la Noche**

*(FRAGRANCE OF THE NIGHT)

Harper's Bazaar, 1928

```
        1       3      4
        2              5
                       6
```

1. Raquel – Goldtone, Pressed Powder Vanity. Book, encased black "Ecrase" leather with stamped gilt Art Moderne lid motif, spine "Classic, Vol. II," no case I.D., framed mirror, 3" x 2⅛" x ½", Ref.: 1928 Ad., $125.00 – 150.00.

2. Raquel – White Metal, Pressed Powder Vanity. Book, encased ivory leather with green grid, lid center oval cameo of femme silhouette, metallic corner guards, no case I.D., framed mirror, 3" x 2⅛" x ½", $100.00 – 125.00.

3. Unmarked – Goldtone, Loose Powder Vanity. Book, encased pink faux pigskin, metallic case guards, stamped gilt oval lid motif of peacock, flange opening, framed mirror, 2¾" x 1" x ⅜", $65.00 – 80.00.

4. Raquel – Goldtone, Pressed Powder Vanity. Book, encased black calf leather with stamped gilt lid crest logo, spine signed "Raquel," framed mirror, 3" x 2⅛" x ½", Ref.: 1928 Ad., $100.00 – 125.00.

5. Raquel – Goldtone, Pressed Powder Vanity. Book, encased black calf leather with stamped gilt lid rococo motif and logo initial, spine signed "Raquel," framed mirror, 3" x 2⅛", Ref.: 1928 Ad., $100.00 – 125.00.
   The Raquels were easily gutted of interior fittings for popular visiting card use. If these cases have mint exteriors, salvage them for about ⅓ above value.

6. Vashé – White Metal, Pressed Powder Triple Vanity. Mini book, encased orchid moire faux leather, gilt and tinted bubble lid motif, no case I.D., box with logo, side hinged double metallic mirrors, exterior square lipstick case, 2" x 1¾" x ½", $100.00 – 125.00.

77

1
2   3
4

5
6

1. Mondaine – White Metal, Loose Powder Vanity. Book, encased tiger stripe brown and tan plastic domed case, cut-out Art Deco femme and cocktail glass lid motif, case signed, framed mirror, embossed "M" on rouge, 3" x 2⅛" x ½" $65.00 – 80.00.

2. Mondaine – White Metal, Loose Powder Vanity. Book, encased white enamel with domed oval lid inset, faux cloisonné black and gilt flora, case signed, framed mirror, papers, embossed "M" on rouge, 3" x 2⅛" x ½", $75.00 – 90.00.

3. La Mode – Goldtone, Loose Powder Triple Vanity. Book, yellow cloisonné flora lid plate, exterior lipstick access, case and box signed, framed beveled mirror, 2½" x 2⅛" x ½", $100.00 – 125.00.

4. Vashé – Goldtone, Pressed Powder Vanity. Book, encased leather with stamped geometric lid motif, no case I.D., embossed logo on rouge and powder, side hinged double metallic mirrors, 1¾" x 1⅝" x ½", $65.00 – 80.00.

5. Unmarked – Gold Wash, Pressed Powder Triple Vanity. Book, Art Moderne cubist case motif, framed mirror, 3" x 2¼" x ⅜", $125.00 – 150.00.

6. D.F. Briggs Co. – Goldtone, Pressed Powder Triple Vanity. Book, case bark finish, flanged borders, lid initialed monogram cartouche, case signed "D.F.B. Co.," framed mirror, 3" x 2" x ⅜", $125.00 – 150.00.

1   3   5
2   4   6

1. Girey – White Metal, Pressed Powder Triple Vanity. Kamra, encased faux guilloché pink vinyl, metal borders, exterior lipstick access, "shutter button" lid release, case signed, framed beveled mirror, 3¼" x 1¾" x ⅜", $65.00 – 80.00.

Some of these cases come without maker mark and are also adapted for loose powder with interior door.

2. Girey – White Metal, Loose Powder Triple Vanity. Kamra, encased green marbled vinyl, metal borders, domed sunray white plastic and Victorian femme portrait, exterior lipstick access, "shutter button" lid release, case signed, puff with logo, framed beveled mirror, 3¼" x 1¾" x ½", $75.00 – 100.00.

3. Unsigned Girey – Goldtone, Pressed Powder Vanity. Kamra, encased black Moroccan leather, Art Moderne lid accents, "shutter button" lid release, same interior as #1, 2⅞" x 1⅞" x ⅜", $100.00 – 125.00.

4. Le Kid (Fr.) – Goldtone, Loose Powder Triple Vanity. Kamra, encased tan embossed leather, "film winders" of lipstick tube and pop-up perfume atomizer, center "lens" compact, case signed "Made in France," framed mirror, 2⅝" x 1¾" x ⅝", $150.00 – 175.00.

5. Zell – White Metal, Loose Powder Vanity. Kamra, encased green marbled vinyl, beveled metal borders, "shutter button" lid release, Art Moderne lid motif, no case I.D., puff with logo, framed beveled mirror, 3¼" x 2" x ½", $65.00 – 80.00.

6. Gwenda (U.K.) – White Metal, Loose Powder Vanity. Kamra, encased blue enamel, coved metal borders, bucolic scene over blue foil ground, "shutter button" lid release, tasseled exterior lipstick access, case signed "Made in England," framed mirror, 3¼" x 1¾" x ⅜", $100.00 – 125.00.

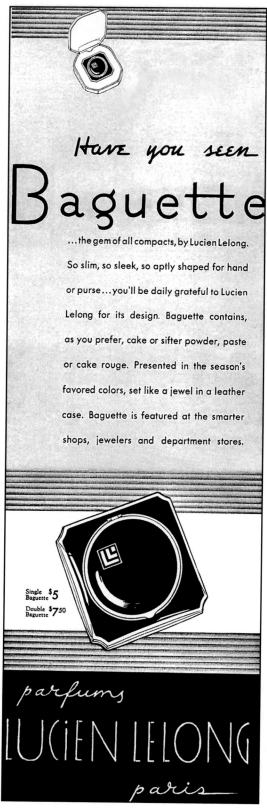

Harper's Bazaar, 1930

```
1    4
2    5
3    6
```

1. Lucien LeLong – White Metal, Loose Powder Vanity. Cushion, encased lavender enamel, "Baguette" case, puff and leather, hinged presentation box with logos, framed mirror, 2¼" sq. x ⅜" Ref.: 1930 Ad., $125.00 – 150.00, with box $175.00 – 200.00.

2. Unmarked – Goldtone, Loose Powder Vanity. Baroque snuff box, encased blue enamel with blue guilloché enameled sunray lid, lunette puff, framed mirror, 3" x 2⅛" x ½", $150.00 – 175.00.

3. Unmarked – White Metal, Loose Powder Vanity. Domed saddlebag, yellow guilloché enameled lid, signed presentation box, lunette framed mirror, 2½" x 2¼" x ½", $150.00 – 175.00.
Presentation jeweler's box, Swenson and Pearson, 935 Belmont Ave., Chicago.

4. Richard Hudnut – White Metal, Loose Powder Vanity. Blue champlevé enamel lid, quartrefoil center, case signed, puff with logo, top hinged double metallic mirrors, 2" sq. x ⅜", Ref.: Pat. 1927, $50.00 – 65.00.

5. Bliss Bros. – Goldtone, Loose Powder Vanity. Snuff box, encased blue enamel with domed porcelain lid inset, no case I.D., gold foil label, papers, embossed rouge, puff and pouch with logo, top hinged double metallic mirrors, 2¾" x 2¼" x ⅝", $75.00 – 90.00.

6. Elmo – Goldtone, Loose Powder Vanity. Snuff box, maroon lid enamel, repoussé flora center, case signed, puffs and embossed rouge with logo, top hinged double metallic mirrors, 3" x 2⅛" x ½", $65.00 – 80.00.

1   3   6
2   4   7
5

1. Reich-Ash – Goldtone, Pressed Powder Vanity. Cushion, encased green enamel with diagonal black lid accent, see P83 #2 for information.

2. Elizabeth Arden – White Metal, Loose Powder Vanity. Domed case, Art Moderne green enameled lid, faux crackled eggshell bands, case signed "Ardenette," puff with logo, top hinged double metallic mirrors, 2⅛" oct. x ½", Ref.: 1933 Ad., $50.00 – 65.00.

3. Unmarked – Goldtone, Loose Powder Vanity. Keystone, Art Moderne encased green enamel lid, lightning bolt decor, center coin-like medallion, lunette framed mirror, 3¼" x 2½" x ⅜", $125.00 – 150.00.

4. Seventeen – Gun-metal, Pressed Powder Vanity. Beveled octagon case, Art Deco flora under plastic, no

case I.D., papers, embossed rose on cosmetics, top hinged double metallic mirrors, See P83 #6 open, 1⅞" oct. x ½", Ref.: 1930 Ad., $100.00 – 125.00.

5. Vanstyle – Goldtone, Loose Powder Vanity. Coved case, Art Moderne bands on black enamel, case signed, bottom hinged double metallic mirrors, 2¼" x 1¾" x ½", $50.00 – 65.00.

6. Lupé – Goldtone, Loose Powder Vanity. Cushion, encased red enamel, lid logo and swirling comet, see P83 #7 for information.

7. Joncaire – Goldtone, Pressed Powder Vanity. Domed case, Art Moderne aqua champlevé lid enameling, case signed, hinged framed lid reverse and embossed powder "Un Peu d"Orient," puff with logo, 2" dia. x ½", see P83 #1 open, $150.00 – 175.00.

1   3   6
2   4   7
     5

1. Joncaire – Goldtone, Pressed Powder Vanity. Aqua champlevé lid enamel, see P82 #7 for information.

2. Reich-Ash – Goldtone, Pressed Powder Vanity. Cushion, encased green enamel, "Deere" lid logo, top hinged framed mirrors, no case I.D., papers, 1¾" x 1¾" x ½", see P82 #1 open, $75.00 – 90.00.

3. Evans – White Metal, Loose Powder Vanity. Domed case, Art Moderne lavender and purple matte enamel lid, case signed, puff with logo, framed mirror, 2¾" dia. x ½", $65.00 – 80.00.

4. Clarice Jane – White Metal, Pressed Powder Vanity. White enameled case, Art Moderne lid motif, coin purse closures, case signed, puffs with script logo, framed mirror, 2" dia. x ⅜", $100.00 – 125.00.

5. Elgin American – White Metal, Loose Powder Vanity. Domed saddlebag, encased black enamel, Art Moderne lid motif, case signed, puff with logo, framed mirror, 3¼" x 2½" x ½", $65.00 – 80.00.

6. Seventeen – Gun-metal, Pressed Powder Vanity. Beveled case, Art Deco lid inset, see P82 #4 for information.

7. Lupé – Goldtone, Loose Powder Vanity. Cushion, encased red enamel, lid logo and swirling comet, puffs with script logo, comet motif is cut out in powder door for powder release, top hinged double metallic mirrors, puffs with logo, 2⅞" sq. x ½", see P82 #6 open, $125.00 – 150.00.

```
1    3    5
2    4    6
```

1. Vee Vanity U.S.A. – Goldtone, Loose Powder Vanity. Domed encased blue enamel, narcissi under lid Lucite bubble, case signed, framed mirror, 2⅜" dia. x ¾", $50.00 – 65.00.

2. Evans – White Metal, Loose Powder Vanity. Domed case to knife-edge, pearlized moss rose lid inset, green champlevè enameled shoulders, case signed, "Mayfair" logo embossed rouge, papers, side hinged double metallic mirrors, 2¼" sq. x ⅜", Ref.: Cat. 1938, $75.00 – 90.00.

3. Elmo – White Metal, Pressed Powder Vanity. Domed case, intaglio lid quatrefoils, Art Moderne lid motif under plastic, top hinged double metallic mirrors, case and presentation box signed, puffs with logo, 2" dia. x ¾", Ref.: Pat. 1926, $150.00 – 175.00.

4. Unmarked – Goldtone, Loose Powder Vanity. Saddlebag, encased white enamel, faux blue guilloché lid enamel, hinged snap closure, lunette framed mirror, 3" x 3" x ⅜", Ref.: Pat. 1927, $125.00 – 150.00.

5. Vee Vanity U.S.A. – Goldtone, Loose Powder Vanity. Domed, black encased enamel, lid goldtone wreathing, case signed, 2¼" dia. x ⅝", $50.00 – 65.00. *Good example by a manufacturer tempting prospective clients to buy the more casual blue (#1) for daytime and use this black case for evening.*

6. Evans – Goldtone, Loose Powder Vanity. Faux ivory guilloché lid enamel, see #2 for similar information.

```
1      3      6
2      4      7
       5
```

1. Unmarked – White Metal, Loose Powder Vanity. Encased black enamel, Art Moderne green enamel lid motif and monogram cartouche, framed mirror, 2¼" sq. x ⅜", $50.00 – 65.00.

2. Silvaray – White Metal, Loose Powder Vanity. Coved case, green champlevè enameled lid, Art Deco dancing femme, stair-step sides, pendant chain hinge ring, top hinged double metallic mirrors, 2" x 1¾" x ⅝", $75.00 – 100.00.

3. Ripley and Gowen Co. – White Metal, Pressed Powder Vanity. Cushion, Art Deco dancing femme silhouette domed lid plaque, top rivet for pendant adaptation, case signed "R.&G. CO.," framed mirror, 2¼" x 1¾" x ½", $65.00 – 80.00.

4. Woodworth – White Metal, Pressed Powder Vanity. Domed case, lid framing over Art Deco femme profile and red flora, exterior flanges for interior compartments, center hinged framed double mirrors, case signed "Karess," puffs with logo, 1¾" dia. x ½", Ref.: 1929 Ad., $225.00 – 250.00.

Major factor which moves this to almost rare is the difficulty finding the case with the lid plating intact. The base goldtone appearance drastically lowers the value.

5. Unmarked – Goldtone, Loose Powder Vanity. Keystone, encased ivory enamel with goldtone borders, lid decal of Edwardian femme, framed mirror, 3¼" x 2¼" x ⅜", $75.00 – 100.00.

6. Clarice Jane – White Metal, Loose Powder Vanity. Cushion, encased black enamel, Art Moderne lid motif, no case I.D., puff with logo, "Elgina" creme rouge, framed mirror, 2¼" sq. x ½", $65.00 – 90.00.

7. Elgin American – White Metal, Loose Powder Vanity. Shield, encased black enamel, Art Deco walking femme and dog on domed lid inset, case I.D. "E.A.M.," side hinged double metallic mirrors, 2¼" x 2¼" x ⅜", Ref.: 1929 Ad., $175.00 – 200.00.

1   4   6
2   5   7
3

1. Richard Hudnut – Goldtone, Loose Powder Vanity. Coved case, encased red enamel, case and box signed, embossed rouge and puffs with logo, framed mirror, 2½" sq. x ⅜", see P87 #4, Ref.: 1936 Ad. – Gemey, $65.00 – 80.00.

2. Geo. W. Luft Co. – White Metal, Pressed Rouge Vanity. Vertical lid bands, monogram cartouche, papers, everything signed "Tangee," glued metallic mirror, 2¼" x 1⅝" x 1", see P87 #7 open, $125.00 – 150.00.

3. Bourjois – White Metal, Loose Powder Triple Vanity. Beveled case, red enameled lid double cartouches, case signed, puffs and embossed rouge "Fiancee," top hinged double metallic mirrors, 2" x 1⅞" x ½", see P87 #1 open, Ref.: 1931 Ad., $75.00 – 100.00.
   1931 Ad. cites "New Garb for Fiancée" – the former Woodworth line. The parent company, International Perfume Inc. of N.Y., decided in 1930 to market all its products under the Bourjois label.

4. Vantine's – Goldtone, Pressed Powder Vanity. Domed octagon case signed "Zanadu," see P87 #2 closed.

5. Unmarked – Goldtone, Loose Powder Vanity. Horseshoe, domed, encased blue enamel, framed round mirror, 2¾" x 2½" x ½", $65.00 – 80.00.

6. Celma – Goldtone, Loose Powder Triple Vanity. Cushion, encased red enamel, black enamel diamond lid motif, case and box signed, top hinged double metallic mirrors, 2" sq. x ½", Ref.: Pat. 1923, $75.00 – 100.00.

7. Lentheric – Gold-plated, Loose Powder Vanity. Encased enamel with circus pony and stars, case signed "14KT Gold Plate," framed mirror, see P87 #5 for reverse design, 3¼" x 2¼" x ⅜", Ref.: 1940 Ad., $65.00 – 80.00.

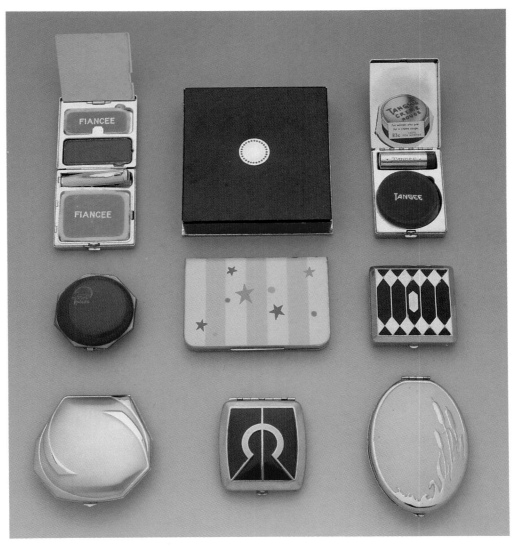

1	4	7
2	5	8
3	6	9

1. Bourjois – White Metal, Loose Powder Triple Vanity. Everything signed "Fiancée," see P86 #3 closed.

2. Vantine"s – Goldtone, Pressed Powder Vanity. Domed octagon case, encased maroon enamel, "Zanadu" lid logo, case signed, embossed logos, top hinged engine-turned reverse frame mirror, 1¾" dia. x ½", see P86 #4 open, $75.00 – 90.00.

3. Clarice Jane – Duralumin, Loose Powder Vanity. Horseshoe, domed beveled case, glossy embossed lid swirls, no case I.D., "Elgina" creme rouge, lunette puff with logo, 2½" x 2½" x ½", Ref.: 1928 Ad., $65.00 – 80.00.

4. Richard Hudnut – See P86 #1 for open Gemey box.

5. Lenthéric – Gold-plated, Enameled Vanity. Reverse case design, see P86 #7 for information.

6. Unmarked – White Metal, Loose Powder Vanity. Domed case, champlevé red lid enamel, geometric motif, pendant chain hinge ring, bottom hinged double metallic mirrors, 2" x 1⅞" x ½", $50.00 – 65.00.

7. Geo. W. Luft Co. – White Metal, Pressed Rouge Vanity. Everything signed "Tangee," see P86 #2 closed.

8. Unmarked – White Metal, Loose Powder Vanity. Beveled case, black champlevé lid enamel, Art Moderne geometric motif, top hinged double metallic mirrors, 1⅞" sq. x ½", Ref.: 1933 Ad., $50.00 – 65.00.

9. Vashé – Silvertone, Pressed Powder Vanity. Domed, oval case, ivory champlevé lid enamel, aquatic scene, no case I.D., embossed powder, framed mirror, 3" x 2" x ½", $75.00 – 90.00.

```
        1
   2        4        5
   3                 6
                     7
```

1. The Lorrette – Goldtone, Loose Powder Vanity. Shield, blue enameled lid side panels, case signed, round framed mirror, 2½" x 2¼" x ⅜", $65.00 – 80.00.

2. Tussy – Goldtone, Loose Powder Vanity. Red enamel lid, case signed, puffs with logo, top hinged double metallic mirrors, 2¼" x 2" x ⅜", $50.00 – 75.00.

3. Renée Thornton, Goldtone, Loose Powder Vanity. Coved black enameled case, enameled lid crest, signed box, pouch, and case, 3" x 2⅛" x ½", Ref.: 1951 Ad. (var), $100.00 – 125.00.
> *This line was founded by Duchess Carafa d'Andria in 1923, N.Y. address.*

4. Elgin American – Gold-plated, Loose Powder Vanity. Clamshell, encased pearlized effect, foil sticker with logo, framed mirror, case signed, 2¾" x 2¾" x ½", Ref.: Cat. 1938, $100.00 – 125.00.

5. André Chenier – White Metal, Loose Powder Vanity. Coved blue enameled case, Art Moderne ivory lid motif, no case I.D., puffs with logo, top hinged double metallic mirrors, 2¼" sq. x ½", Ref.: 1940 Ad., $75.00 – 100.00.

6. Helena Rubinstein – Goldtone, Loose Powder Vanity. Coved case, ivory enameled lid, center cartouche, case signed, embossed rouge and puffs "rose" logo, 2¼" x 2" x ½", Ref.: 1937 Ad., $65.00 – 80.00.

7. Elgin American – Goldtone, Loose Powder Triple Vanity. Encased blue champlevé enamel, Arts and Crafts lid framing, hinged spring action lipstick tube, case signed, framed mirror, 3⅛" x 2" x ⅜", $150.00 – 175.00.
> *Arts and Crafts movement identified with Roycroft, is almost never displayed in women's cosmetics. The designs ran concurrently with Art Nouveau, but this seems to be a much later case.*

1   3   4
  2   5

1. Yardley – Goldtone, Pressed Powder Vanity. Mirror Pact, mechanical slide mirror top with hinged case for access to powder and rouge, embossed reverse with logo and assorted flora, case signed "London," framed beveled mirror, 3⅞" x 2" x ⅜", Ref.: 1936 Ad., $100.00 – 125.00.

2. Kreisler – Bimetal, Loose Powder Vanity. Coved case, Art Moderne lid motif, top and bottom spring release, case signed, bottom hinged double metallic mirrors, 2¾" x 2¼" x ½", $65.00 – 80.00.

3. Langlois – Goldtone, Loose Powder Triple Vanity. Side spring action, diagonal lid motif and monogram cartouche, stepped sides, case and box signed "Cara Nome," puffs with logo, framed mirror, 3¼" x 2⅜" x ⅜", $100.00 – 125.00.

4. Lenthéric – Goldtone, Loose Powder Triple Vanity. Coved case with top and bottom spring action, ivory and cream case enamel, lid logo, case signed, puffs with logo, bottom hinged double metallic mirrors, 2⅞" x 2¼" x ½", $65.00 – 80.00.

Function did not follow form with this case; very nail unfriendly. Watch for cranky spring action.

5. Zell – White Metal, Loose Powder Vanity. Streamline, encased pearloid ivory vinyl with metal borders, hidden spring lid opener, beveled case, no case I.D., box and puffs with logo, papers, framed beveled mirror, 3½" x 2½" x ½", $75.00 – 90.00.

89

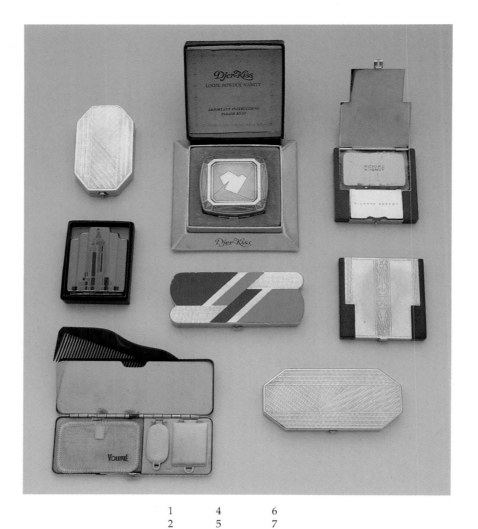

1	4	6
2	5	7
3		8

1. Houbigant – Silvertone, Pressed Powder Vanity. Art Moderne cross diagonal lid motif, case signed, puffs with logo, framed mirror, 2⅞" x 1¾" x ½", Ref.: 1929 Ad., $75.00 – 90.00.

2. Volupté – White Metal, Pressed Powder Vanity. "Skyscraper," gray enameled lid with black building silhouette, stepped case, lettered reverse "Empire State – World"s Tallest," box and case signed, papers and original tag, hinged double metallic mirrors, 2" x 1⅝" x ½", preview Ad. – 12/30, Rare.

> *Provenance is that this boxed case might be the building dedication souvenir, May 1931.*

3. Volupté – Duraluminum, Loose Powder Triple Vanity. See P91 #3 closed for information.

4. Djer-Kiss – Nickel Silver, Loose Powder Vanity. Art Moderne case and presentation box, intaglio lid motif, sloped borders, case and box signed, papers, side hinged framed mirrors, puffs with logo, 2" sq. x ⅝", Ref.: 1926 Ad., see P91 #1 closed, $225.00 – 250.00.

> *The outstanding Art Moderne presentation box in mint condition calls for these prices.*

5. Zanadu – White Metal, Pressed Powder Triple Vanity. Art Moderne lid motif of champlevè blue enamel scalloped case, framed mirror, case signed, 3⅝" x 1½" x ⅜", see P91 #2 open, $125.00 – 150.00.

6. Richard Hudnut – Bakelite, Pressed Powder Vanity. "Skyscraper," Art Deco lid, green base, 2⅜" sq. x ¼", see #7 closed, $150.00 – 175.00.

7. Richard Hudnut – Bakelite, Loose Powder Vanity. This case has red base and powder well, otherwise similar to #6.

> *The nickel plating precludes polishing, however, as a rare design classic a damaged case should be included in a tolerant collection. It also comes with a black base and silver foil box; values may double on these mint boxed sets.*

8. Houbigant – "Platinum Tone," Pressed Powder Triple Vanity. Art Moderne chevron lid panels, case signed, see P91 #4 open, 3⅝" x 1¾" x ⅜", Ref.: 1929 Ad., $125.00 – 150.00.

1   4
2   5
3   6

1. Djer-Kiss – Presentation Box. See P90 #4 open.

2. Zanadu – White Metal, Pressed Powder Triple Vanity. See P90 #5 closed and information.

3. Volupté – Duraluminum, Loose Powder Triple Vanity. Baton, lid bijou of rhinestones and faux coral beads, case signed, bottom hinged metallic mirrors as lid for comb storage, see P90 #3 open, 4⅛" x 1½" x ⅜", Ref.: 1934 Ad., $100.00 – 125.00.

Solved the lack of lipstick tube room by using creme rouge as lip coloring.

4. Houbigant – "Platinum Tone," Pressed Powder Triple Vanity. See P90 #8 closed and information.

5. Lenthéric – Goldtone, Loose Powder "Triplikit" Vanity. Chameleon, calligraphy and crowned circle lid motif, case signed, framed mirror, 3⅜" x 2⅝" x ¾", Ref.: 1940 Ad., $50.00 – 65.00.

See Vol. I – P124 (1951 Ad.), for Wadsworth clone. But eleven years later? Wadsworth the case maker, might have decided to market its own version after W.W.II.

6. Clarice Jane – White Metal, Loose Powder Vanity. Domed shield with encased black enamel, monogrammed lid display, no case I.D., creme rouge refill paten "Clarice Jane, Elgin, Ill.," framed mirror, 3½" x 3½" x ⅜", $50.00 – 65.00.

Some of these plain enameled cases required elaborate initialing as the focus decoration, and were designed for this type of artisan engraving.

Marie Earle considers the gift-seeker

with less than Five dollars

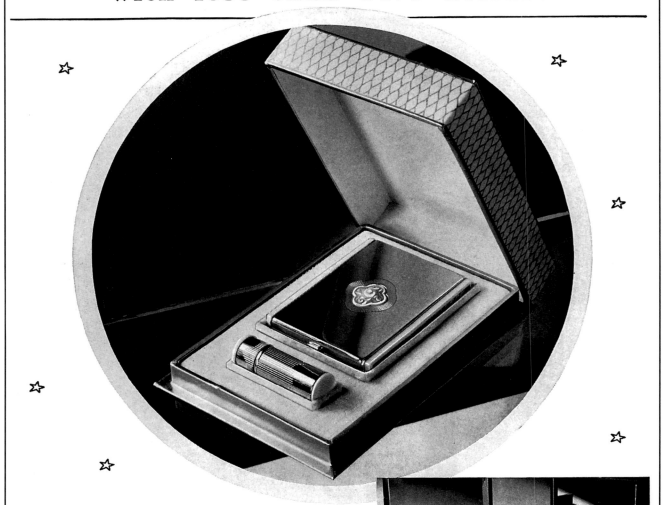

If you'd like to give a present of jewel-like splendor... and have less than $5 to spend for it... don't despair. Marie Earle has the solution, in this exquisite Double Compact and Lipstick set. The case is of polished gold-tone metal, with sides and medallion that look exactly like carved ivory. The compact is flat and slim, as compacts should be. And contains powder and rouge in really smart shades, as compacts should, but seldom do. The mirror is exceptionally large, and exceptionally good! All quite in the Marie Earle tradition... for only $4.25.

Marie Earle

Travel Luxury—*Lovely and practical... a large travel case in genuine leather in soft brown, lined throughout with cream leather. May be initialed in gold at no extra expense. Contains a complete home treatment of Marie Earle preparations. Notice the large mirror top. $25. A baby sister of the larger size $12.50*

Harper's Bazaar, 1935

1   4
2   5
3   6

1. Frances Denney – Goldtone, Loose Powder Vanity. Sunray lid motif with recessed gilt stars on faux ivory inset panel, case signed, puffs with gilt stars, top hinged double metallic mirrors, box with "North Pole, 1940," 1937 Ad. "Starglow," 2¼" sq. x ⅜", $65.00 – 90.00 with box.

2. Evans – Goldtone, Loose Powder Vanity. Oval yellow cloisonne lid disk, faux Bakelite ivory enameled sides, case signed, framed mirror, 3½" x 2⅛" x ⅜", Ref.: 1938 Cat., $65.00 – 80.00.

3. Richard Hudnut – Gold-plated, Loose Powder Vanity. Chameleon, deep chased beveled case framing, case signed "14K Gold Plated," puffs with logo, framed mirror, 3¼" x 2½" x ½", $75.00 – 90.00.

4. Marie Earle – Goldtone, Loose Powder Vanity. Sunray enameled border lid, faux ivory quatrefoil inset, presentation box and case signed, puffs with logo, "scissors" mechanical powder dispenser, top hinged double metallic mirrors, papers, 2½" sq. x 1", Ref.: 1935 Ad., complete $100.00 – 125.00.

5. Coty – Goldtone Bakelite, Loose Powder Vanity. Coved ivory Bakelite base with metallic case inset, Art Moderne gothic lid motif, case signed, puffs with logo, framed beveled mirror, 3¾" x 2⅜" x ½", $75.00 – 100.00.

6. La Mode – Goldtone, Loose Powder Triple Vanity. Domed case with rose tints, lid initialed monogram cartouche, dual exterior lipsticks, case signed, right hinged double metallic mirrors, 2¾" x 1¾" x ¼", $45.00 – 60.00.

1   4
2   5
3   6

1. Unmarked – Goldtone, Loose Powder Vanity. Faux burled walnut case, sides with chased wreathing, framed mirror, 2¾" dia. x ⅜", $50.00 – 65.00.

2. Unmarked – Goldtone, Loose Powder Vanity. Faux yellow cloisonné dog and child bucolic lid scene, top hinged double metallic mirrors, 2½" sq. x ⅜", $45.00 – 60.00.

3. Unmarked – Bakelite, Loose Powder Vanity. Goldtone and blue enameled case inset, center monogram cartouche, reverse initials "LIC NY" (Long Island College, New York?), glued metallic mirror, 3" x 2¼" x ½", $75.00 – 100.00.

4. Evans – White Metal, Loose Powder Vanity. Pouch, green leather, domed lid Art Moderne motif, right hinged double metallic mirrors, "Mayfair" logo embossed on rouge, no case I.D., puff with logo, 2½" dia. x ½", Ref.: 1938 Cat., $65.00 – 80.00.

5. Rex – Goldtone, Loose Powder Vanity. Needlepoint and lace lid inset under plastic, no case I.D., acanthus powder door motif, framed beveled mirror, 2¾" sq. x ⅜", $35.00 – 50.00.

6. Tu-Adore – Bakelite, Loose Powder Vanity. Cushion, domed lid inset of silver foil and black bucolic scene, goldtone frame, case signed, right side hinged double metallic mirrors, 2" sq. x ½", $75.00 – 100.00.

```
       1      3      5
       2             6
              4
```

1. Bonita – Goldtone, Loose Powder Triple Vanity. Encased mustard enamel, decreasing pewter ball bottom flange opener, case signed, puff with logo, framed beveled mirror, 3½" x 2¼" x ½", $65.00 – 80.00.

2. Coty (Fr.) – White Metal, Pressed Powder Vanity. Art Moderne lid crest, Bakelite inset, stepped panels, case signed, puffs with logo, French papers "L'Origan," framed mirror, 2¾" x 2¼" x ⅜", $75.00 – 90.00.
Many of the Coty products of this genre have goldtone cases.

3. Nymfaun – Bimetal, Pressed Powder Vanity. Coved case, silvertone etched to base goldtone, Art Nouveau box with design logo, goldtone interior, case signed, "Feb. 22, 1928" engraving, case framed mirror, 4" x 2½" x ½", Ref.: 1924 Ad., complete $125.00 – 150.00.

4. Prince Matchabelli – Goldtone, Loose Powder Vanity. Black enameled lid, crown lid logo, case signed, puff with logo, top hinged double framed mirrors, 2½" x 2⅜" x ½" Ref.: Pat. 1933, $50.00 – 65.00.
Powder control engineering is so tight, the interior has metal manicure tool scratch marks at access points.

5. Max Factor – Goldtone, Loose Powder Vanity. Stepped lid, Art Deco logo motif, case signed, unmarked fleece puffs, slide powder dispenser, 2¾" x 2" x ½", Ref.: 1937 Ad., $100.00 – 125.00.

6. Richard Hudnut – White Metal, Pressed Powder Vanity. Art Deco ivory and black champlevé enameled lid motif, silver foil presentation box (clear celluloid cover removed), case signed "Gemey," framed mirror, 2¾" x 1¾" x ⅜", Ref.: 1931 Ad., $65.00 – 80.00.

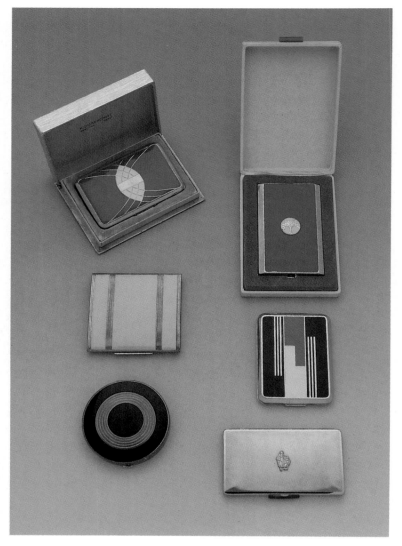

1   4
2   5
3   6

1. Richard Hudnut – White Metal, Loose Powder Triple Vanity. Coved blue enameled case, Art Moderne blue and white champlevé enameled lid, center cartouche, gold foil presentation box and case signed, puffs with logo, framed metallic mirror, 3" x 2" x ⅜", Ref.: 1936 Ad., complete $75.00 – 100.00.

2. Foster – Goldtone, Loose Powder Vanity. Coved pink enameled case, strap lid bars, case signed, framed mirror, 2¾" x 2⅝" x ⅜", $50.00 – 65.00.

3. Daggett and Ramsell – Goldtone, Loose Powder Vanity. Black enamel domed lid, box and case signed "Dagelle," fleece puffs, top hinged double metallic mirrors, 2½" dia. x ½", $45.00 – 60.00.

4. Langlois – White Metal, Loose Powder Triple Vanity. Blue enameled beveled case, lid flower basket logo, presentation box not signed, case signed "Cara Nome," framed mirror, 3¼" x 2" x ½", complete $100.00 – 125.00.

5. Richard Hudnut – White Metal, Pressed Powder Triple Vanity. Beveled case, Art Moderne white, rose, and black champlevè lid enamel, case signed "DuBarry," framed mirror, 3" x 2¼" x ⅜", $65.00 – 80.00.

6. Yardley – White Metal, Pressed Powder Vanity. Beveled case, "The Lavender Seller" goldtone lid logo, red plastic push piece, case signed, puffs with paper logos, framed mirror, 3⅜" x 2" x ⅜", $50.00 – 65.00.

```
1        4
2        5
3        6
```

1. Foster – Goldtone, Loose Powder Triple Vanity.
Pierced domed lid framing with faceted faux collet
mounted gemstones, case signed, framed beveled mirror, 2¾" x 2⅜" x ½", $125.00 – 150.00.
*Foster was arbitrary on case I.D. A partner to this
case is unsigned as is pouch and box (#3565). Look
for the case format, but unsigned will drop the price.*

**2. Charles of the Ritz – Goldtone, Loose Powder
Vanity.** Stepped concentric circled lid, monogram cartouche, case signed, puff with logo, framed mirror,
3¼" dia. x ⅜", $45.00 – 60.00.

**3. Richard Hudnut – Goldtone, Loose Powder Triple
Vanity.** Beveled case, rhinestone and faux emerald lid
bijou, case signed, puffs with logo, framed mirror, 3¼"
x 2¼" x ½", $65.00 – 90.00.

4. Volupté – Bimetal, Loose Powder Vanity. Silvertone sleeve case over goldtone interior, mesh faux belt

buckle lid bijou, baguette rhinestone inset, exterior
"Lip Lock" lipstick, case signed, puff signed, case
glued beveled mirror, 3¼" x 2⅜" x ¾", Ref.: 1949 Ad.
(var.), $125.00 – 150.00.

5. Max Factor – Goldtone, Loose Powder Vanity.
Chevron lid, red logo mask, case signed, framed mir-
ror, 3½" x 2½" x ½", Ref.: 1939 Ad., $50.00 – 65.00.
*This case appears in a 1940 trade ad with Bridgeport
Metal Goods Mfg. Co. as the maker. Cosmetic
houses did not make, as a rule, their own cases.*

6. Briggs – Goldtone, Loose Powder Vanity. Shield,
domed lid with repoussé rose and green tinted flora,
heart monogram cartouche, no case I.D., puff with
logo, framed round metallic mirror, 2½" x 2⅜" x ⅜",
$125.00 – 150.00.

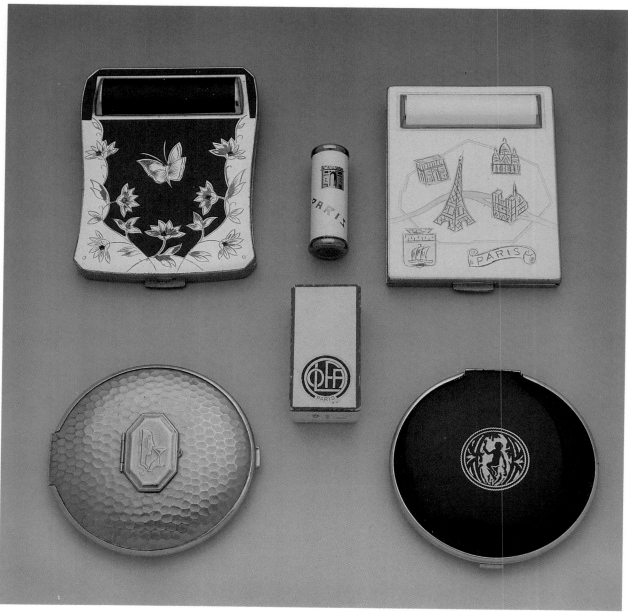

1
2   3   4
                      5

1. Unmarked OLFA (Fr.) – Goldtone, Loose Powder Vanity. Encased black enamel, flora and butterflies lid motif, pink faux ruby insets, roll-top interior lipstick tube storage, no case I.D., see #4 for identical interior, framed beveled mirror, 4" x 3" x ¼" (tube case ⅞"), $125.00 – 150.00.

2. Unmarked Mondaine – Bimetal, Loose Powder Triple Vanity. Goldtone honeycomb domed case, white metal overlay, Art Deco creme rouge well, beveled hinged lid, femme head with cocktail glass, framed mirror, 3¼" dia. x ½", Ref: 1935 Ad. (var.), $75.00 – 100.00.

3. OLFA (Fr.). Engraved refill box and lipstick for #4.

4. OLFA (Fr.). See Vol. I – P109 #1 for case in black, lipstick refill, box, and pouch with logo, complete $125.00 – 150.00.

5. Unmarked Mondaine – White Metal, Loose Powder Vanity. Metallic blue enamel domed case, Art Deco faun design etched through to case metal, 3¼" dia. x ½", Ref: 1935 Ad. (var.), $100.00 – 125.00.

3
1   4   5
   2   6

1. Evans – Goldtone, Loose Powder Vanity. Roll-top case, hatch and vertical ribbed lid design, monogram cartouche, case signed, framed mirror, 2¾" x 2" x ½", Ref.: 1938 Ad., $65.00 – 90.00.

All roll-top cases must have matching interior lipstick tubes or prices tumble.

2. Bourjois – Goldtone, Loose Powder Triple Vanity. Lid cut out for interior lipstick tube placement, scalloped lid border, case signed, fleece puffs with logo "Evening in Paris," framed metallic mirror, 3¼" x 2⅜" x ⅜", Ref.: 1938 Ad., $75.00 – 90.00.

3. A W (U.S.) – White Metal, Loose Powder Triple Vanity. Black enameled case, Art Moderne sunrise stenciled on lid, large exterior hinge houses a lipstick tube, case signed with initials only, 2½" x 2¼" x ⅜" (with hinge 2¾"), $100.00 – 125.00.

4. K and K – Goldtone, Loose Powder Vanity. White enamel lid, cut-out lid bijou, rhinestones, faux coral beads, and green enameled leaves, lipstick tube acts as lid release, framed mirror, see Vol. I – P111 #2 and 6 for identical cases, 3" x 2¼" x ¾", $75.00 – 100.00.

Slip case is not missing, lid bijou is too high and wide for fit.

5. Elgin American – Goldtone, Loose Powder Vanity. Lid cut-out for interior lipstick fit, vertical rib lid motif, case signed, puff, pouch and powder lid with "American Beauty," framed mirror, 2⅞" x 2⅝" x ⅜", Ref: 1950 Ad., $50.00 – 65.00.

6 Elizabeth Arden – Goldtone, Loose Powder Vanity. Double access to exterior pressed rouge compartment, doors have faux emerald collet push bars, chevron engine-turned case motif, case signed, puffs with logo, framed mirrors, 3½" x 2⅝" x ¼", $75.00 – 100.00.

1 4
2 5
3 6

1. Mondaine – Goldtone, Pressed Powder Combination Case. "Cig-Vanette," padded red faux alligator leather book, Art Moderne stamped gilt motif, lid, spine, and presentation box with logo, bottom well for cigarettes, papers, 3" x 2" x ¾", 1st Pat. 1924, 3rd 1929, $100.00 – 125.00.

2. Evans – Goldtone, Loose Powder Combination Case. Double access, hatch case design with rib lid inset, coved case signed, puff with logo, affixed metallic mirror, spring clips in bottom well, 2⅞" x 2⅛" x ¾", Ref.: 1938 Ad., $45.00 – 60.00.

3. Unmarked – Goldtone, Loose Powder Combination Case. Luggage, ivory enamel with goldtone straps, faux jade cabochon lid ornament, see Vol. 1 – P114 #3 for information, $75.00 – 90.00.

4. Mascot (A.S. Brown/U.K.) – Goldtone, Loose Powder Combination Case. Double access, flap lid spring release, pseudo cigarette case motif, case signed, framed mirror, 3¼" x 2¼" x ¾", $65.00 – 80.00.

5. Mondaine – Goldtone, Pressed Powder Combination Case. Tan padded leather book, Art Deco green tinted flora lid display, leather coin purse in bottom well, see #1 for information, $65.00 – 80.00.

6. Bliss Bros. – Goldtone, Loose Powder Combination Case. Double access, black enameled case, oval sunray and quatrefoil green tinted flora lid motif, case signed, puff with logo, beveled case glued mirror, 3" x 2½" x ⅝", $150.00 – 175.00.

This is one of the finest examples of American case artistry. It's regrettable that the artist is unknown.

```
1       4
2       5
3
```

1. Leading Lady – Goldtone, Loose Powder Combination Case. Double access, black Lucite lid with port hole, hinged goldtone framed beveled top mirror and case glued interior mirror, bottom well has cigarette spring clip, no case I.D., puff with logo, 3½" sq. x ½", see #4 open, $75.00 – 100.00.

2. Volupté – White Metal, Loose Powder Combination Case. Double access, encased ivory enamel with beveled border, domed blue cloisonné lid bijou, cigarette spring clip in top section, slide-out bottom compact with pop-up hinged double metallic mirrors, case signed, 3⅛" sq. x ⅝", $125.00 – 150.00.

> *A rare failed design for Volupté. There is no catch or lock on the bottom tray, which slides out as the case is handled and the mirrors, puff, and powder pop out.*

3. Unmarked – Goldtone, Loose Powder Combination Case. Double access, encased black enamel – ala La Mode, oval M.O.P. compact lid bijou, case glued mirror, cigarette spring clip in interior compartment, 4⅛" x 3" x ⅜", Ref.: Pat. 1932, $75.00 – 100.00.

4. Leading Lady – Goldtone, Loose Powder Combination Case. See #1 closed for information.

5. Unmarked (Fr.) – Goldtone, Loose Powder Combination Case. Encased mottled brown enamel with intaglio lid inset of eighteenth century femme, hinged flap closure, interior hinged beveled framed mirror, cigarette spring closure in lid compartment, 3⅜" x 3" x ¾", $150.00 – 175.00.

1 3 4
2   5

1. Zell Fifth Avenue – Goldtone, Loose Powder Vanity Kit. Pocket watch case, lid mirror, diamanté circlet, silk tassel, black velvet and gold lamé "tulip" carrier, faux tortoise shell diamanté topped comb, exterior lipstick, no case I.D., puff with logo, case glued interior mirror, 2½" dia. x ½", $100.00 – 125.00.

2. Avon – Goldtone, Loose Powder Vanity Kit. Plinth and column case lid motif, hinged flap closure, black faille carrier, aqua liner, exterior lipstick, everything signed, case glued beveled mirror, 2¾" sq. x ⅜", $75.00 – 100.00.

3. Ciner – Goldtone, Loose Powder Vanity Kit. Black enameled case lid and lipstick, affixed oriental scene, faux gemstones, black faille carrier with gold satin liner, everything signed, framed mirror, 2" sq. x ⅜", $250.00 – 275.00.

4. Max Factor – Goldtone, Pressed Powder Vanity Kit. "Regency Case," coved, encased weave design, diamanté hinged lid closure, black/lurex damask carrier, papers, exterior lipstick with diamanté circlet, everything signed, case glued mirror, 3" x 2¼" x ½", Ref.: 1965 Ad., $65.00 – 80.00.

5. Zell Fifth Avenue – Goldtone, Loose Powder Vanity Kit. Vertical rib case, triangle lid diamanté bijou, black faille and gold lamé carrier, exterior lipstick with diamanté circlet, no case I.D., puff with logo, case glued beveled mirror, 2¼" x 2⅛" x ⅜", $75.00 – 100.00.

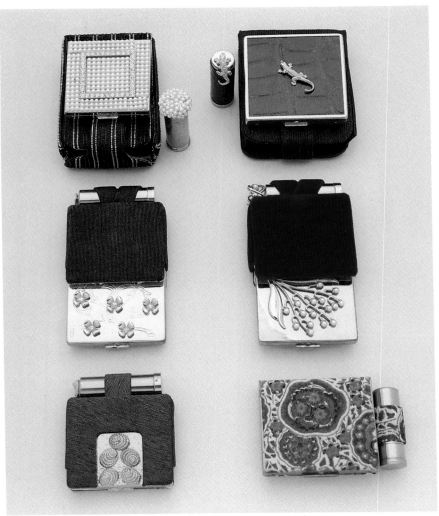

1   4
2   5
3   6

1. Dorset Fifth Avenue – Goldtone, Loose Powder Vanity Kit. Faux pearl pavé lid panel with center rhinestone frame, lipstick with top floret cluster, black and lurex faille carrier, flap snap, signed blue satin liner, no case I.D., puff with logo, case glued beveled mirror, 2¼" sq. x ½", $50.00 – 65.00.

A failed clone attempt at the majestic Ciners.

2. Flato – Goldtone, Loose Powder Vanity Kit. Affixed rhinestone centered Dogwood blooms, exterior lipstick tube with bloom, black faille carrier, ivory liner, everything signed, framed mirror, 2½" x 2⅛" x ⅜", Ref.: 1948 Ad., $175.00 – 200.00.

3. Flato – Goldtone, Loose Powder Vanity Kit. Affixed sea shells and bubbles lid motif, exterior lipstick with sea shell, green barkcloth carrier, ivory faille liner, everything signed, framed mirror, 2½" x 2⅛" x ⅜", Ref.: 1948 Ad., $200.00 – 225.00.

4. Ciner – Goldtone, Loose Powder Vanity Kit. Brown alligator lid and lipstick tube, goldtone alligator affixed to case and lipstick tube, brown faille carrier, satin liner, everything signed, framed mirror, 2¾" sq. x ½", $150.00 – 175.00.

5. Flato – Goldtone, Loose Powder Vanity Kit. Affixed faux pearl lily-of-the-valley bijou, exterior lipstick with tiara (lacquer shadow on case), red velvet carrier, ivory faille liner, everything signed, framed mirror, 2½" x 2⅛" x ½", $125.00 – 150.00.

A slippage in classic Flato quality and design.

6. Britemode – Goldtone, Loose Powder Vanity Kit. Encased Madras fabric, exterior lipstick, no case I.D., puff with logo, case glued mirror, 2¾" x 2⅜" x ⅝", $50.00 – 65.00.

1
3
2

1. Atomette – Goldtone, Loose Powder Purse Kit. Affixed faux sapphire and diamanté circlet bijou, lipstick and perfume atomizer with circlet, black faille carrier, tan liner, everything signed, framed mirror, carrier 4⅜" x 2¾" x 1⅛", Ref.: Pat. 1941. $275.00 – 300.00.

2. Richard Hudnut – Goldtone, Loose Powder Purse Kit. "Tree of Life," faux cabochon emerald affixed bijou, lipstick with like design, ivory and gold Lurex damask carrier, ivory satin liner, snap flap, everything signed, framed mirror, carrier 4¼" x 3" x 1", $175.00 – 200.00.

3. Coty – Goldtone, Loose Powder Purse Kit. Five-piece set of compact, lipstick ,and rouge case, etched glass perfume flacon with cord attached prong mounted emerald, "Emeraude," plastic comb, coin purse, red, blue, and green Lurex balls on black faille carrier, black satin liner, framed mirrors, everything signed, carrier 5" x 3¼" x 1½", Ref.: 1951 Ad., $250.00 – 275.00.

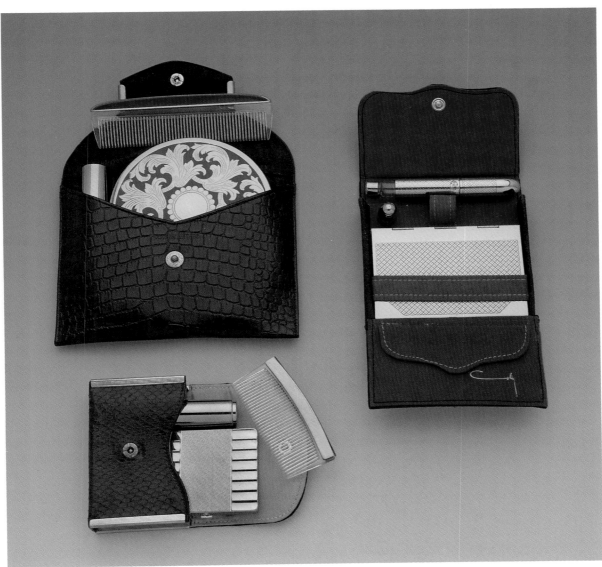

1
2　3

1. Rex Fifth Avenue – Goldtone, Loose Powder Purse Kit. Three-piece set of red enameled rococo flapjack, lipstick, and red topped comb, black alligator embossed leather carrier, black moiré liner, goldtone monogram flap snap, no case I.D., carrier signed, puff with logo, case glued beveled mirror, carrier 5¾" x 4¼" x ½", $100.00 – 150.00.

2. Majestic – Goldtone, Loose Powder Purse Kit. Three-piece set of compact, lipstick, and goldtone topped comb, navy blue snakeskin carrier, with ribbed sides, ivory liner, everything signed, case glued mirror, carrier 3½" x 2¼" x 1⅛", $75.00 – 100.00.

3. Coty – Goldtone, Loose Powder Purse Kit. Memo book, woven texture with corner guards and spine cartouche, tube breaks at center for lipstick and glass perfume flacon, "Chypre," navy faille carrier with red liner, everything signed, framed mirror, carrier 4" x 3½" x 1", Ref.: 1950 Ad. (var.), $250.00 – 275.00.

Coty had huge splashy Christmas ads with many of their designer cases repackaged into these kits while adding containers for their popular perfume and lipstick lines.

The Delineator, 1925

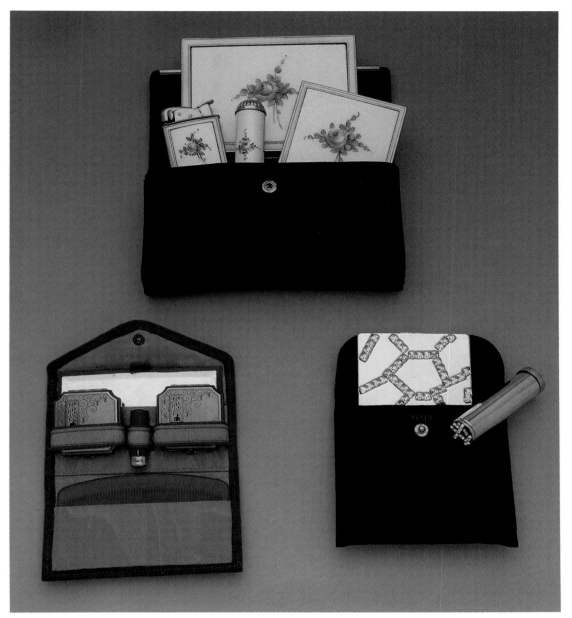

2

1   3

1. Lanchère – Goldtone, Pressed Powder Purse Kit.
Five-piece set of compact, rouge, lipstick, suede backed beveled mirror, and faux tortoise-shell comb, cases and lipstick signed "Flair," tan suede carrier, beige watered silk liner, box: # X100 tan, carrier 4¼" x 1¾" x ¾", $225.00 – 250.00.

2. Evans – Goldtone, Loose Powder Purse Kit.
"Clutchette," five-piece set of compact, lipstick, cigarette case, lighter, and comb, white cloisonne enameling with white enameled borders, everything signed, framed mirror, black satin carrier with goldtone snap flap bar, carrier 6" x 3½" x 1", Ref.: 1950 Ad., $250.00 – 300.00.

3. Flato – White Metal, Loose Powder Purse Kit.
Two-piece set of compact and lipstick tube, lid has random strands of emerald-cut baguettes, repeated on lipstick top, everything signed, framed mirror, black faille coin purse carrier, carrier 4" x 3½" x 1", $250.00 – 275.00.

A Flato digression from the classic "sleeve" carriers and abstract case design; no reference date – yet.

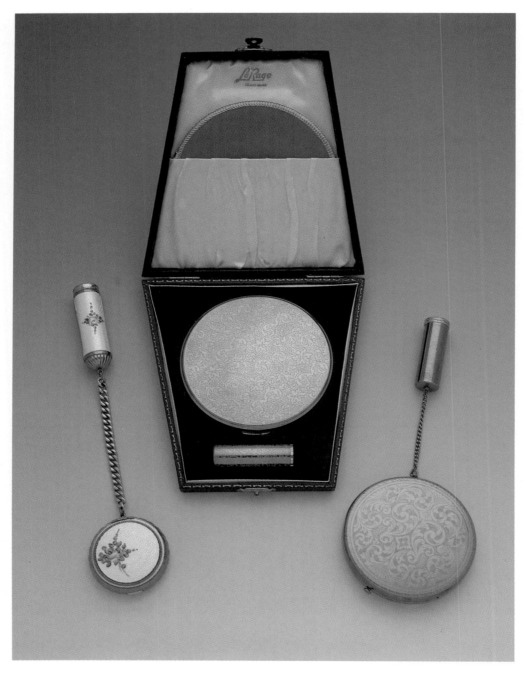

1   2   3

1. Evans – Goldtone, Loose Powder Pendant Vanity. White cloisonné with pink rosebud motif, heavy link chain, convex ribbed case sides, double paneled lipstick, no case I.D., puff with logo, case glued mirror, 2" dia x ⅝", Ref.: 1952 Ad., $125.00 – 150.00.

2. Le Rage (U.K.) – Goldtone Presentation Box. Two-piece set of white lace lid transfer on flapjack and lipstick, everything signed, faux black leather presentation box, gilt trim, brass lock, ivory taffeta and maroon liners, pocket for pouch, flapjack 4" dia. x ⅜", boxed 6¼" x 6" x 3¾" x 1⅜", $200.00 – 225.00.

3. Dorset Fifth Avenue – Goldtone, Loose Powder Pendant Vanity. Domed case with link chain, unadorned lipstick, case signed, puff with logo, case glued mirror, 3⅛" dia. x ⅝", $75.00 – 100.00.

Carson Pirie Scott 1928 catalog

1
2   3
4

5
6

1. Elgin American – Bimetal, Pressed Powder Pendant Vanity. 14K gold filled lid, moiré effect, broad bar link chain, gold wash interior, lipstick and eyebrow crayon tubes, case signed "E.A.M.," framed mirror, 2½" sq. x ½", see #5 open, $100.00 – 125.00.

2. Unmarked – Goldtone, Pressed Powder Pendant Vanity. See P111 #5 closed.

3. Unmarked – Goldtone, Pressed Powder Pendant Can. Sphinx and pyramids with lotus flower lid design, traces of green and yellow enamel, ball wrist chain, replacement tassel, framed mirror, 2½" dia. x ⅝", $175.00 – 200.00.

> *Although Egypt had been a popular European winter resort since the 1880s, with Howard Carter"s tomb find in 1922, the cosmetic industry joined the design craze with various pseudo-Egyptian products.*

4. Marathon – White Metal, Loose Powder Pendant Vanity. Saddle bag, center affixed faux jade and marcasite bijou, broad bar link chain, gold wash interior, lipstick and eyebrow crayon tubes, puffs with embroidery, case signed, framed mirror, 3¼" x 2¼" x ⅝", $175.00 – 200.00.

5. Elgin American – Bimetal, Pressed Powder Pendant Vanity. See #1 closed for information.

6. Marathon – White Metal, Loose Powder Pendant Vanity. Shield, encased red and black champlevé enamel, beveled shoulders, medium bar chain, gold wash interior, lipstick tube, case signed, framed metallic mirror, see P111 #1 open, 3⅝" x 2¼" x ⅝", Ref.: 1928 Cat., $225.00 – 250.00.

```
1        3        5
2        4        6
                  7
```

1. Marathon – White Metal, Loose Powder Pendant Vanity. See P110 #6 closed for information.

2. Unmarked – White Metal, Pressed Powder Pendant Vanity. Gold wash finish, domed blue cloisonné lid bijou, link chain, framed mirror, 2⅛" sq. x ⅜", Ref.: 1927 Cat., $35.00 – 50.00.

3. Evans – White Metal, Loose Powder Pendant Vanity. Art Deco green champlevé enamel motif, domed beveled case, ring link chain, no case I.D., molded metallic mirror with rouge disk inset, 2⅛" dia. x ⅜", Ref.: 1932 Cat., $65.00 – 90.00.

4. Unmarked – Goldtone, Pressed Powder Pendant Can. Oriental lid scene in black and red tints, black braided wrist cord, silk tassel, framed mirror, 2⅜" dia. x ½", $175.00 – 200.00.

5. Unmarked – Goldtone, Pressed Powder Pendant Vanity. Saddle bag, domed case, woven lid motif, link chain with ring, swivel framed mirror, see P110 #2 open, 2½" x 2" x ¾", Ref.: 1926 Pat., $100.00 – 125.00.

6. Bliss Bros. – Goldtone, Loose Powder Pendant Vanity. Encased ivory enamel, chinoiserie lid design, domed case, small bar chain with ring, gold wash interior, side hinged double metallic mirrors, case signed "BBCo," 1¾" dia. x ⅜", $65.00 – 80.00.

7. Norida – Goldtone, Loose Powder Pendant Vanity. Domed engine-turned case with vertical black accents, small link ring chain, no case I.D., puff with logo, framed mirror, 2" dia. x ½", $45.00 – 60.00.
A very early Norida case without their much advertised "Can't Spill" powder control apparatus.

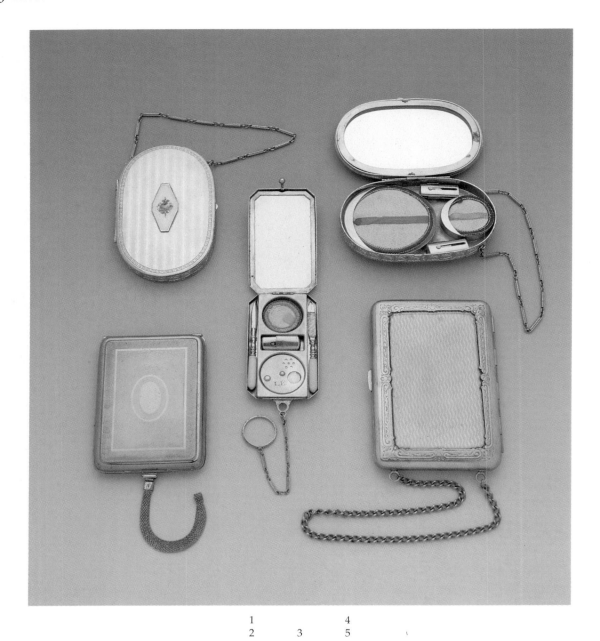

1
2   3   4
         5

1. D.F. Briggs Co. – White Metal, Pressed Powder Pendant Vanity. Oval case, cloisonné lid bijou, lipstick and eyebrow crayons, broad bar chain, case signed "D.F.B.," framed mirror, see #4 open, 4⅛" x 2⅝" x ⅜", $150.00 – 175.00.

2. Vivaudou – Goldtone, Pressed Powder Pendant Vanity. Moiré pattern with borders, oval lid cartouche, mesh wrist chain, hinged rouge well signed "Pattie Duette – Flat – Vivadou," framed mirror, 3⅝" x 2¾" x ½", see P113 #1 open, Ref.: 1923 Pat., $150.00 – 175.00.

3. Unmarked – White Metal, Loose Powder Pendant Vanity. Scenic cloisonne lid plaque, medium bar ring chain, see P113 #3 closed for information.

4. D.F. Briggs Co. – White Metal, Pressed Powder Pendant Vanity. See #1 closed for information.

5. Unmarked – Goldtone, Loose Powder Pendant Vanity. Lid insets of peach faux guilloché enameled panels under celluloid, gold wash finish, link chain, purple leather card case in lid, three coin holders, hinged powder well with pleated silk puff, Ivorene writing slate, framed mirror, 4½" x 3" x ½", see P113 #4 open, $275.00 – 300.00.

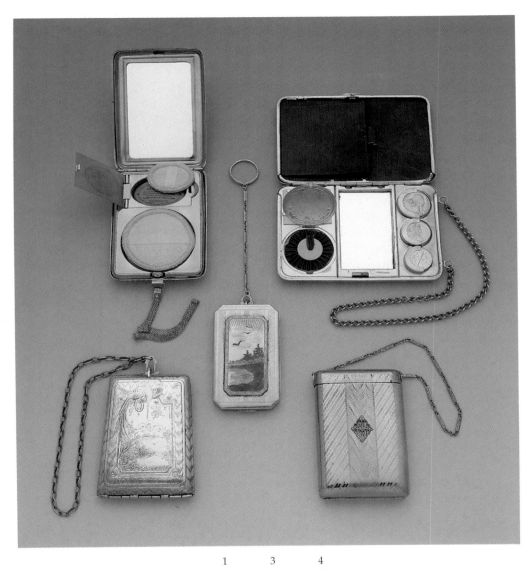

1   3   4
2   5

1. Vivaudou – Goldtone, Pressed Powder Pendant Vanity. See P112 #2 closed for information.

2. Unmarked – White Metal, Loose Powder Pendant Vanity. Tropical lid scene with bird of paradise, link chain, two coin holders, powder chamois hinged compartment, affixed framed oval mirror, 2½" x 3¼" x 2¼" x ½", $100.00 – 125.00.

3. Unmarked – White Metal, Loose Powder Pendant Vanity. Scenic cloisonné lid plaque, medium bar ring chain, ivory handle nail file and knife, oval lipstick tube, framed metallic mirror, see P112 #3 open, 3" x 1¾" x ⅜", $250.00 – 275.00.

4. Unmarked – Goldtone, Loose Powder Pendant Vanity. See P112 #5 closed for information.

5. Terri – White Metal, Pressed Powder Pendant Vanity. Coved case with spring action top opener, center moiré motif panel, marcasite bijou, gold wash finish, square moiré patterned lipstick, card case behind framed mirror, broad bar chain, embossed rouge and powder with logo, no case I.D., 3½" x 2¼" x ⅝", $125.00 – 150.00.
Several older cases have a gold wash. As fads go the silver cases became passé for a short time and the local jeweler dipped many a fine case. The wash now looks like tarnish but should not be cleaned as such.

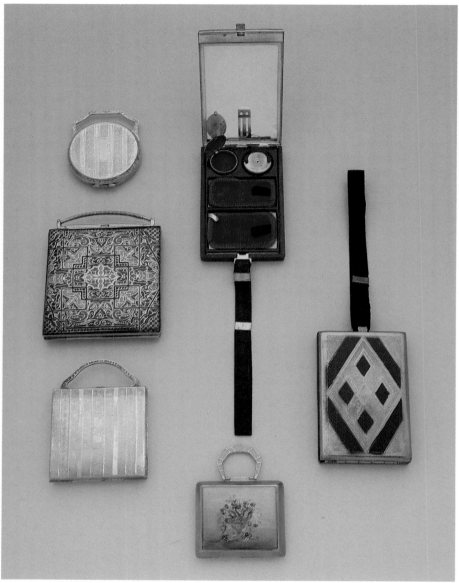

```
1      4      6
2
3      5
```

1. Unmarked Elgin American – White Metal, Pressed Powder Rigid Handle Case. Encased vertical bands, monogram cartouche, framed mirror, 2¼" dia. x ½", $50.00 – 65.00.

2. Unmarked – Goldtone, Loose Powder Spring Handle Case. Padded leather, multicolor and gilt stamped lid, green reverse, handle acts as opener, paper framed affixed mirror, 3½" x 3¼" x ⅝", $75.00 – 90.00.

3. Elgin American – White Metal, Pressed Powder Rigid Handle Vanity. Vertical case bands, monogram cartouche, case signed "E.A.M.," see P110 #5 open, 2½" sq. x ½", $45.00 – 60.00.

4. Terri – Bakelite, Pressed Powder Pendant Vanity. See #6 closed for dimension and price information.

5. La Mode – Goldtone, Loose Powder Rigid Handle Vanity. Green cloisonné lid with flower urn, white faux guilloché reverse, beveled shoulders, cloisonné handle, hinged lipstick case, side hinged double metallic mirrors, case signed, rouge with logo, 2¼" sq. x ½", $200.00 – 250.00.

6. Terri – Bakelite, Pressed Powder Pendant Vanity. Goldtone lid with black enamel accents, grosgrain wrist ribbon (this interior varies with #4, round pressed powder, rouge and lidded creme rouge, and no coin holder), framed mirror, no case I.D., logo on pressed cosmetics, 3¾" x 2⅜" x ⅝", $100.00 – 125.00.

1	2	4	6
	3	5	

1. Evans – Goldtone, Pressed Powder Pendant Vanity Can. Rococo lid motif, triangular monogram cartouche, small link wrist chain and tassel, interior double access, hinged framed mirrors, papers "Mayfair London," no case I.D., 2½" dia. x ¾", $175.00 – 200.00.

2. Evans – White Metal, Pressed Powder Pendant Vanity. Triangular case, rococo lid motif with center crest, snake wrist chain, mesh tassel, side hinged framed mirrors, no case I.D., 2⅞" tri. x ⅝", $100.00 – 125.00.

> *The Evans pendant Vanity Cases are usually unsigned, but can be identified by the embossed woven reverse pattern. Also Mayfair is the Evans trademark.*

3. Blackinton – Sterling Silver, Pressed Powder Pendant Vanity Can. Double access, black enameled lid, flower basket motif, flanged case, rod link wrist chain, mesh tassel with faceted cap, pressed patens affixed by snap action, double framed mirrors, hallmarked, 2" dia. x ⅝", $225.00 – 250.00.

4. Evans – White Metal, Pressed Powder Pendant Vanity. Snuff box, domed case, monogram cartouche, link ring chain, mesh tassel, felt and Ivorene topped puffs, no case I.D., framed mirror, 2¾" x 1½" x ⅝", $100.00 – 125.00.

5. Evans – Goldtone, Pressed Powder Pendant Vanity Can. Champlevé lid enameled rosettes, center blue/silver glass disk, link wrist chain, hand-painted wood teardrop, no case I.D., hinged framed mirror, 2" dia. x ⅝", Rare.

6. Evans – White Metal, Pressed Powder Pendant Vanity Can. Intaglio lid design of Egyptian motifs of winged falcon (son of Horus), pyramid, lotus border, mesh wrist chain, matching tassel, papers "Mayfair London," no case I.D., 2½" dia. x ¾", $250.00 – 275.00.

1	4	7
2	5	8
3	6	9

1. Unmarked Ripley and Gowen Co. – White Metal, Loose Powder Pendant Vanity. Baroque, hinged lid inset, cloisonné center oval disk, medium bar ring chain, chased beveled sides, no case I.D., framed mirror, 2⅛" x 1⅞" x ⅜", $65.00 – 80.00.

R. & G. Co. does not always have a flat surface for a logo; compare with other signed cases.

2. Unmarked – Silver-plated, Pressed Powder Pendant Can. Domed hammered case, lid crest, ring link chain, original glass paten and ribboned felt puff, framed mirror, 1½" dia. x ¾", $75.00 – 100.00.

3. E.B.M.Co. – White Metal, Loose Powder Pendant Vanity. Gold wash case, Art Deco femme and dog lid motif, beveled borders, single bar ring chain, signed, framed mirror, 2¼" x 1¾" x ½", $125.00 – 150.00.

4. E.B.M.Co. – White Metal, Loose Powder Pendant Vanity. Art Moderne geometric case motif, beveled borders, small link wrist chain, case signed, case affixed metallic mirror with rouge circle inset, 2" sq. x ⅜", $100.00 – 125.00.

5. Unmarked – White Metal, Pressed Powder Pendant Vanity. Pierced rococo lid crown, guilloché lunette scenic lid panel, broad bar wrist chain, framed mirror, 3" x 2⅛" (w/crown 2⅝") x 1", $100.00 – 125.00.

6. Evans – White Metal, Loose Powder Pendant Vanity. Domed case, niello beveled borders, guilloché lid inset, small bar ring chain, framed lunette mirror with rouge circle inset, 2¼" dia. x ⅜", Ref.: 1929 Cat., $75.00 – 100.00.

7. R.M.Co. – White Metal, Loose Powder Pendant Vanity. Shield, guilloché scenic lid panel, gold airplane fillip, coved sides, small bar ring chain, case signed, framed mirror, 2¼" x 2" x ⅜", $150.00 – 175.00.

8. Ballou Mfg. Co. – Gold-filled, Loose Powder Pendant Can. Domed case, initialed lid cartouche, link ring chain, case signed "B. Mfg. Co.," framed convex metallic mirror, 1½" dia. x ⅜", $125.00 – 150.00.

9. Wightman and Hough Co. – White Metal, Pressed Powder Pendant Vanity. Snuff box, flange opener, monogram cartouche, mesh wrist band, slide-out exterior lipstick tube, case signed "W & H Co.," framed mirror, 2¾" x 1¾" x ½", $65.00 – 90.00.

1	3	5
2	4	6

1. Unmarked – White Metal, Pressed Powder Pendant Vanity. Cloisonné lid panel, link wrist chain, framed mirror with pressed rouge and coin insets, 2⅛" sq. x ⅜", Ref.: 1927 Cat., $50.00 – 65.00.

2. Evans – White Metal, Pressed Powder Pendant Vanity. Silhouette duo scene, celluloid cover, champlevé enameled border, link ring chain, papers "Mayfair Evans," no case I.D., lunette framed mirror, pressed rouge inset, 2" dia. x ½", $75.00 – 100.00.

3. Finberg Mfg. Co. – White Metal, Loose Powder Pendant Vanity. White and black cloisonné lid panels, link wrist chain, signed "FMCO," framed lunette mirror, oval rouge inset, 2½" sq. x ½", $125.00 – 150.00.

4. International Silver Co. – Sterling, Pressed Powder Pendant Vanity. Domed octagon case, double access, bar link wrist chain, femme lid silhouette, rouge top case, framed mirror, gold wash powder interior, round framed affixed mirror, hallmarked, 2" oct. x ¾", $225.00 – 250.00.

5. Evans – Sterling, Loose Powder Pendant Vanity. Cloisonné domed case, baroque engraved lid inset, link wrist chain, "Tap-Sift" interior, side hinged double metallic mirrors, case signed, 2¼" sq. x ½", Ref.: 1932 Cat., $250.00 – 275.00.

6. E.B.M.Co. – White Metal, Loose Powder Pendant Vanity. Saddlebag, Art Deco lid motif of walking femme, stars, and enameled flora, beveled border, bar ring chain, 2⅞" x 2" x ½", $125.00 – 150.00.

```
        1           5
        2     4     6
        3           7
```

1. Elgin American – White Metal, Loose Powder Pendant Vanity. Shield, Art Moderne lid, enameled side panels, bar link wrist chain, case signed "E.A.M.," bottom hinged double metallic mirrors, 2¼" x 2¼" x ⅜", Ref.: 1929 Cat. (var.), $125.00 – 150.00.

2. Elgin American – White Metal, Loose Powder Pendant Vanity. Art Moderne cerise and pink enameled lid motifs, bar link wrist chain, case signed "E.A.M," framed mirror, 2⅛" x 1¾" x ⅜", Ref.: 1930 Cat., $150.00 – 175.00.

3. Unmarked Evans – White Metal, Loose Powder Pendant Vanity. Multicolor cloisonné lid bands, link wrist chain, lunette framed mirror, rouge inset, 2⅛" sq. x ½", $150.00 – 175.00.

4. Elgin American – White Metal, Loose Powder Pendant Vanity. Art Deco bird-of-paradise enameled lid motif, bar link wrist chain, hinged comb holder, case signed "E.A.M.," framed mirror, 3" x 1¾" x ½", Ref.: 1930 Cat., $225.00 – 250.00.

5. Elgin American – White Metal, Loose Powder Pendant Vanity. Art Deco enameled opposing birds-of-paradise, lid panels, bar link wrist chain, case signed "E.A.M.," bottom hinged double metallic mirrors, 2" sq. x ⅜", $200.00 – 225.00.

6. Volupté – White Metal, Loose Powder Pendant Vanity. Art Moderne encased red enamel, multicolor accents, scalloped domed case, detachable bar ring chain, no case I.D., papers, lunette framed mirror, rouge inset, 2⅛" sq. x ⅜", Ref.: 1932 Cat., $200.00 – 225.00.

7. Elgin American – White Metal, Loose Powder Pendant Vanity. Art Moderne champlevé enameled lid, bar link wrist chain, case signed "Elginite," framed mirror, 3" x 2¼" x ⅜", Ref.: 1930 Cat., $250.00 – 275.00.

```
1    3    5
2    4    6
```

1. J.M. Fisher – White Metal, Loose Powder Pendant Vanity. Lid scene of "The Mutt," crimped link ring chain, 2¼" dia. x ½", Ref.: 1929 Cat., $275.00 – 300.00.

2. J.M. Fisher – White Metal, Loose Powder Pendant Vanity. Lid scene of "Viking Ship," single bar ring chain, oval lipstick tube, 2¼" x 2" x ½", Ref.: 1929 Cat., $275.00 – 300.00.

3. J.M. Fisher – White Metal, Loose Powder Pendant Vanity. Lid scene of stylized flora with femme silhouette figure, broad bar ring chain, attached mauve and black lipstick tube, blue velvet lined Art Moderne patterned box, no box, foil sticker, or name I.D., 2¾" x 2⅛" x ½", $350.00 – 375.00.

4. J.M. Fisher – White Metal, Loose Powder Pendant Vanity. Saddlebag, lid scene of "When Knighthood Was in Flower," chased border, broad link wrist chain, oval lipstick and solid perfume tubes, 2⅞" x 2¼" x ½", Ref.: 1932 Cat., $250.00 – 275.00.

5. J.M. Fisher – White Metal, Loose Powder Pendant Vanity. Lid scene of "Mary Wa Lee," single bar ring chain, oval lipstick, 2¾" x 1¾" x ½", Ref.: 1932 Cat., $250.00 – 275.00.

6. J.M. Fisher – White Metal, Loose Powder Pendant Vanity. Art Moderne geometric lid scene, single bar ring chain, 2½" x 1⅞" x ½", $275.00 – 300.00.

All the cases have multicolor champlevé enameled lids and engine-turned banded reverse, framed metallic mirrors, no case I.D. other than through cat. views. The company christened those cases which have names. Enamel is very fragile.

1   2   4
3

1. Evans – White Metal, Loose Powder Pendant Vanity. Domed case, brown enameled lid and lipstick tube, cloisonné oval disk, crimped chain, bottom hinged double metallic mirrors, papers "Mayfair Evans," no case I.D., 2¼" x 2⅛" x ½", $100.00 – 125.00.

2. Richard Hudnut – White Metal, Pressed Powder Pendant Vanity. Guilloché case lid and lipstick tube, broad bar detachable chain, case signed "Deauville," puffs with logo, bottom hinged framed mirror, signed damask and paper presentation box, see P121 #1 closed box, 2⅛" dia. x ⅝", Ref.: 1924 Pat., $175.00 – 200.00.

3. Evans – White Metal, Loose Powder Pendant Vanity. Cushion, champlevé enameled case, faux moon-

stone capped enameled lipstick carrier containing oval tube, crimped chain, Art Moderne lid inset, side hinged double metallic mirrors, no case I.D., 2¼" sq. x ⅜", Ref.: 1932 Cat., $125.00 – 150.00.

4. Finberg Mfg. Co. – Goldtone, Loose Powder Pendant Vanity. Domed guilloché case, cloisonné lid inset and paneled lipstick tube, small bar chain, lunette framed mirror, rouge inset, case signed "FMCO," 2" dia. x ½", $250.00 – 275.00.

Another outstanding example of American artistry. Case might be vermeil, but no sterling markings.

1
2   3   4
5

1. Richard Hudnut – Deauville Presentation Box. See P120 #2 open.

2. Unmarked – White Metal, Loose Powder Pendant Vanity. Enameled domed case and lipstick tube, champlevé enamel tiger lily lid motif, framed mirror, 2" dia. x ⅜", $50.00 – 65.00.

3. Evans – White Metal, Loose Powder Pendant Vanity. Domed beveled case, enameled lipstick tube and lid, bas relief love birds, crimped chain, rouge with embossed "Mayfair Evans," side hinged double metallic mirrors, no case I.D., 2⅛" dia. x ½", Ref.: 1932 Cat., $75.00 – 100.00.

4. Evans – White Metal, Loose Powder Pendant Vanity. Domed case, enameled lid inset and oval lipstick tube carrier, niello effect on center flower urn and sloped borders, crimped chain, no case I.D., side hinged double metallic mirrors, 2¼" dia. x ½", Ref.: 1931 Cat., $125.00 – 150.00.
Very transitional case — classic front and modern reverse. Any of these Evans cases missing the oval lipsticks in the carrier should be decreased by $25.00.

5. Evans – White Metal, Loose Powder Pendant Vanity. Enameled lid and lipstick carrier, Art Deco femme silhouette lid motif, crimped chain, no case I.D., side hinge double metallic mirrors, 2⅛" sq. x ⅜", Ref.: 1932 Cat., $125.00 – 150.00.

Parfums — of particular choice • Parfum LE DEBUT...
A perfume from Paris — a new creation in fragrance. Four separate and distinct *odeurs* to express the four loveliest of feminine moods. Created, sealed and packaged in the Paris *laboratoire* of Richard Hudnut.

Le *Début* Bleu ○ *in blue flacon* ○ *Romance*
Le *Début* Vert ○ *in green flacon* ○ *Adventure*
Le *Début* Blanc ○ *in white flacon* ○ *Gaiety*
Le *Début* Noir ○ *in black flacon* ○ *Sophistication*

THREE SIZES: $3.75—$7.50—$12.50

le Début

The new vogue for colorful compactes • Compacte LE DEBUT expressing the smart vogue for colorful compactes to blend with the costume. Finished in gold or silver, their tops are in four colors of genuine *cloisonné*: Blue, black, jade green and ivory white. Refills of powder and rouge in the popular shades... in a delightful blend of the four *odeurs* of *Parfum* LE DEBUT.

PRICE $5.00
(enameled dotted top $2.50)

NEW THINGS ... *for the lovely lady of fashion!*

New things ... Lovely things ... Quite as adorable, as utterly charming and graceful as the new mode itself! ... Now they are ready for you:

A trig little compacte with a colorful top to blend smartly with the costume ... Perfume in the gay modern manner of Paris and the other capitals of fashion ... a caressing *nuance* of *scent* to catch up and express the spirit of a mood, whatever the mood may be!

Or, if you wish, the new colorful creation in lip sticks—to blend happily with the four colors of *Compacte* LE DEBUT ... A happy family these—*compacte* and *parfum* and *lip stick* LE DEBUT—in tune with the new vogue that completes the *ensemble* of costume ... A happy family that lovely ladies everywhere will adore!

You will find them at the better shops.

A new creation in lip sticks • Lip Stick LE DEBUT ... Four lip sticks with the wit to be charming and colorful ... to blend happily with the four colors of *Compacte* LE DEBUT ... in the popular shades.

PRICE $2.50
... And refills, too! ... A unique, completely new feature.

RICHARD HUDNUT • *Parfumeur* • NEW YORK • PARIS

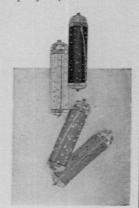

Harper's Bazaar, 1928

1   2   4
3

1. Richard Hudnut – Goldtone, Pressed Powder Pendant Vanity. "DuBarry Beauty Box," center monogram cartouche, detachable ring chain, carrier for removable lipstick tube and eyebrow crayon, silk lined presentation box, everything signed, case 3⅜" x 1⅜" x ⅝", box 4½" x 3" x 1", Ref.: 1930 Ad., $150.00 – 175.00.

2. Richard Hudnut – Goldtone, Pressed Powder Vanity. "le Début," stepped octagon case, black and gold cloisonné lid, logo embossed powder and rouge, top hinged framed mirror, gold foil presentation box, everything signed, case 2" oct. x ⅝", box 3" oct. x 1", Ref.: 1928 Ad., $175.00 – 200.00.

3. Richard Hudnut – Goldtone, Pressed Powder Pendant Vanity. "le Début," stepped octagon case, green

and gold cloisonné lid and attached lipstick tube, bar wrist chain, same interior, size and reference as #2, $150.00 – 175.00.

4. Richard Hudnut – White Metal, Pressed Powder Pendant Vanity. "le Début," cushion, octagon, enameled case, champlevé lid inset and lipstick panels, wind rose motif, ring carrier, spring action lid and interior framed mirror, logo embossed powder and rouge, leather topped puffs with logo, navy blue leather presentation box, ivory silk moiré liner, everything signed, case 2¼" oct. x ½", box 6¼" x 3¼" x ¾", $300.00 – 350.00.

This case does not appear in the le Début 1928 Ad. blitz. The patent date is 1926, and the case design is different; might have been included later in the salon sales.

1   3

2   4

1. Richard Hudnut – White Metal, Pressed Powder Pendant Vanity. "le Début," "Chatelaine," blue and ivory cloisonné lid inset, bar ring chain, same interior, size and reference as P123 #2, blue flocked silver foil lined presentation box, everything signed, box 6½" x 3¾" x 1⅜", $225.00 – 250.00.

2. Richard Hudnut – White Metal, Pressed Powder Vanity. "le Début," ivory and green cloisonné, same interior, size, and reference as P123 #2, gray flocked silver foil presentation box, everything signed, box 2¾" sq. x 1⅛", $150.00 – 175.00.

This also comes in a rare ivory and white center combination.

3. Richard Hudnut – White Metal, Pressed Powder Pendant Vanity. See #1 for case information, silver foil presentation box 4" x 3¼" x 1⅛", $175.00 – 200.00.

4. Richard Hudnut – Goldtone, Pressed Powder Pendant Vanity. See #1 for case information, $125.00 – 150.00 (without box).

le Début

Double Compacte le Début • *finished in gold or silver, topped with genuine cloisonné, of four colors: blue, black, green or white. Practical refills of powder and rouge. Price $5.00.*

Chatelaine le Début • *Double Compacte and Lip Stick . . . green, blue, white or black . . . joined by a graceful chain . . . refills for both . . . powder loose or compact. Price $10.00. Lip Stick alone $2.50; Compacte alone—with chain—$7.50.*

Parfum le Début • *four individual odeurs, each expressing a lovely feminine mood—Romance, Adventure, Gaiety, Sophistication . . . each in a flacon of symbolic hue. And Compacte le Début, in blue or green. Price $20.00.*

RICHARD HUDNUT PARFUMEUR

NEW YORK PARIS

Gifts . . .

THAT FASHION HAS A FINGER IN!

Here are gifts that women love to give . . and hope to *get*— (with implicit faith in their own particular Santa Claus!)

There is a whole happy family of things called *le Début* (remember that name!) — offered in varied gift ensembles in attractive gift packages.

A perfume created, sealed and packaged in Paris . . . in four individual *odeurs* to express the four loveliest of feminine moods. Compactes with gay, colorful tops of *cloisonné* in four smart colors that will harmonize with every frock. And a gay little lip stick (refillable) in the same four colors.

Each blends happily with each — and all complete the smart perfection of the *ensemble* . . . You will find all of these and other lovely *le Début* gifts at any of the better shops.

Ladies' Home Journal, 1928

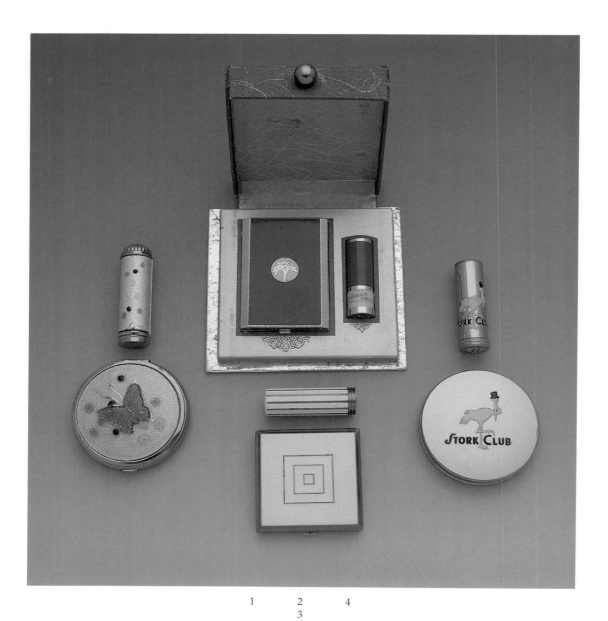

1   2   4
3

1. Evans – Goldtone, Loose Powder Compact and Lipstick. Domed case and paneled lipstick, cloisonné enameled multicolored dots and raised butterfly, case only signed, puff with logo, case glued mirror, no lipstick I.D., case 2½" dia. x ⅝", set $100.00 – 125.00.

2. Langlois – White Metal, Gift Presentation Set. Beveled enameled loose powder vanity and lipstick, ivory champlevé enameled lid logo, signed "Cara Nome," framed mirror, Art Moderne presentation box, silver foil and blue padded lid, no I.D., case 2⅞" x 2" x ½", box 4" x 3" x 1¼", complete $150.00 – 175.00.

3. Lorie, Inc. – Goldtone, Loose Powder Vanity and Lipstick. Ivory champlevé enameled lid and paneled tube, everything hinge signed or labeled "Adrienne," top hinged double metallic mirrors, case 2⅜" dia. x ½", set $75.00 – 100.00.

4. Cigogne, Inc. – Goldtone, Pressed Powder Compact and Lipstick. Embossed white enameled stork, black accents and lettering, items signed and labeled "Cigogne and Stork Club," puff with Stork Club motif, case glued mirror, case 2¼" dia. x ⅝", set $175.00 – 200.00.

A New York night club with many souvenirs. Paramount Studios in 1945 used it for a thinly plotted movie.

1   2
3

1. Shulton – Goldtone, Gift Presentation Set. Three pieces consisting of pressed rouge and creme cases, and lipstick, scalloped white enameled lid motifs with flower girl lid logo, signed "Old Spice – Shulton – Desert Flower," framed mirrors, everything signed, cases 1½" dia. x ⅜" and 1⅛" dia. x ⅜", water colored waffle patterned box, box 4¼" sq. x ¾", complete $50.00 – 65.00.

2. Vivienne – Goldtone, Gift Presentation Set. Three pieces consisting of pressed powder compact, rouge case, and oval lipstick with label, dried flora with but-terfly decal under celluloid lid inset, "Ambre de Russie" papers, framed mirrors, cases 2½" dia. x ½" and 1½" dia. x ½", labeled mauve papered box 5½" x 3½" x ¾", complete $75.00 – 100.00.

3. Hampden – Goldtone, Pressed Powder Gift Presentation Set. Three pieces consisting of loose powder compact, rouge case, and lipstick, domed faceted emerald green Lucite rhinestone circlets, all signed or labeled "Passion Flower," powder puff with logo, framed mirror, cases 3" dia. x ¾" and 1⅜" dia. x ½", box 5¾" sq. x 1", complete $100.00 – 125.00.

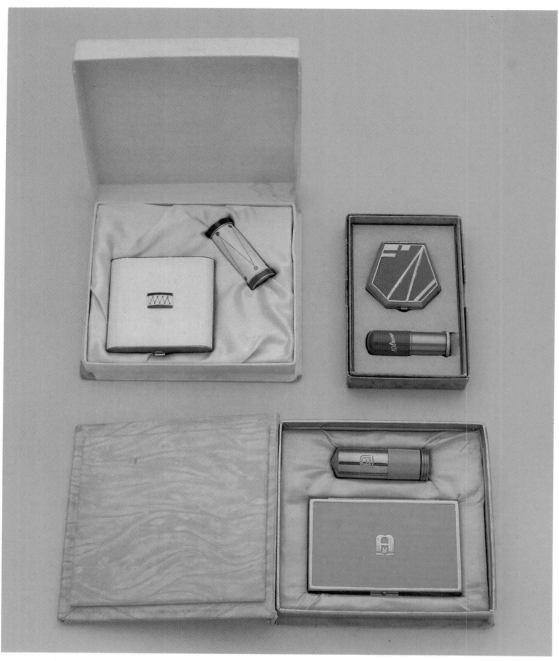

1   2
           3

1. Charbert – Goldtone, Gift Presentation Set.
Encased white enamel coved loose powder compact
and lipstick, raised drum motif, sliding powder compartment, framed mirror, marching soldier box logo,
everything signed "Drumstick," case 2¼" sq. x ¼", box
4½" x 4¼" x ⅞", Ref.: 1937 Ad., complete $125.00 –
150.00.

*This is the fifth cosmetic house in the collection that
has the pat.ed sliding powder dispenser.*

2. Milrone – White Metal, Gift Presentation Set. Saddlebag, loose powder vanity and lipstick, Art Mod-

erne champlevé enameled lid, both pieces signed, no
box I.D., top hinged double metallic mirrors, case 1¾"
x 1¾" x ½", box 4" x 2½" x ¾", complete $100.00 –
125.00.

3. Avon – Goldtone, Gift Presentation Book Set.
Loose powder vanity and lipstick, aqua enameled lid
and lipstick with "A" logo, center box lid silver seal,
everything signed, framed mirror, case 3" x 2" x ⅜",
box 4¼" sq. x 1", Ref.: 1937 Ad., complete $150.00 –
175.00.

1. THREE GIFT PERFUMES IN FAMOUS DRUM 3.00
2. PANIER ENSEMBLE. PERFUME, COLOGNE, LIPSTICK 5.00
3. MAJOR SET. PERFUME, COMPACT, LIPSTICK 5.50
4. FLORAL BOUQUET. EAU DE COLOGNE IN THREE ODORS 3.25
5. COMPACT JUNIOR AND DRUMSTICK LIPSTICK SET 2.00
6. DRUMSTICK LIPSTICK, VANITY SET, SINGLE 3.50. DOUBLE 4.00
7. BATH SET. EAU DE COLOGNE AND DRUM OF BATH POWDER, ALL ODORS 3.50

AVAILABLE AT BETTER SHOPS OR WRITE CHARBERT, 27 WEST 56th STREET, N. Y.

CHARBERT

Stage Magazine, 1937

129

1

2   3

1. Linda Lee – White Metal, Gift Presentation Set.
Three pieces consisting of loose powder vanity, rouge
case, and lipstick, domed black enameled cases,
everything signed, box with abstract logo, framed
rouge mirror, vanity with top hinged double metallic
mirrors, cases 2" dia. x ½" and 1½" dia. x ⅜", box 8" x
4¼" x ¾", Ref.: 1944 Ad., complete $125.00 – 150.00.

**2. George W. Luft Co. – Plastic, Tin, and Cardboard
Gift Presentation Set.** Three pieces called "Beauti-
Set" consisting of loose powder cardboard box, rouge
tin, and plastic lipstick, everything signed "Tangee,"
box "Mad.e in Canada," no mirrors, cases 2½" dia. x

⅝" and 1¼" dia. x ¼", box 4¾" x 3½" x ⅞", complete
$75.00 – 100.00.
    *A truly W.W. II gift set with exempt tin as the only
metal.*

**3. Richard Hudnut – White Metal, Gift Presentation
Set.** Three pieces consisting of silver foil powder box,
rouge can with framed mirror, and logo puff, paneled
Art Moderne lipstick, Art Deco votary femme logo, all
items signed "Marvelous," powder box 2⅞" dia. x
1½", rouge 1½" dia. x ⅜", box 6" x 5¼" x 1⅞", Ref.:
1937 Ad., complete $150.00 – 175.00.

Saturday Evening Post, 1933

Artist signed

Chapter Three

CARRYALLS

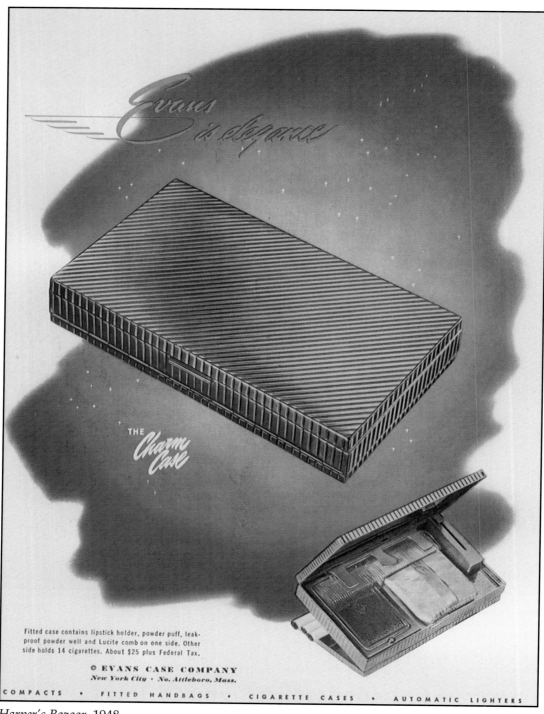

Fitted case contains lipstick holder, powder puff, leak-proof powder well and Lucite comb on one side. Other side holds 14 cigarettes. About $25 plus Federal Tax.

EVANS CASE COMPANY
New York City · No. Attleboro, Mass.

COMPACTS · FITTED HANDBAGS · CIGARETTE CASES · AUTOMATIC LIGHTERS

Harper's Bazaar, 1948

"...IT HOLDS COMPACT, LIPSTICK, LARGE WELL FOR CIGARETTES, FULL SIZE MIRROR AND A SWANSDOWN PUFF. BETTER HAVE IT MONOGRAMMED FOR IT IS A TEMPTATION."

WOMAN'S HOME COMPANION, 1934

One of the earliest manufacturers of carryalls preferred to use the slogan: "...New Ensemble Vanity — so very Parisienne!" The cases are signed "M.M.R.'S." A 1926 ad reveals that this company, *Morris–Mann & Reilly*, was out of Chicago on Wells St. Their artistry and design is superb in different mediums, from Bakelite to porcelain and the remarkable hand engine-turning work on the carryall interiors. Although a case maker, the ad states that, "...powder, lip and face rouge and 2 velvet puffs...are available at any Drug, Department or Jewelry Store." The complete refill kit was $4.75. (Not cheap for 1926!) This information gives a clear picture on how case makers were able to serve their clients. At present nothing more is known, their cases are identified only by a paper powder protector.

Terri and Mondaine carryalls went in totally different design directions. Terri also went from Bakelite to metal. The earlier cases have exterior lipstick and perfume tubes and are solidly made. Their flagship was the coved case which contained a compartment for cigarettes, finely engineered and advertised with confidence: "A Complete Vanity." The word "carryall" was not yet in the industry's lexicon.

Mondaine's carryall had few variations. They had one design per category, i.e. the book case, the round triple vanity (a rare digression in the beauty kits), and the carryall. By merely changing colors, lid insets, and case fabrics, they are easily identifiable, with or without a signature. This stodgy attitude and lack of storage kept carryalls from becoming the premier accessory until after W.W.II.

Evans, the master inventor of the carryall with variations and such elan, has almost become a generic name for the post-war carryalls. If one studies the basic design patterns that Evans used, the variations might be only in the low teens. Evans also developed the sleeve technique, whereby the core interior was interchangeably slipcased with the current decor choice. The cores were goldtone and were either single or double access depending on the price range. The top of the line had a larger core case with a lighter and a side graduated chain handle. Lastly, the "Petite" box carryall arrived still using the same slipcase concept.

The Evans sunray case was surely the favorite with many an ingenious design variation, always a surprise at its ability to change and yet be recognizable. The one sidestep was the use of leathers and snakeskin not only as case cladding but as handles. These cases are not common.

Of the big three U.S. carryall makers, Elgin is an anomaly. Almost first out of the gate, in 1929, with its magnificent early E.A.M. carriers, Elgin did not reenter until 1952 with a totally different carrier concept.

Instead of rotating its few good designs, Elgin offered too many options, different combinations of handles, finishes, and carrier cases, trying to create a custom item. Like an automobile with numerous optional features, the delay in compiling these cases might have discouraged the buyer when Volupté and Evans were waiting with boxed ready merchandise at hand.

Volupté deserves a mention for their consistency of design and handsome presentation boxes, but also in using ill-fitting cloth carriers that were glued rather than sewn and not always suited to its case. They also had a poor track record for lacquering that did not hold up to extensive handling. Considering Volupté was the only U.S. maker of the super carryall, which was carried as a clutch purse, the lacquer should have been impervious to non-gloved hands.

After World War II, Europe began to produce an amazing collection of carryalls; almost too late for a role in the market dominated by Evans and Volupté. The éclat of these cases is the complete break with U.S. images, polka dots, padded leather, black lace exteriors, silk tassels, unusual shapes, and full of clever interior fittings. Form truly follows function with these cases.

The Parklanes severe exteriors surprise with piquant interiors. Clever use of the space is evident — built-in rouge refill storage, clips for stamps, lidded well for collapsible lipstick holder, and where room is lacking for powder, a pli is used. Stratton did not stray from its conservative image and with a few others went big time with purse-like party cases and clutches. The lithographic finishes and lacquer have a tendency to become unstable with time.

The carryall story can't be complete without a comment on the aristocratic cases. Several hand-crafted cases are in view. One hallmarked sterling mini clutch has exquisite engraving both inside and out (as yet unknown). This contrasts with a highly commercial case, using costly materials to carry the artistic load with much status hype and little imaginative design.

For sheer imagination the Ostertag sterling triptych case is awesome. The Paris salon of Ostertag rivaled Cartier in producing magnificent jewelry and objets d'art during the twenties and thirties. Every item has numerous hallmarks. The gemstone ornamentation is cut out so when the lid is raised the light shines through gemstones. Unfolding the triptych is also a trip. Finely tooled to perfect balance, the mirror panels swing out and hold position. There are no exterior tabs or flanges. Imagine the gasps when this case was opened at the Ritz. It is so heavy that adjusting the mirrors by hand is not possible and any attempt might cause a case to back flip into a nearby vichyssoise.

'Tis a Pleasure to Give—

Terri Vanities will please *her* with their chic, fascinating air of exquisite smartness. Trim, dainty accessories to charm that will harmonize with *every* alluring mood of her ensemble.

If your favorite dealer cannot supply you, order direct. Write Dept. T.

TERRI, *Incorporated*
4 West 40th Street   New York

Closed

Open

Terri Oval Vanity

Exquisite leather-effect case with white or green gold plated striped design. Fitted compartments with full face mirror, face rouge, face powder, lipstick, concealed comb and place for cigarettes, keys and coins.

Price, $7.50 each

Terri VANITY

Theatre Magazine, 1925   Artist signed

1   3

2   4

1. Terri – Bakelite, Vanity Carryall. "Lido," beveled case, inset lid cartouche, silk braided wrist cord, removable exterior Bakelite lipstick in cord loop, pressed powder and rouge, side hinged metallic backed mirror, lid card case, case signed, 3¼" x 2½" x ⅞", Ref.: 1925 Ad., $150.00 – 175.00.

2. Mondaine – White Metal, Demi Carryall. Cream encased enamel, coved, raised oval deep yellow lid inset, white braided silk wrist cord, pressed powder and rouge with embossed "M," hinged compartment, case signed, framed mirror, 4" x 3" x ⅜", Ref.: 1935 Ad. (var.), $125.00 – 150.00.

3. D.F. Briggs Co. – White Metal, Demi Carryall. Center affixed plate of silhouette ballet duo, detach-able bar link ring chain, pressed powder and rouge, twin lipstick and eyebrow crayon tubes, hinged framed mirror, lid card case, signed "D.F.B. Co.," 3" x 2" x ¾", $125.00 – 150.00.

4. Terri – White Metal, Demi Carryall. Oval luggage case, faux Moroccan leather finish, black silk braided wrist cord, exterior recessed comb, pressed powder and rouge embossed signature, no case I.D., square brown Bakelite lipstick tube, hinged metallic backed mirror, 3¾" x 2½" x 1", $150.00 – 175.00.

The mint case has the original sales slip dated 7/2/30. One wonders if this case was either too treasured to use or exiled?

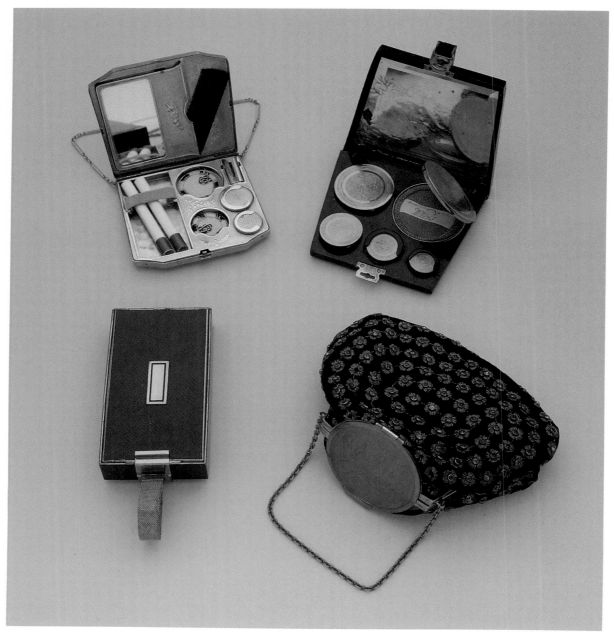

1   3
2   4

1. Elgin American – Gold-filled, Demi Carryall. See P137 #4 closed.

2. Park Lane (U.K.) – Goldtone, Demi Carryall. Black enameled case, double access, mesh wrist strap, clip closures, loose powder and pressed rouge compartments, comb, lipstick (not included) well, beveled framed mirror, reverse shown open P137 #3, postage stamp and money or card clips, cigarette well, compartment for telescoping cigarette holder, no case I.D., 4⅜" x 2½" x 1", Ref.: 1937 Pat., $300.00 – 350.00.

3. Morris–Mann & Reilly – Bakelite, Demi Carryall. See P137 #2 closed.

4. Evans – Goldtone, Pouch Carryall. Black satin pouch, rhinestone centered gold thread florets, link chain, rosetone bucolic vanity lid scene, see P137 #1 open, loose powder, rouge with "Mayfair" logo, papers, side hinged double metallic mirrors, no case I.D., pouch 4½" dia., case 2½" dia., $150.00 – 175.00.

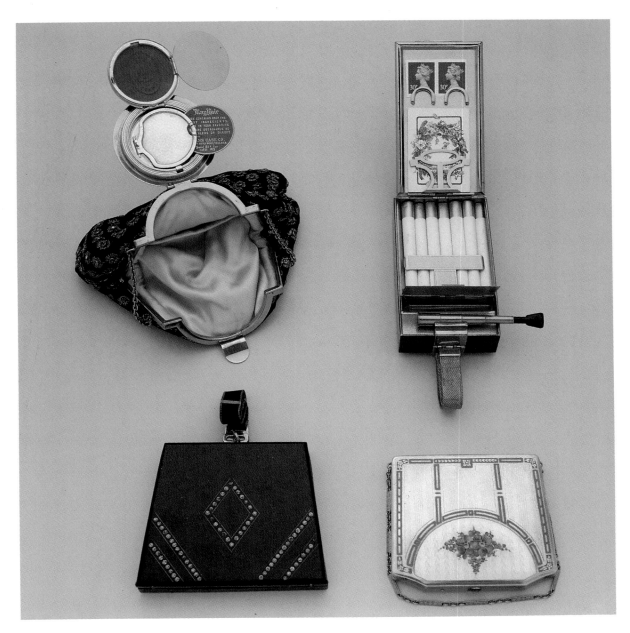

1 3
2 4

1. Evans – Goldtone, Pouch Carryall. See P136 #4 closed.

2. Morris–Mann & Reilly – Bakelite, Demi Carryall. Black case, faux citrine lid bands, black grosgrain adjustable wrist strap, pressed powder and rouge, pill box, coin holders, beveled case glued mirror, no case I.D., puffs and papers with logo "M.M.R.'s," see P136 #3 open, 4¼" x 3¼" x 3½" x ⅝", Ref.: 1926 Ad. (var.), $475.00 – 500.00.

3. Park Lane (U.K.) – Goldtone, Demi Carryall. See P136 #2 closed.

4. Elgin American – Gold-filled Demi Carryall. Lunette cloisonné lid plate, green enamel accents, broad bar link wrist chain, comb, coin holders, pressed powder and rouge, oval lipstick tube, case framed mirror, case signed, see P136 #3 open, 3¾" x 3¼" x ½", Ref.: 1929 Cat., $275.00 – 350.00.

1   3
2   4

1. Unknown (For.) – Goldtone, Clutch Carryall.
Encased white enamel and black polka dots, loose powder, pressed rouge, replacement lipstick, top hinged metallic framed beveled mirror with comb slot, ⅔ lid compartment and spring clip, hallmarked "foreign Pat.," see P139 #1 open, 4¼" x 2¼" x ⅞", $275.00 – 300.00.

2. Unmarked – White Metal, Clutch Carryall.
Padded red leather case, exterior lipstick with silk tassel (does not act as case carrier), double access, spring releases, beige kid leather lined compartment, lidded loose powder and rouge, case glued beveled mirror, 4¾" x 3¼" x ⅝", $150.00 – 175.00.

3. AGME (SW) – Goldtone, Clutch Carryall. See P139 #3 closed.

4. La Mode – Goldtone, Cylinder Carryall. Double access, top lid shell motif, large link wrist chain, attached telescoping cigarette holder tube, loose powder, no case I.D., 3½" x 1½" dia., see P139 #5 open, $225.00 – 250.00.

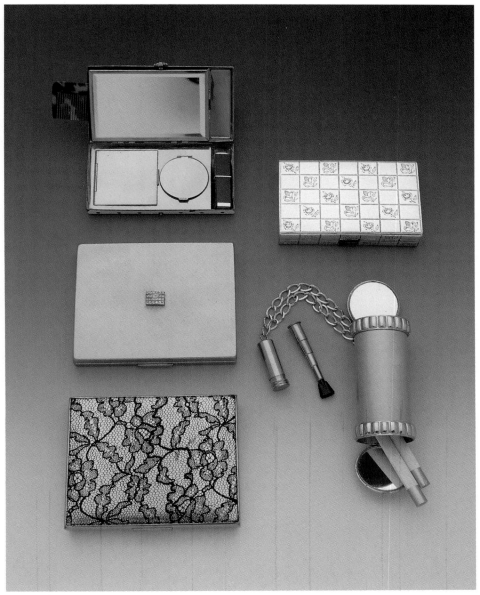

1
2
3

4
5

1. Unknown (For.) – Goldtone, Clutch Carryall. See P138 #1.

2 AGME (SW.) – Goldtone, Clutch Carryall. "Vanite Deluxe," rhinestone lid bijou, loose powder, lipstick, comb clip, framed beveled mirror, case signed "Made in Switzerland," 4¼" x 3½" x ⅝", see P138 #3 open, $250.00 – 275.00.

3. AGME (SW.) – Goldtone, Clutch Carryall. Padded gold lurex and black case, see #2 for identical information.

4. Unknown (For.) – Sterling, Clutch Carryall. Hand-chased case, squares design with diagonal rosebuds and thistles, design repeated on interior duo lids, spring action malachite topped lipstick opener, loose powder, framed beveled mirror, touchmark of snake in lozenge cartouche, 4" x 2½" x ⅞", $350.00 – 400.00.
Outstanding workmanship with hidden hinges, balance, and each flora is slightly different.

5. La Mode – Goldtone, Cylinder Carryall. See P138 #4 closed.

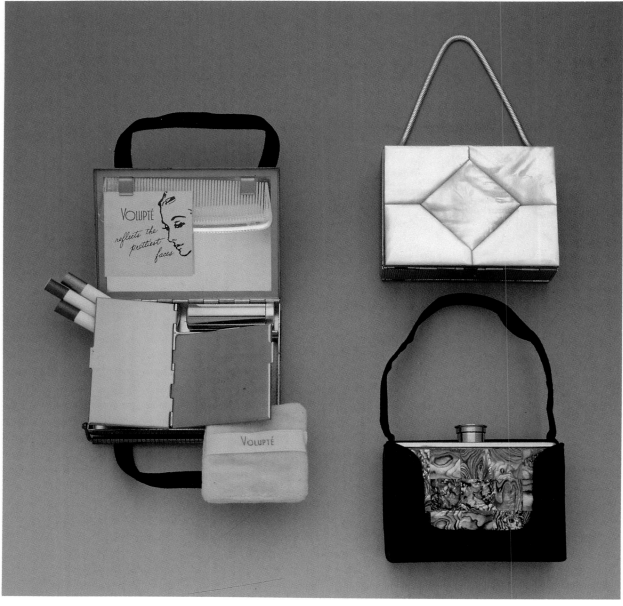

1 2
3

1. Volupté – Goldtone, Demi Carryall. Encased black suede, "Swinglok," narrow handles, no exterior ornamentation, lipstick, comb clip, papers, puff with logo, framed mirror, case signed, 4¼" x 3¼" x 1", Ref.: 1951 Ad., $65.00 – 90.00.

2. Zell Fifth Avenue – Goldtone, Demi Carryall. Double access, beveled M.O.P. lid panels, snake wrist chain, ribbed sides, lipstick, comb clip, no case I.D., puff with logo, case glued beveled mirror, 4" x 3" x 1⅜", $75.00 – 100.00.

3. Elgin American – Goldtone, "Carryette." Abalone lid panels, exterior spring action lipstick opener, black faille carrier, back pocket and comb, case signed, puff with logo, case glued mirror, 3½" x 2¼" x 1", Ref.: 1957 Ad., $100.00 – 125.00.

1   3
2

1. Volupté – Goldtone, Demi Carryall. "Matchstick shade" lid motif, hinged closure, faux sapphire affixed plate, link wrist chain, lipstick, top hinged double metallic mirrors, case signed, puff with logo, 4¼ x 3⅛" x 1", $75.00 – 90.00.

2. Elgin American – Goldtone, Purse Carryall. Post Deco inscribed lid motif, gold lurex carrier with strap and back pocket, hidden spring case opener, lipstick, case signed, puff with logo, case glued mirror, 3½" x 2⅜" x ⅞", $100.00 – 125.00.
Back to the drawing board for this idea. The case

must be squeezed with some force to open (putting the mirror at risk) and doesn't care to close.

3. Zell Fifth Avenue – Goldtone, Purse Carryall. Double access, affixed pavé rhinestone lid bijou, ribbed sides, black faille carrier, swivel rigid handle and snake chain, back pocket, lipstick, comb and money clips, case glued beveled mirror, no case I.D., puff with logo, 4¼" x 3¼" x 1¾", $100.00 – 125.00.
Undated ad explains the two handles either the "Princess Carryall" or "Handbag Cassette."

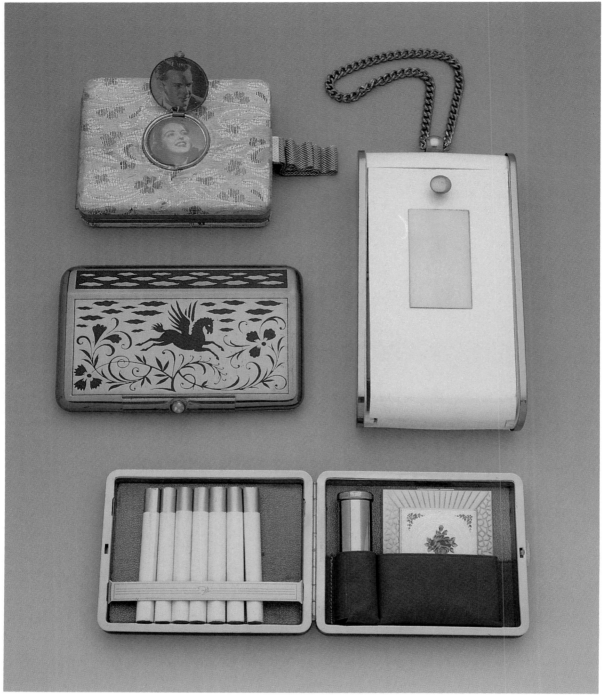

1
2
3
4

1. Zell – Goldtone, Demi Carryall. "Round Towner," encased multicolored lurex damask, mesh wrist strap, lid locket, gilt vinyl interior, affixed coin purse, lipstick and compact, only I.D. on coin purse, case glued mirror, box information, 4" x 3¼" x 1", $50.00 – 65.00.

2. Yardley (U.S.) – Goldtone, Clutch Carryall. Post Deco beveled lid, black champlevé enameled Pegasus and cloud motif, hinged closure with faux coral inset, loose powder and pressed rouge, lipstick, glass perfume flacon, spring lid clip, coved case signed, puff with logo, framed mirror, See P143 #4 open, 5" x 3¼" x

⅝", Ref.: 1941 Ad., $150.00 – 175.00.

3. Unmarked Wadsworth – Bakelite, Standard Carryall. Goldtone panels, lipstick and link wrist chain, white case and interior, loose powder, case attached beveled mirror, 6¼" x 3¼" x 1¼", Ref.: W.W.II (var.) 1948 Ad., $75.00 – 90.00.

4. Zell – Goldtone, Portmanteau. "Round Towner," encased red leather, gold leather interior, cloisonné compact lid plate, case glued beveled mirror, everything signed 4" x 3¼" x 1", $75.00 – 100.00.

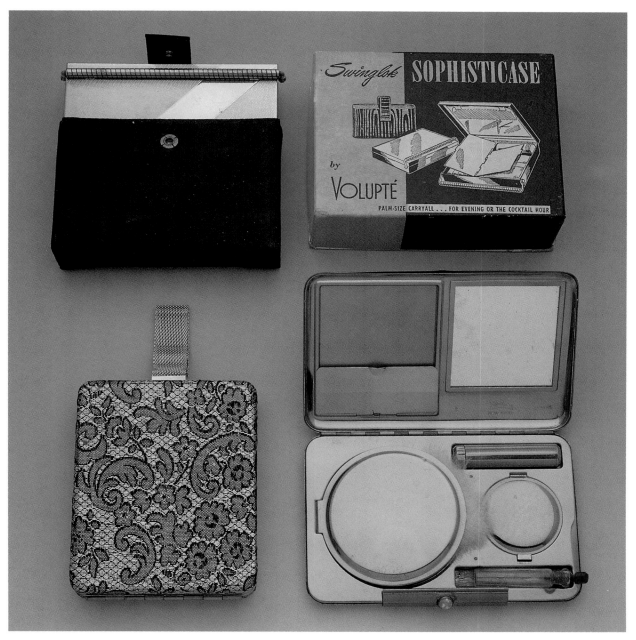

```
1        3
2        4
```

1. Volupté – Goldtone, Purse Carryall. "Sophisticase," "palm-size," diagonal lid motif, "Swinglok" closure, black moire slip carrier, lipstick, comb clip, case signed, puff and box with logo, framed mirror, 4¼" x 3¼" x ¾", Ref.: 1949 Ad., see #3 for box, $100.00 – 125.00.

2. Zell – Goldtone, Demi Carryall. "Round Towner," encased black and lurex damask, mesh wrist strap, black moiré interior, loose powder compact, lipstick,

comb, no case I.D., puff with logo, case glued mirror, cigarette case clip, 4" x 3¼" x 1", $75.00 – 90.00.
The Zell "Round Towners" must be complete for these prices.

3. Volupté – Presentation Box. See #1.

4. Yardley (U.S.) – Goldtone, Clutch Carryall. See P142 #2 closed.

Harper's Bazaar, 1948

1

2

3

1. Evans – Trimetal, Clutch Carryall. Basketweave case motif in rose, silver, and gold tones, double access, loose powder, case signed, puff with logo, case glued mirror, see 1948 ad for similar interior, 5½" x 3⅛" x 1", $125.00 – 150.00.

2. Unmarked – Goldtone, Clutch Carryall. Copper enameled case plates, Zodiac signs, reverse has opposite color scheme, loose powder, lipstick, coin purse and comb, bottom hinged double metallic mirrors, 5¼" x 3⅛" x ¾", $150.00 – 175.00.

3. Evans – Goldtone, Clutch Carryall. "The Park Lane," double access, post Deco case ribbed sunrays, faux ruby bijou, ribbed sides, gilt stamped logo on mirror "bienen davis" (sic), Ref.: 1948 Ad., $175.00 – 200.00.

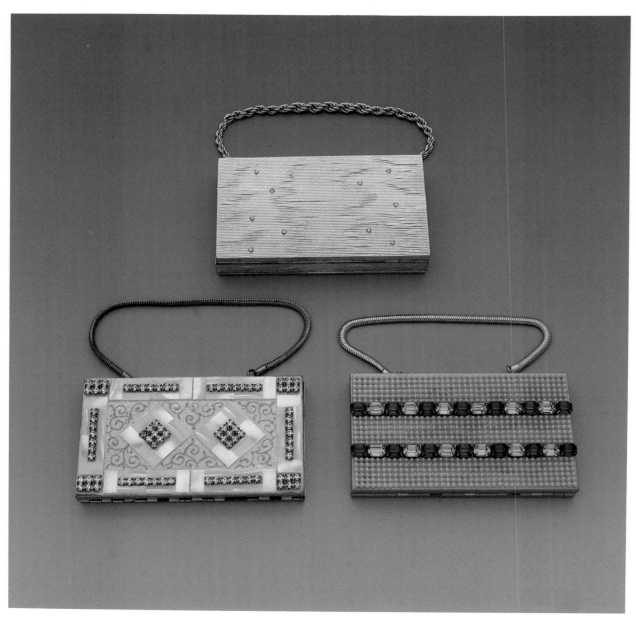

2

1   3

1. Unmarked – Goldtone, Standard Carryall. M.O.P. lid plaque, bars of prong mounted rhinestones and gilt rococo spangled ground, snake wrist chain, loose powder, coin purse, comb, lipstick, bottom hinged metallic backed beveled mirror, 5¼" x 3" x ¾", $75.00 – 100.00.

2. Evans – Bimetal, Standard Carryall. Double access, encased silvertone moiré pattern, scattered prong mounted rhinestones, tapered link wrist chain, gold-

tone interior, loose powder, lipstick, comb clip, case signed, puff with logo, case glued beveled mirror, 5½" x 3⅛" x 1", Ref.: 1955 Cat., $75.00 – 90.00.

3. Weisner of Miami – Goldtone, Standard Carryall. Faux pearl lid panels, faceted faux sapphire bands, snake wrist chain, loose powder, coin purse and comb, lipstick, bottom hinged double metallic mirrors, no case I.D., box information, 5¼" x 3" x ⅞", $75.00 – 100.00.

1
2

1. Volupté – Bimetal, Purse Carryall. Keyboard lid border motif, goldtone bas-relief grand piano, silvertone case, black faille carrier, back pocket, exterior lipstick, goldtone interior, music box plays "Let Me Call You Sweetheart," loose powder, case signed, puff with logo, hinged double metallic mirrors, 5¼" x 3" x ½", Rare.

The rarity rating is based on finding a mint case with the silvertone finish unmarred and a working music box.

2. Evans – Bimetal, Standard Carryall. Double access, "Sunburst" silvertone case, lattice lid motif, faux emerald cut rhinestones at junctures, goldtone interior, loose powder, comb clip, lipstick, case signed, puff with logo, case glued beveled mirror, 5½" x 3⅛" x 1¼", Ref.: 1948/1955 Ads., $75.00 – 100.00.

Like the Elgin "Heart" and the Coty "Envelope," this Evans sunburst design appearing on all manner of their cases, probably kept the business going in the waning fifties.

2

1 3

1. Evans – Goldtone, Standard Carryall. Double access, "Coronation," rhinestone enhanced crown lid plaque, mesh wrist band, see #3 for similar interior and 1950 ad, also Vol I – P139 for 1949 Ad.var., 5½" x 3⅛" x 1", $150.00 – 175.00.

2. Unmarked – Goldtone, Standard Carryall. Double access, chameleon, mesh wrist band, loose powder, lipstick, coin purse and comb, money clip, case glued beveled mirror, 5⅜" x 3⅛" x ¾", $125.00 – 150.00.

3. Evans – Goldtone, Standard Carryall. Double access, "Adonna," sunburst case with affixed Valjean 17 jewel watch with second hand, mesh wrist band, see 1950 ad for interior, case signed, puff with logo, 5½" x 3⅛" x 1", $175.00 – 200.00.

Note ad — watch is featured as 15 jewel, while the case has a 17 jewel watch; the customer might have had a choice. This is not a replacement. The 15 jewel wasn't inexpensive when new, wonder if the 17 jewel was higher.

Cigarettes stay fresh and sweet in separate compartment, away from powder and perfume scent.

VIRGINIA MAYO

glamorous star of the

WARNER BROS. PRODUCTION

"BACKFIRE"

proudly owns and uses the fitted Adonna carryall, by EVANS. You, too, will enjoy this EVANS masterpiece. At leading jewelry and department stores 60.00 plus tax. Other carryalls, by EVANS, from 25.00

Evans is elegance

Shimmering Entrance Piece

for your evening glamour, in the gracious, supremely beautiful Adonna carryall by EVANS...with 15-jewel watch...thoughtfully fitted for make-up needs, with space for cigarettes, coins, lipstick and powder...has full size mirror, comb and velour puff.

EVANS ● FINEST FITTED HANDBAGS, POWDER BOXES, CIGARETTE CASES, AND THE SENSATIONAL NEW EVANS AUTOMATIC LIGHTERS

Vogue, 1950

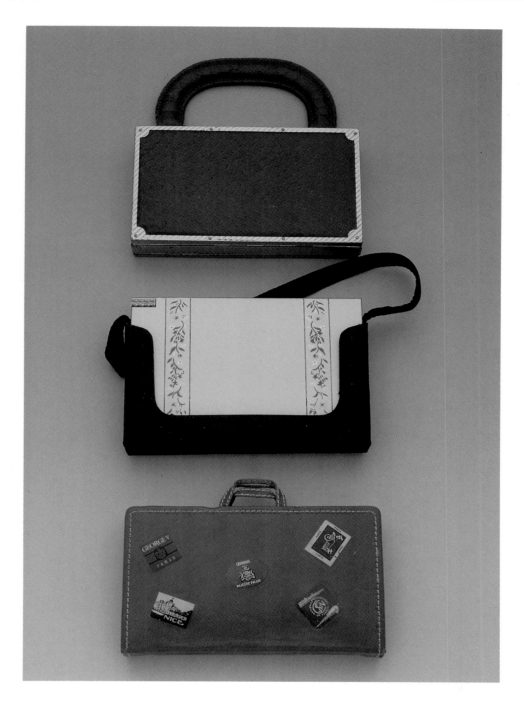

1
2
3

1. Evans – Goldtone, Standard Carryall. Double access, padded red snakeskin case, rigid snakeskin handle, similar interior to 1950 ad on page 149, 5½" x 3⅛" x 1", $125.00 – 150.00.

2. Volupté – Goldtone, Purse Carryall. Yellow linen-textured lid enamel, flora banding, black faille carrier, back pocket, exterior lipstick access, yellow taffeta coin purse, comb, loose powder, case signed, puff with logo, bottom hinged double metallic mirrors, 5¼" x 3" x ½", $175.00 – 200.00.

Cases for daytime use are unusual; the carryalls were mainly designed for evening wear. Also the use of yellow enamel required dress color coordination which meant that one carryall did not fit all.

3. Unmarked – Goldtone, Standard Carryall. Suitcase, encased tan leather with travel decals, small leather handles, loose powder, lipstick, coin purse and comb, bottom hinged double metallic mirrors, 5½" x 3¼" x 1" (mid-fifties), $150.00 – 175.00.

Decals are merely glued-on paper and very frail.

1
2

1. Volupté – Goldtone, Super Carryall. "Lip–Lock" exterior lipstick closure, lid diamanté bijou, loose powder, comb clip, case glued mirror, no case I.D., puff with logo, 6" x 4¾" x ¾", Ref.: 1955 Cat., $350.00 – 400.00.

This case may also come with a suede carrier, if found in mint condition increase price by $50.00.

2.Volupté – Goldtone, Super Carryall. Encased lithographed flowers and urn petit-point decor, loose pow-der, signed case, coin purse with oval lipstick and comb, puff with logo, case glued beveled mirror, 6" x 4¾" x ⅝", Ref.: 1939 and 1946 interiors, $300.00 – 350.00.

The pre-W.W. II cases have "Leak Proof" powder wells. This was not used in the post-war cases although the interiors stayed the same for a time until the "Lip–Lock" design was introduced in the early fifties.

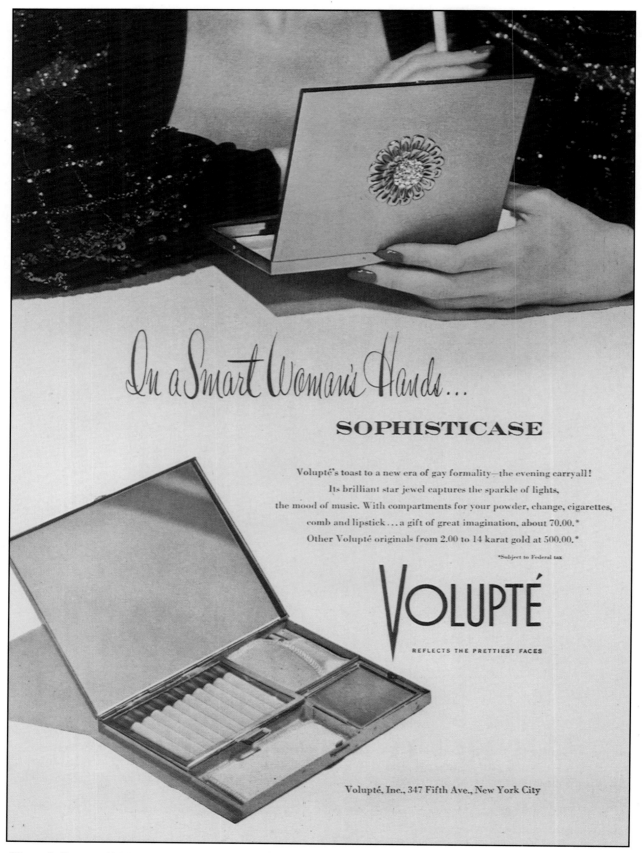

In a Smart Woman's Hands...

SOPHISTICASE

Volupté's toast to a new era of gay formality—the evening carryall!
Its brilliant star jewel captures the sparkle of lights,
the mood of music. With compartments for your powder, change, cigarettes,
comb and lipstick...a gift of great imagination, about 70.00.*
Other Volupté originals from 2.00 to 14 karat gold at 500.00.*

*Subject to Federal tax

VOLUPTÉ

REFLECTS THE PRETTIEST FACES

Volupté, Inc., 347 Fifth Ave., New York City

Harper's Bazaar, 1946

1
2

1. Volupté – Goldtone, Super Carryall. Encased champlevé enameled motif of Persian horses and tendrils, loose powder, signed case, coin purse with oval lipstick and comb, puff with logo, case glued beveled mirror, 6" x 4¾" x ⅝", Ref.: 1939 and 1946 interiors, $300.00 – 350.00.

Finding this case with its enamel intact is the challenge. The finish reacts adversely to hand moisture.

2. Volupté – Goldtone, Super Carryall. Affixed lid bijou of curled petals set with faux aquamarines and diamonds, loose powder, case signed, puff with logo, see 1946 ad for interior view and case ornament variation, 6" x 4¾" x ⅝", $250.00 – 300.00.

1
2

1. Rex Fifth Avenue – Mock Tortoise-shell, Purse. See P155 #2 closed.

2. Elgin American – Goldtone and Lucite, Baton Carryall. Mock tortoise-shell case with interior goldtone demi carryall inset, lipstick, loose powder, case signed "American Beauty," puff with logo, bottom hinged metal framed mirror, side case glued mirror duo, see P155 #1 open, 8½" x 2⅝" x 1⅜", $300.00 – 350.00.

1
2

1. Elgin American – Goldtone and Lucite, Baton Carryall. See P154 #2 closed.

2. Rex Fifth Avenue – Plastic and Goldtone, Purse. "Clear View," mock tortoise-shell, large link wrist chain, metal capped coin purse closures and side bands, two interior hinged compartments, loose pow-der, no case I.D., puff with logo, papers, comb clip, lipstick, case molded framed mirror, 6½" x 4½" x 1⅜", see P154 #1 open, $175.00 – 250.00.

Lipstick compartment is too large for containment — tube rattles noisily. A supply-your-own lipstick design intent?

1
2

1. Unknown (Fr.) – Goldtone, Purse Carryall. Encased black enamel, see P157 #1 closed.

2. Ostertag (Fr.) – Sterling, Clutch Triptych Carryall. Lid and push bar of diamonds and tourmalines set in yellow gold, exterior lighter access, linear and star engraved interior, hinged lipstick and pill boxes with tourmaline buttons, loose powder compact, tortoise- shell comb, lid cigarette compartment with clip, hinged six-sided metallic mirror triptych, case hall- mark "Arginal," #64495, French (crab and Minerva touchmarks), see P157 #2 open, 5¾" x 3½" x ⅞", $3,000.00 – 5,000.00.

Ostertag was a famous Parisian jeweler on the place Vendôme during the twenties and thirties.

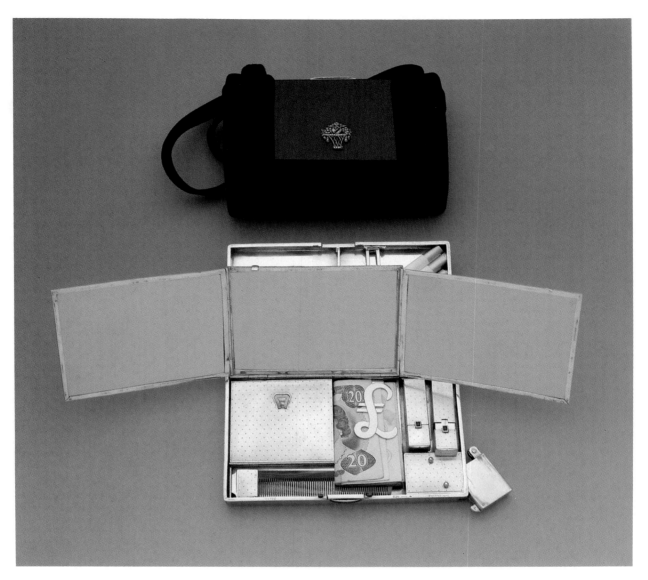

1
2

1. Unknown (Fr.) – Goldtone, Purse Carryall.
Encased black enamel, sterling and marcasite affixed lid bijou, black suede duo handled carrier, enameled interior, two compartments, loose powder, lipstick, tortoise-shell comb, case framed mirror, hallmark boxed WW and "Paris, Made in France" marabou puff, 5⅜" x 3⅞" x ⅞", see P156 #1 open, $650.00 – 1,000.00.

2. Ostertag (Fr.) – Sterling, Clutch Triptych Carryall.
See P156 #2 closed.

1   3
      2

1. Jeanne Bernard (Fr.) – Suede, Novelty Carryall. Double access, black suede "canopic jar" carrier, affixed rhinestone accented case bowknots, black braided silk wrist cord with tassel, goldtone top compact, loose powder, case signed in powder well gold foil Eiffel Tower and ribboned logo in lower case, 7" x 3⅜" dia., $175.00 – 200.00.

2. Unknown – White Metal, Super Carryall. Black enameled lid, ribbed center panel, four interior compartments, one with expansion band for cigarettes,

case signed on exterior side "La Minaudiere," case affixed beveled mirror, 6" x 4¾" x ⅝", Rare.

3. Blum's Vogue (Fr.) – Suede, Novelty Carryall. Double access, black suede ball, gold struts and banding, rope suede handle, hinged latch closures, top lid mirror and loose powder well, tan kid leather lower case lining, case signed "Made In France For Blum's Vogue Chicago," 3" round, 3¾ " handle, $250.00 – 275.00.

1. Van Cleef & Arpels – 18K Gold, La Minaudiere. "Woven Gold" basketweave case, 32 diamonds set in platinum on lid clasp, hinged interior compartments, loose powder compact and glass lidded well, matched lipstick tube with 16 diamonds set in platinum crown, gold capped tortoise-shell comb, framed mirror, everything signed, 5½" x 3⅛" x ⅞", Ref.: 1952 Ad., current auction prices between $12,500.00 and ? depending on number of diamonds and style of lid clasp.

Chapter Four

MILITARY, PATRIOTICS & NON-METALS

Vogue, 1945

"...VOLUPTÉ SUGGESTS ITS ELLIPTICAL METAL CASES AS SUGAR CARRYING ITEMS — NAMING THEM 'SHUG' CASES. THEY HOLD A WEEK-END'S SUPPLY OF SUGAR CUBES."

AMERICAN PERFUMER, 1942

The lead quote from the *American Perfumer* trade magazine in 1942 was not as humorous then as it is today. War rationing of food and commodities was no laughing matter — although humor was never rationed. If one had the gasoline coupons for travel and the tire tread to dare it, the ration book or actual materials were packed with the clothes. The weekend hostess expected her guests to bring their own sugar, coffee, soap, etc., so containers were devised out of what was left after the metal scrap drives had made their quotas. Once again the compact case rose from snuff, sewing items, rosaries, coin purse, and calling card storage, answered the call and became a sugar bowl.

A comment from Volume I still holds: "This category of non-metals and patriotics crosses over the previous categories by including all forms of cases (compacts, vanities, carryalls etc.) because the emphasis is in the material rather than the form...."

Since the first recognition of military and patriotic cosmetic cases in this series, there has been an active interest both in book publications and articles concerning this new collectible. A major W.W.II cross-over market is developing, and with the introduction here of international cases, yet another scramble will begin. It is doubtful, however, that any interest in "shug" compact cases will create another cross-over.

There are two distinct categories in W.W. II compact cases. One is the generic patriotics that have no specific identifications, i.e. eagles, flags, slogans. The second is the military case which splits into two units — branch of service with eagle Army insignias, wings, anchors, ball and anchor of the Marines, etc., and the unit which features the actual names of forts, camps, ships (not in this chapter), mottos, names or number of ground or naval forces, service rank or position. Research is required to decode these various regimental or division insignias.

Some are so well known that identification is instant — 8th Air Force, camp names, airborne division. Others may take a little effort to identify. The introduction of several women's insignias should shake loose a very neglected category.

Rosie the Riveter for some reason became the personification of the woman's role in W.W.II. Rosie's poster with her bulging biceps and rivet gun should have been matched with posters showing the activity of women who ferried B-17 bombers and fighter planes as WAFS and WASPS, Army WACS, Navy WAVES, Coast Guard SPARS, combat nurses (who were torpedoed, shot up or down), Red Cross, and those women who manned the home front with volunteer service. Uniform insignia accompanies several of these groups as hat or lapel pins; try to maintain this union in collecting the case.

The U.K. patriotics which were sold in New York during the Battle of Britain prior to the United States' abrupt entry after Dec. 7, 1941, also have pins and badges with cases. This new entry is bound to be a cross-over and varies in quality, quantity, and variety. Mugs, plates, posters, etc, are now appearing at shows. Again the compact collector should assemble the lapel pins with the appropriate case presentation; the dinnerware is best left to the U.K. dinnerware collectors.

For the first time carryalls are introduced in this chapter. These military cases are interesting in their own right. The Henriette carryall is one of the earliest examples of Lucite and the phrase: "Sapphire Air-Glass," in 1939, hints at the timorous use of plastic by the industry as a term for future marketing. The eagle emblem serves as another disguise.

An attempt to revive the flapjacks in the sixties resulted in the Revlon Honey Buns — designed by Van Cleef & Arpels — and are a series; up to four at this publication.

One of the foreign carryalls is non-metal and handmade — almost crudely — but it wanted its day in this volume so it took passage from a U.K. collectibles show to an Ohio show without visible means. It is made of tortoise shell, which is banned (old or otherwise) by the U.S. for import. There was some serious talk by the author with the U.K. dealer about the U.S. Customs problem and reasons for the case rejection; sadly the case was left behind. It stayed in the author's mind like a lost pet. One year later at a local show there it was — cracks, loose hinges, and stubborn powder door — no question, same case. The dealer said it came from a recent auction and had no idea who the previous owner was, or history of the "plastic what-ever." Do inanimate objects have a life of their own? It makes one wonder.

The Mappin & Webb jewelers presentation box does seem askew in this category, but tortoise shell was considered intrinsically valuable in the twenties.

Several of the biggies are hand painted and might have one-of-a-kind status. International dealers are snapping these up because of the uniquely U.S. flavor and W.W. II ambiance. The bigger, the better seems to be the criteria. The Lucite cases are also under siege by suddenly becoming a craft item and in the process are being vandalized and their value eroding. The cases in this volume that have personal lid depictions, such as faces, photographs, insignias, or places are original to the case and have a legitimate value. When the non-metals are at last extinct because of lack of judgment, there will be no revival by current case markers and like the dodo bird will be seen only in books.

```
                    1              5
              2         4     6
                 3                7
```

1. Crest – Bimetal, Loose Powder Compact. Silver-tone lid inset, RCAF emblem, no case or box I.D., pouch with logo, framed mirror, 2¾" x 2½" x ⅜", $125.00 – 150.00.

2. Stratnoid (U.K.) – Goldtone, Loose Powder Compact. Lid crest "Lord Strathcona's Royal Canadian Horse," case signed, framed mirror, 2" dia. x ⅜", Rare.
> *Prominent Canadian who formed this troop for the Boer War.*

3. Elgin American – Bimetal, Loose Powder Compact. Encased silvertone, crest "Royal Canadian Mounted Police," engraved "Regina, Sask. 1961," case signed, puff with logo, framed mirror, 2¾" square x ⅜", $150.00 – 175.00.

4. Unmarked – Goldtone, Loose Powder Compact. Flapjack, lid crest "Canadian Medical Corps," flanged case, framed mirror, 3¾" dia. x ⅜", $100.00 – 125.00.

5. Stratton (U.K.) – Goldtone, Loose Powder Compact. RAF regimental insignia (unicorn and crown), 3⅞" x 3" x ⅜", $125.00 – 150.00.

6. Unmarked (U.K.) – Goldtone, Loose Powder Compact. Domed case, RAF emblem, framed mirror, 2⅜" dia. x ⅜", $100.00 – 125.00.

7. Elgin American – Goldtone, Loose Powder Compact. White enameled case, lid emblem "Scottish Horse," case signed, puff with logo, framed mirror, 2¾" x 2¼" x ⅜", Ref.: 1953 Ad. (Vol. I P170), $75.00 – 100.00.
> *Issued to honor the Coronation of Queen Elizabeth II.*

1
2   4
3   5

1. M.A. Vendig Co. – Plastic, Loose Powder Compact. Mock tortoise-shell domed case, Ohio 37th Buckeye Division/148th Infantry lid insignias, khaki pouch (G.I. issue?) with division patch stitched on, no case I.D., puff signed "MAVCO," case glued beveled mirror, 3⅞" dia. x ¾", pouch 4½" x 4", Rare.

A poignant example of W.W. II handiwork. Was it made by the soldier as a gift, or was it a home front memento? The case has never been used.

2. Zell – White Metal, Beauty Box. White metal beveled case, WASPs "Fifinella" emblem, case with loose powder, rouge, eyebrow pencil, mascara and brush, eyeshadow, lip paste, hinged double metallic mirrors, case signed, 3" x 1⅞" x ½", $275.00 – 300.00.

*The **W**omen **A**irforce **S**ervice **P**ilots of W.W.II, formerly WAFS, flew out of Avenger Field, Sweetwater, Texas, as the first U.S. women to fly military planes. "Fifinella" was their good luck gremlin and guarded the front gate to Avenger Field.*

3. Wadsworth – Goldtone, Loose Powder Compact. Lid motif engraved parachutes, wings, and emblem of 82nd Airborne Division, case signed, puff with logo, case glued beveled mirror, sticker "Not Subject to Federal Tax," 3" sq. x ⅜", $250.00 – 275.00.

4. Unmarked – Goldtone, Loose Powder Compact. Chameleon, lid cross-hatch, WAAC officer insigna Athena (Greek goddess of wisdom and victory), "touch lock opener," case glued mirror, 2¼" sq. x ⅜", $275.00 – 300.00

*The **W**omen's **A**rmy **A**uxiliary **C**orps. of W.W.II, later changed to WAC, dropping the auxiliary.*

5. Zell – Goldtone, Loose Powder Compact. Flanged case with red, white, blue lid bands, U.S.A. tank model, case signed "Z," puff with logo, 3¼" sq. x ⅜", $75.00 – 100.00.

```
1      4      6
2      5        7
3              8
```

1. Unmarked – White Metal, Pressed Powder Vanity.
M.O.P. lid inset, hand-painted floral spray, "Camp
Perry, Ohio," hinged metallic framed mirror, 2" oct. x
1¾", Rare.
*The Ohio National Guard Reservation is located on
Lake Erie. It has been home of the National Rifle
Matches since 1907.*

2. Henriette – Goldtone, Loose Powder Compact.
Enameled ivory case, red and blue bands with stars,
U.S. Army eagle emblem, "Camp Croft" (S.C.), case
signed, framed mirror, 3" sq. x ⅜", $75.00 – 100.00.

**3. Dorset Fifth Avenue – Goldtone, Loose Powder
Compact.** Coved case, lid insignia, "U.S. Naval
Amphibious Base, Little Creek, Virginia," case signed,
framed mirror, 3¼" sq. x ¼", $175.00 – 200.00.

4. Henriette – Lucite, Loose Powder Compact. Snuff
box, scalloped case, goldtone side bands, mirrored lid,
U.S. Army eagle emblem, "Fort Knox" (KY), case
signed, fleece puff with logo, case glued mirror, 2¾" x
2¼" x ¾", $150.00 – 175.00.

5. Unmarked – Goldtone, Loose Powder Vanity.
Manned tank and fighter aircraft lid display, "Fort
Ord Calif.," framed mirror, 3" x 2⅜" x ⅜", $175.00 –
200.00.

**6. Immortelle – White Metal, Pressed Powder Com-
pact.** M.O.P. lid inset, hand-painted U.S. Army eagle
emblem, "Camp McCoy" (Wisc.), stepped lid, no case
I.D., puff and powder with logo, framed mirror, 3" x
1¾" x ½", $125.00 – 150.00.

7. Unmarked – Goldtone, Loose Powder Compact.
Enameled lid scene U.S. Army emblem and sentry,
tents with flag, "Indiantown Gap" (Reservation, PA),
framed mirror, 3" sq. x ⅜", $150.00 – 175.00.

8. Henriette – Goldtone, Loose Powder Compact.
U.S. Army Armoured Division lid display, "Camp
Campbell" (KY), box, case, and puff signed, framed
mirror, 3¼" dia. x ⅜", $75.00 – 100.00.

Short-wave WAC

"SERGEANTS were never like this!" G.I.'s say, as a slim young WAC swings into the cabin of the big C-46 training plane at Reno Army Air Base.

But men taking advanced radio work at this ferry division installation of the Air Transport Command know Sergeant Dorothy Capling rates her sergeant's stripes and flight pay. As a qualified radio instructor with official flying status, she trains radio operators who fly ATC routes all over the world.

Sergeant Capling's a soldier ...but a woman, too. So she keeps pretty and feminine despite many long hours of strenuous duty.

Wartime living has taught many women to simplify their beauty care with DuBarry Beauty Preparations. These are the preparations that have achieved such notable results for more than 150,000 students of the famous DuBarry Success School...because they're *co-related*...each scientifically formulated for its special purpose, yet all blended so they work together for greater loveliness.

Du BARRY
BEAUTY PREPARATIONS
by RICHARD HUDNUT

Featured in the Richard Hudnut Salon and DuBarry Success School
693 Fifth Avenue, New York 22, N.Y....and at better cosmetic counters everywhere

For lovelier make-up... begin with creamy, protective DuBarry Foundation Lotion to keep the skin soft. Then DuBarry Face Powder...light, but clinging...*perfect* for every skin type.

Add glowing color... DuBarry Lipstick has always been known for its wonderful texture, its long-lasting qualities. DuBarry Rouge Parfait complements your lipstick shade.

All this excitement in one festive package! Foundation lotion, powder, rouge and lipstick, boxed to make a glamorous Christmas gift. So attractive, you'll want one, too. Complete, $4.25 *plus tax.*

Charm, 1944

Postcard, 1943

1. Volupté – Goldtone, Loose Powder Vanity. "Lip-Lock" exterior lipstick closure, Daughters of America service emblem, case signed, puff with logo, framed mirror, 3¼" x 2¼" x ¾", $65.00 – 80.00.

A patriotic organization with interest in good citizenship founded in 1891 as a helping hand. Not a part of D.A.R.

2. Unmarked – Goldtone, Loose Powder Compact. Portrait, green metallic finish, "E For Production" sterling emblem, interior portrait frame, side hinged metal framed beveled mirror, 2¾" x 2⅜" x ⅝", $125.00 – 150.00.

3. Elgin American – Goldtone, Loose Powder Compact. Black enameled case, international flags lid display, case signed, puff with logo, case glued mirror, 3" dia. x ¼", $50.00 – 65.00.

4. A.W.V.S. See #8 for case. Uniform pin worn " ...Left side of Overseas Cap 1½" off center...," 1¾" x 1⅛".

5. Clarice Jane – Goldtone, Loose Powder Vanity. Domed saddlebag, black encased enamel, Red Cross cloisonné emblem, no case I.D., puff with logo, 2½" x 2½" x ½", $125.00 – 150.00.

6. In-Service W.W.II Faille Bracelet. NFS.

7. Unmarked – Goldtone, Pressed Powder Compact. Lotus bud border, rivet affixed Ivorene lid plaque, faux ruby enhanced Daughters of America emblem, framed mirror, 2½" dia. x ⅝", $75.00 – 100.00.

8. Volupté – Goldtone, Loose Powder Compact. Encased blue enamel, American Women's Voluntary Services emblem, see #4 for AWVS uniform pin, case signed, puff with logo, framed mirror, 3" sq. x ⅜", Ref.: 1943, set $150.00 – 175.00.

Founded in 1940 this uniformed organization performed over twenty W.W. II duties including motor transport, fingerprinting, canteens and blood banks, and emergency radio service.

9. Elgin American – Goldtone, Loose Powder Compact. White enameled case, "V for Victory" lid symbols, case signed, puff with logo, case glued mirror, 3" dia. x ¼", $50.00 – 65.00.

```
1    4    7
2    5    8
3    6    9
```

1. Elgin American – Goldtone, Loose Powder Compact. Stars on enameled lid, goldtone crossed cannon, paper label on case glued mirror "Coast Artillery," case signed, puff with logo, 3" dia. x ¼", $75.00 – 100.00.

2. Alexandra Markoff – White Metal, Loose Powder Compact. Encased black enamel, U.S. Army Air Force sterling wings lapel insignia, case signed, sliding powder dispenser, framed broad beveled mirror, 1¾" x 2¼" x ⅝", $150.00 – 175.00.

3. Unmarked – Goldtone, Loose Powder Compact. Lid motif blue cloudy sky, unfurled flag, goldtone mottos, case framed mirror, 3½" sq. x ⅜", Ref.: 1941 Cat., $125.00 – 150.00.

4. Unmarked Zell – Goldtone, Loose Powder Vanity. Kamra, beveled case, encased gold spangled vinyl, chintz lid inset under celluloid, army crossed infantry rifles, 3¼" x 2" x ½", $100.00 – 125.00.

5. Unmarked – Goldtone, Loose Powder Vanity. Black enamel stepped lid, exterior comb, broad bar opener, center cartouche affixed U.S.N. pilot wings, framed beveled mirror, 3¼" x 2¼" x ½", Ref.: 1938 Cat., $175.00 – 200.00.

6. Girey – White Metal, Loose Powder Vanity. Kamra, encased gold spangled vinyl, exterior lipstick, lid inset naval officer's emblem on gold ground, case signed, puff with logo, framed beveled mirror, 3¼" x 1¾" x ⅜", $150.00 – 175.00.

7. Elgin American – Goldtone, Loose Powder Compact. Blue, red and white sergeant chevrons and infantry rifles on white enameled lid, paper label "U.S. Infantry," case signed, puff with logo, case glued mirror, 3" dia. x ¼", $75.00 – 100.00.

8. Unmarked – Goldtone, Loose Powder Compact. Red enameled lid border, U.S. Army eagle on white ground, case framed mirror, 2¼" sq. x ¼", $75.00 – 100.00.

Case also comes in blue and white borders.

9. Unmarked – Copper, Loose Powder Compact. Lid scene of assault landing force and U.S. Marine emblem, puff signed "Aloha From Hawaii," framed mirror, 3" x 2⅜" x ⅜", $225.00 – 250.00.

1   3

2

1. & 2. Henriette – Goldtone, Three Piece Set. "Sole authentic case for British War Relief Society and Bundles for Britain." Gold foil label on case mirror, ivory enameled cases with heraldic lid display. Case — loose powder, case signed, framed mirror, 3" sq. x ⅜". Cigarette Case — signed, 5¼" x 3" x ⅜". Pin — signed "Official R.W.R.S. & B.B. by Accessocrat." Complete $250.00 – 300.00.

All these accessories were sold in New York City at the start of the Battle of Britain, 1940. Note the smaller variations that were also available without the cases. The smaller pins and letter opener are NFS.

3. Unmarked – Goldtone, Two Piece Set. "British War Relief Society." Case and pin have Union Jack motif with affixed heraldic emblems (case looks Evans-like), no claims to official status such as #1 and #2. Case — loose powder, case glued mirror, 2⅝" sq. x ½". Pin — signed "Cartier" and legend, 1¾" x 1¼". Complete $225.00 – 250.00.

Miscellaneous Pin, British Legion – Womens (sic) Section. Blue enamel, sterling mounted lion's head, signed "J.R. Gaunt – London #11397," NFS.

All these items belong to the author and some were gifts, hence the Not for Sale (NFS) notations.

Sure Fire for Sweet Romance

your Luscious lovely Face

Wear your Alluring Alix-Styled Shade of the

New Jergens Face Powder

YOUR LOOK-ALIVE LOOK

You need a new kind of beauty today—have that look-alive look or you lack allure. And the shades of the New Jergens Face Powder were styled by Alix, famous fashion designer and color genius, to give that gorgeous, young, *alive tone*. Her dresses made even plain women glorious. Her shade for you can make hearts spin with your fresh glamour!

YOUR VELVET-SKIN CHEEK

Yes! That Dream-Boy in uniform will be yours for keeps when he sees your new complexion. Here's why: the texture of exquisite Jergens Powder is velvetized—by an exclusive process. Result—it makes your skin look smoother, finer, more flawless (it helps hide tiny skin faults). Wear your enticing Jergens shade today—see him stop, look and adore!

CHOOSE YOUR SHADE

Peach Bloom (for fair or medium skin)—to give a colorful, dewy look. **Rachel** (for creamy-fair skin)—to give clear, striking glamour. **Naturelle** (for blonde-fair skin)—to give fragile, delicate beauty. **Brunette** (for medium or dark-toned skin)—to give dramatic, radiant allure. **Dark Rachel** (for medium or dark-toned skin)—to give a tawny, vivacious look. **Big Boudoir Box $1.00...Try-it sizes 25¢, 10¢.**

Photoplay, 1943   Artist signed — Varga

1	4	6
2	5	7
3		8

1. Henriette – Plastic, Loose Powder Compact. Hat, U.S.N. white and blue, metallic brim crest, case glued mirror, no case I.D., 3" dia. x 1⅜", Ref.: 1944 Ad., $75.00 – 100.00.

2. Unmarked – Bimetal, Loose Powder Compact. Goldtone case, brass hat with U.S. Army crest, bar opener, case glued mirror, 2¼" sq. x ⅜", $45.00 – 60.00.

3. American Can Co. – Goldtone, Pressed Powder Can. Case signed "Beauté Box — Canco," lid inset W.W. I U.S. Army soldier photo under celluloid, 2½" dia. x ⅝", Rare.
   Legend: company advertised service: "...send in photo and company will mount photo"; photo identity unknown.

4. Unmarked – Bimetal, Loose Powder Compact. Brass hat, Corps of Engineers sweetheart lid bijou, goldtone case, U.S. Army brim crest, case glued mirror, 3" dia. x 1¼", $100.00 – 125.00.

5. Unmarked – Goldtone, Loose Powder Compact. Saddlebag, chameleon, U.S. Army Infantry sweetheart bijou, parade gun, chain and tassel, enameled accented hat and crest, 3" x 2¾" x ½" (with pin 1"), $150.00 – 175.00.

6. Henriette – Plastic, Loose Powder Compact. Hat, U.S. Army, red, *pink*, and blue, gold foil brim crest, case glued mirror, no case I.D., 3" dia. x 1¼", Ref.: 1944 Ad., $65.00 – 75.00.

7. Cara Mia – Goldtone, Loose Powder Compact. Snuff box, damask case motif, M.O.P. U.S. Army hat with metallic crest, no case I.D., puff with logo, 2⅞" oval x 2¼" x ½", $125.00 – 150.00.

8. Elgin American – Goldtone, Loose Powder Vanity. Domed saddlebag, encased aqua enamel, center lid photo inset with removable U.S. Army model picture, case signed, puff with logo, framed mirror, 2½" x 2½" x ½", $75.00 – 90.00.

1   4
2   5
3   6

1. Zell Fifth Avenue – Leather and Metal, Loose Powder Novelty Compact. Billfold, faux ostrich embossed leather, coin purse, snap latch with U.S. Army crest, brown moiré interiors, goldtone compact, no case I.D., puff with logo, framed mirror, 3¼" sq. x ¾", $75.00 – 90.00.

2. Unmarked – Ebonite, Loose Powder Compact. Saddlebag, black case, U.S.N. metallic wings, 3¼" x 2⅝" x ½", $125.00 – 150.00.

3. Lady Vanity – Plastic, Loose Powder Compact. Leather oval case, "In-Service" sweetheart U.S. Quartermaster crest, tan plastic interior, no case I.D., puff with logo, case glued mirror, 4" x 2¾" x ½", $125.00 – 150.00.

4. M.A. Vendig Co. – Lucite, Loose Powder Compact. Domed clear case, mirror reverse lid inset, goldtone U.S. Army emblem on silver foil ground, no case I.D., puff signed "Mavco," case glued mirror, 3⅞" dia. x ⅝", $75.00 – 100.00.

5. Unknown (For.) – Alligator, Loose Powder Compact. Brown skin, zipper closure, case signed "Made in Cuba," goldtone U.S. Marine emblem, tan suede liner, case glued mirror, 3¼" x 2¾" x ¾", $100.00 – 125.00.

6. Unmarked – Goldtone, Loose Powder Compact. Maple veneer case panels, lid inlay U.S. Coast Guard rank, anchor, and wood burned initials, framed mirror, 2⅞" sq. x ⅜", $65.00 – 80.00.

```
        1                 6
    2        4        7
  3        5        8
```

1. Wand Art – Wood, Loose Powder Compact. "Hand Decorated" duo with legend, no case I.D., box with logo, case glued mirror, 3" x 2¾" x ¾", $75.00 – 100.00.

2. Zell – Goldtone, Loose Powder Vanity. "Knapsack," exterior lipstick on closure flange, blue enameled lid, U.S. Army emblem gilt lid transfer, no case I.D., papers, case glued beveled mirror, 2¾" sq. (w/lipstick 3¼") x ½", $65.00 – 80.00.

3. Unmarked – White Metal, Loose Powder Vanity. Portrait of General Eisenhower, celluloid cover, top hinged double metallic mirrors, 2" x 1¾" x ½", Rare.
Time Magazine did a portrait series on General Eisenhower. This "4 star" portrait was emphasized in the 1948 Draft Eisenhower campaign.

4. Carrel, LTD. (U.S.). All wood lipstick, signed "Leon Laraine," 2½" x ⅞" dia., $25.00 – 35.00.

5. Zell – White Metal, Two-Piece Set. Aqua enameled signed comb and loose powder compact case, both display U.S. Army gilt insignias, no case I.D., case glued mirror, 2⅞" x 2⅛" x ½", comb 4⅜" x 1⅜", complete $50.00 – 75.00.

6. Valdor – Ivorene, Boxed Two-Piece Set. Rouge and lipstick with U.S. Navy emblem decals and stickers, no mirror, case 1⅞" dia. x ½", tube 2" x 1" dia. , complete $75.00 – 100.00.
Decals are barely hanging on, hence the price.

7. Unknown – Wood, Loose Powder Compact. All wood case, case glued mirror with gold foil sticker "Victory Compact – warranted hand made," 3⅝" x 3⅜" x ⅝", $45.00 – 60.00.

8. Unmarked – Plastic, Loose Powder Compact. Ribbed lid, mirror reverse display of red flocking with white stars, gilt U.S. Army pilot wings, 3½" x 2¾" x ⅜", $25.00 – 40.00.

1
2

1. Park Lane (U.K.) – Goldtone, Loose Powder Clutch Carryall. Aqua enameled case, sterling RAF wings, side compartment holds gray silk coin purse and lid comb clip, case glued beveled mirror, no case I.D. (interior decor similar to case in carryall collection), see P175 #1 open, 5½" x 3½" x ⅞", $275.00 – 300.00.

Supply-your-own lipstick paper in well. This tube happens to be a handsome rosetone Dorothy Gray Ltd.

2. Unmarked (For.) – Sterling, Loose Powder Clutch Carryall. Lid dragon motif with flora and U.S. Marine emblem, initialed cartouche, interior with two lidded compartments and a well (which is too shallow for lipstick), hinged lids, interior lid replication, no mirror, lid well, obviously handmade, no hallmarks so not for export, 5" x 3⅜" x ¾", Rare.

1
2

1. Park Lane (U.K.) – Goldtone, Loose Powder Clutch Carryall. See P174 #1 closed.

2. Henriette – Lucite, Loose Powder Clutch Carryall. "Sapphire Air-Glass" case, metallic U.S. Army emblem, two hinged interior compartments and lipstick well, plastic comb clip, lipstick replacement, case signed, case glued beveled mirror, 5¼" x 3¼" x 1", Ref.: 1939 Ad., $250.00 – 275.00.

This was one of the early domestic uses of Lucite. However the term didn't seem glamorous enough for the cosmetic industry. This Henriette sobriquet should have lasted longer; a truly stunning case.

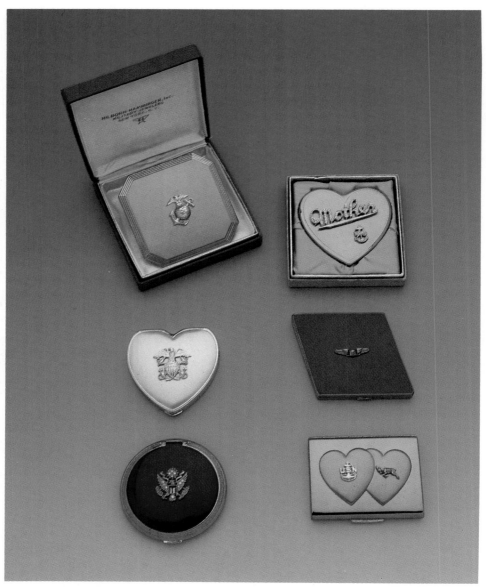

1	4
2	5
3	6

1. Wadsworth – Goldtone, Loose Powder Compact. Stepped case, sterling and vermeil Marine Corps emblem, red leather box, case signed, puff with logo, framed mirror, 3⅛" oct. x ⅜", $125.00 – 150.00.

2. Hingco – Sterling, Loose Powder Compact. Domed heart case, U.S. Navy emblem, case signed, framed mirror, 2¾" x 2⅝" x ⅝", $150.00 – 175.00.

3. Unmarked – Goldtone, Loose Powder Compact. Domed red metallic finish, U.S. Army sweetheart bijou, framed mirror, 2⅞" dia. x ½", $65.00 – 80.00.

4. Unmarked – Goldtone, Loose Powder Compact. Heart, rhinestone script "Mother" and U.S.N. emblem, framed mirror, 3" x 2¾" x ½", $75.00 – 90.00.

5. Unmarked – Goldtone, Loose Powder Vanity. Rhombic, red metallic finish, U.S.N. wings, framed mirror, 2¾" rhom. x ⅜", $65.00 – 80.00.

6. Stratton (U.K.) – Goldtone, Loose Powder Compact. Coved case, twin hearts in relief, Annapolis U.S. Naval Academy emblem and goat mascot, case signed, puff with logo, framed mirror, 3" x 2⅜" x ½", $125.00 – 150.00.

To Ellen—with Love!

One girl loves a soldier . . . one loves a sailor . . . one loves a lad in the Marines. But, they all adore the gift which says, "You're first in my heart."

Typical of the gorgeous Evening in Paris gift sets. Set illustrated sells at $2.95 plus tax.

Evening in Paris BOURJOIS

Evening in Paris gift sets to thrill her heart...and priced to suit every pocketbook...$1.00 to $15.00 *(all prices plus tax)*

Ladies' Home Journal, 1943

1   2   3

1. Unmarked – Cardboard, Pressed Powder Pendant Vanity. Orange silk and gold band covered case, gold cord with finger ring, black tassel, blue Peking glass beads, two interior gold papered fitted boxes, celluloid topped felt puffs, cardboard framed mirror, 3¼" x 1⅞" x ¾", $150.00 – 175.00.

2. Jeunesse de Fleur – Bakelite, Pressed Powder Pendant Vanity. Double access, black wrist cord, silk tassel with black enameled goldtone oval lipstick tube, green case and black center divider, cosmetic and card sides, case signed, Ivorene framed mirror, 3" x 2" x 1", tassel 5½", $175.00 – 200.00.

3. Unmarked – Cardboard, Pressed Powder Pendant Vanity. Black silk covered case, celluloid lid with goldtone overlay Oriental duo, gold wrist cord and tassel, pink Peking beads, see #1 for similar information.

Although now unmarked these cases are probably Vantine's with missing paper I.D. labels. The lid legend has no meaning.

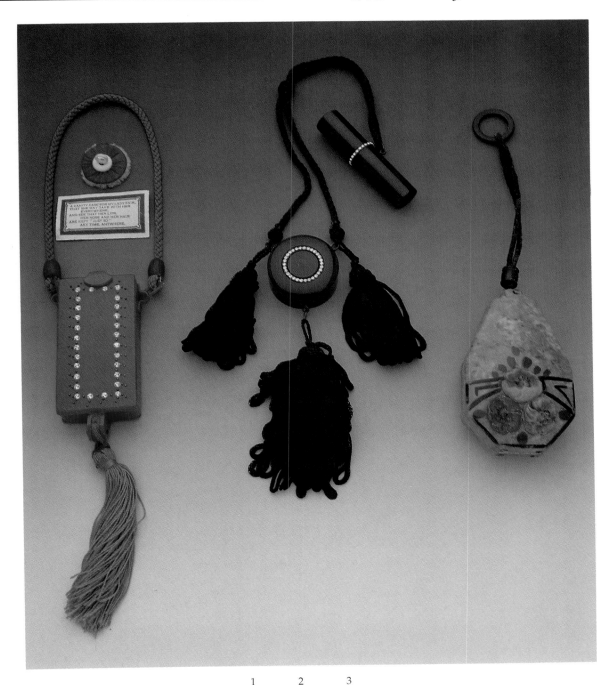

1   2   3

1. Unmarked – Bakelite, Pressed Powder Pendant Vanity. Orange case, diamanté lid inset, silk cord and tassel, Bakelite beads, silk topped puff, lipstick,, case affixed round mirror, card with poem, 3⅛" x 1⅝" x ¾", $250.00 – 275.00.

> *"A vanity case for my lady fair,*
> *that she will take everywhere,*
> *And see that her lips,*
> *Her nose and her hair*
> *Are kept 'just so'*
> *Anytime, anywhere."*

2. Unmarked – Bakelite, Powder Vanity. Diamanté lid inset screw top case, three silk braided loop tassels, silk wrist cord, tube with removable glass perfume flacon, diamanté ring, fleece puff, case glued mirror, case 1½" dia. x ¾", cord 9", tube 2¾" x ⅝" dia., $475.00 – 500.00.

> *Evidence of powder but no screen or paten; may have been a nose puff carrier only. None of the tassels were made to have concealed items, such as a lipstick tube.*

3. Unmarked – Celluloid, Pressed Powder Pendant Vanity. Green domed teardrop case, molded lid flora, hand-painted accents, cotton braided cord, wood slide and ring, case framed mirror, 3½" x 2¼" x 1¼", $225.00 – 250.00.

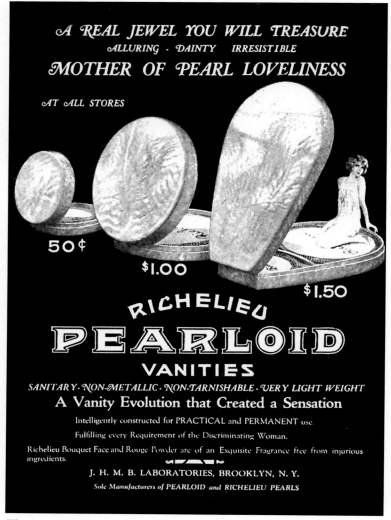

Theatre – 1924

1. Unmarked – Ivorene, Pressed Powder Vanity. Triangle case, full skirted femme lid imprint, framed mirror, 2⅞" x 2¾" x ¾", $65.00 – 80.00.

2. Fuller – Pearloid, Loose Powder Combination Compact. Horseshoe, comb in reverse pocket, case signed, framed mirror, 2¼" x 2¼" x ⅝", $45.00 – 60.00.

3. Fuller – Ivorene, Pressed Powder Combination Can. Reverse shown, circle cartouchè "Hazel," lid without detail, framed mirror, 2½" dia. x ¾", $50.00 – 65.00.

4. Blum-Pak – Plastic, Loose Powder Hand Mirror Compact. Molded design, interior mirror backing acts as exterior lid inset, hand-painted flora, reverse case glued mirror, no case I.D., puff with logo, 2½" dia. x ½", with handle 4¼", $50.00 – 65.00.

5. Unmarked – Ivorene, Pressed Powder Compact. Triangle case with green lid and reverse flanges, see #1 for information.

6. Unmarked – Celluloid, Loose Powder Hand Mirror Compact. Exterior framed mirror, hollow handle, 1¾" dia. x ½", with handle 3¼", $45.00 – 60.00.

7. Fuller – Pearloid, Loose Powder Combination Compact. Horseshoe, reverse with logo, see #2 for information.
   1925 patent information lists Wm. J. Hines as designer for Fuller Brush Co., Hartford, Conn.

8. Purse Hand Mirror. N.F.S.

```
            1         5
    2           4     6
        3               8
                    7
```

```
1      4      6
2      5      7
3             8
```

1. Victoria Vogue – Plastic, Loose Powder Compact. Mock tortoise-shell coved case, molded Spanish femme head lid inset with cardboard frame and foil ground, case signed "VV's," papers, case glued mirror, 3⅛" dia. x ¾", $25.00 – 35.00.

2. Victoria Vogue – Plastic, Loose Powder Compact. Domed case, coin purse closure, papers, no mirror, 2⅜" dia. x ⅜", $15.00 – 20.00.

3. Geo.W. Luft Co. – Plastic, Loose Powder Compact. Snuff box, marbled "air stream" form, case signed, puff and powder packet with logo "Tangee," framed mirror, 3" x 2⅛" x ¾", $50.00 – 60.00.

4. Coty – Bakelite and Metal, Lipstick. "Periscope" tube, oval molded ribbed case, pivoting metal cap, label, 2⅛" x ¾", Ref.: 1939 Ad., $15.00 – 25.00.

5. Lucinda of Hollywood – Lucite, Loose Powder Compact. Case signed, puff "Ziegfeld Creations," case glued beveled mirror, 3" x 2½" x ½", $25.00 – 40.00. *The puff is not a replacement — fits exactly in mint case.*

6. Unmarked – Plastic, Loose Powder Compact. Oval domed marbled case, coin purse closures, flora sterling lid inlay, case glued round mirror, 3½" x 3" x ⅜", $40.00 – 65.00.

7. N L O C R – Plastic, Loose Powder Compact. Cushion black and pink case, molded femme lid cameo, case signed, metallic framed mirror, thumb nail opening, 2½" x 2½" x ½", $15.00 – 20.00.

8. Lenthéric – Lucite, Loose Powder Vanity. Book, lid decal motif on interior mirror foil backing, goldtone lipstick, case signed, puff and lipstick with logo, case glued mirror, 3⅜" x 2½" x ⅞", Ref.: 1942 Ad. (var.), $75.00 – 90.00.

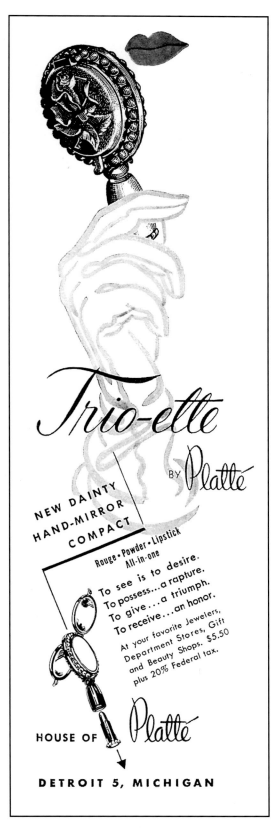

Trio-ette BY *Platté*

NEW DAINTY
HAND-MIRROR
COMPACT

Rouge • Powder • Lipstick
All-in-one

To see is to desire.
To possess...a rapture.
To give...a triumph.
To receive...an honor.

At your favorite Jewelers,
Department Stores, Gift
and Beauty Shops. $5.50
plus 20% Federal tax.

HOUSE OF *Platté*

DETROIT 5, MICHIGAN

Harper's Bazaar, 1945

1
2

4
5

3

1. Schiaparelli – Plastic, Pressed Powder Disk Compact. "Shocking Pink" case, lid signature, foam rubber puff, reverse paper label, case framed mirror, 2¾" dia. x ⅝", $35.00 – 50.00.

2. Marie Earle – Plastic, Pressed Powder Compact. Framed box, embossed Cupid and branches under domed plastic lid, case signed "Marie Earle Make-Up by Lilly Dache," box and reverse case information, puff with M.E. logo, papers, 2¾" dia. x ¾", complete $75.00 – 125.00.

3. Woodbury – Plastic, Pressed Powder Can. Molded femme and legend overlay on blue lid plate "Dream Stuff," reverse information, no mirror, 2¾" dia. x ⅝", Ref.: 1952 Ad., $45.00 – 60.00.

4. Platé – Plastic, Loose Powder Hand Mirror Vanity. "Trio-Ette Cameo," "Reuben Blue," double access, exterior reverse mirror, molded case design, lipstick tube in handle, case and lipstick signed, puff with logo, case glued mirrors, 2½" dia. x 4⅞", box 5¼" x 4" x 1⅜", Ref.: 1945 Ad., complete $150.00 – 175.00.
There are seven colors — ivory, ebony, cornelian, tortoise, briar rose, Nile green, and Reuben blue. Price can vary widely with certain colors, boxed and mint case condition. (Note ad typo: platté)

5. Colonial Dames Co. – Plastic, Pressed Powder Can. Lid logo intaglio effect with orange accents, reverse paper information "Campus Make-Up," "smooth on with wet sponge," no mirror, 3⅜" dia. x ⅝", Ref.: 1945 Ad., $35.00 – 50.00.

Screenland, 1952

```
1        5
2    4   6
3        7
```

1. Charles Blair (Fr.) – Cloth, Loose Powder Compact. Fold over case (no hinges), padded gold and silver thread damask, white faux kid leather liner, plastic ring lid ornament, case signed, framed glued mirror, 3¾" x 2¾" x ½", $35.00 – 50.00.

2. Henri Bendel – Beaded, Loose Powder Compact. Encased black bead work, embroidered bird of paradise and flora, white faux kid leather liner, no case I.D., case glued mirror, Ref.: 1951 Ad. (var./"Made in France"), 3" x 2½" x ⅝", $75.00 – 100.00.

3. Unknown (Fr.) – Cloth, Loose Powder Pouch Compact. Encased multicolored damask, coin purse closure, marabou puff with pink ribbon and sticker "Fluffi Puff – France," ivory kid leather liner, case glued mirror, 3¾" dia. x ¾" (squashed), $75.00 – 90.00.

4. Unmarked (For.) – Cloth and Metal, Pressed Powder Vanity. Horseshoe, encased damask, snap flap, goldtone tray for powder and hinged oval lipstick, case glued mirror, 2½" x 2½" x ¾", $35.00 – 50.00.

5. Unknown (Ch.) – Cloth and Metal, Loose Powder Compact. Silk damask case, Oriental scenes, white metal mirror frame, case signed "China," 4¼" oval x 3½" x ⅜", $50.00 – 65.00.

6. WA mae [sic] – Cloth and Metal, Loose Powder Pouch Carrier Compact. Black faille case, small link wrist chain, ivory moiré liner and hinged mirror, no case I.D., puff with logo, 2⅞" dia. x ¾" (squashed), $50.00 – 65.00.

7. Boots (U.K.) – Cloth, Loose Powder Compact. Silk petit point flower basket lid design, snap flap, ivory faux kid leather liner, product brochure "La Question," no other case I.D., case glued beveled mirror, 2⅞" x 2½" x ½", $30.00 – 45.00.

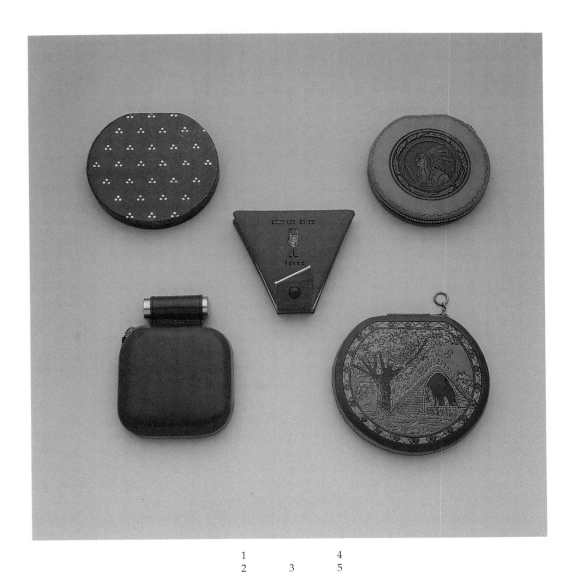

1   4
2   3   5

1. Rothena – Leather, Loose Powder Compact. Horseshoe, encased brown leather, lid stamped gilt dots, no case I.D., puff with logo, case glued mirror, 3¾" x 3⅝" x ½", $45.00 – 60.00.

2. Trix (Ger.) – Leather, Loose Powder Vanity. Maroon leather padded case, zipper closure and tab signed, goldtone exterior lipstick, Ivorene interior, no case I.D., case framed beveled mirror, 4" x 3" x ¾", $35.00 – 50.00.

3. Unknown (Sp.) – Leather, Loose Powder Compact. Trianglar red leather case, snap flap, lid gilt stamped "Gonzalez Byass – Jerez" and wine glass, ivory paper interior, case glued beveled mirror, 3½" x 3¼" x ⅝", $50.00 – 65.00.
    Jerez, Spain, is the home of Sherry wine.

4. Unknown (U.S.) – Leather, Loose Powder Compact. Tan leather case, embossed bonneted Plains Indian lid motif, zipper closure and signed "Merita U.S.A.," faux ivory kid leather interior, case glued mirror, 3½" x 3½" x ⅝", $65.00 – 80.00.

5. Unknown – Leather, Loose Powder Compact. Horseshoe, tan leather with stamped Oriental scenes, reverse with Forbidden City temple, zipper closure has illegible mark, white faux kid leather interior, case glued mirror, 4¼" x 4" x ⅝", $50.00 – 65.00.

1   4

2   3   5

1. Bliss Bros. Co. – Wood, Loose Powder Compact. Hand-carved intaglio clipper ship lid scene, exterior hinge toggle closure, papers, puff with logo "Bliss," case glued round mirror, W.W.II sticker "Not subject to Federal tax," 2⅞" sq. x ⅝", $75.00 – 90.00.

2. Unmarked – Wood, Loose Powder Compact. Cushion, hand-painted lid scene of eighteenth century duo, case glued round mirror, 3⅛" sq. x ⅝", $50.00 – 65.00.

3. Zell – Wood and Plastic, Loose Powder Compact. Flapjack, wood base, plastic lid, hand-painted flamingo scene, no case I.D., puff with logo, case glued mirror, 4" dia. x ¾", $45.00 – 60.00.

4. Bourjois – Wood, Loose Powder Compact. Coved case, lid transfer of dancing duo, no case I.D., puff with logo "Evening in Paris," case glued beveled mirror, 3" x 2½" x ¾", $75.00 – 90.00.

5. Unknown (Aus.) – Wood, Loose Powder Compact. Carved ivory Bakelite horse and jockey, goldtone closure knobs, signed "Made in Austria," case glued mirror, 2⅞" dia. x ⅜", $45.00 – 60.00.

These W.W.II "Woodies," with the exception of #3, are all wood including hinges, hence the tax advice.

1
2

3
4

1. Belle – Goldtone and Lucite, Loose Powder Compact. "Porthole," beveled Lucite base, goldtone frame, faux burled walnut plastic lid plate, case signed, case glued mirror, 3½" sq. x ½", Ref.: 1946 Ad., $65.00 – 80.00.

2. Unmarked – Sterling and Lucite, Loose Powder Compact. Blue lid, round inset of dove duo in high relief, clear base, 2⅞" sq. x ⅝", $125.00 – 150.00.
The sterling lid ornament also appears as a jewelry set of pin and earrings, 1943 U.S. patent.

3. Unmarked – Lucite, Loose Powder Compact. Reverse mirror lid design, whirling comet on black ground, case glued round mirror, 3" sq. x ½", $75.00 – 90.00.
The center of this case is not removable. Any attempt to personalize it for contemporary reasons by removing the lid display, completely negates the case value and destroys a part of scarce W.W. II compact history.

4. Saks Fifth Avenue – Lucite, Loose Powder Compact. Molded domed case, silvered lid ground, no case I.D., signed foil mirror logo label and "Not Returnable if This Sticker is Removed," 3½" dia. x ½", with label $75.00 – 100.00.

1   3

2

1. Bell Deluxe – Lucite, Loose Powder Compact.
Reverse mirror lid design, blue flocked ground, no
case I.D., puff with logo, case glued mirror, 3¾" sq. x
⅝", $75.00 – 100.00.

2. Unmarked – Lucite, Loose Powder Compact.
Reverse mirror lid design, floral basket on white disk,
case glued mirror with plastic framing, 3¾" sq. x ⅝",
$100.00 – 125.00.

3. Unmarked – Lucite, Loose Powder Compact.
Reverse mirror lid design, sunray blue foil, case glued
mirror, 4" x 3½" x ⅝", $75.00 – 100.00.
   None of these case have removable lid displays or
   mirrors.

1

2

3

1. Revlon – Plastic, Pressed Powder Compact. Flap-jack, aqua case, coin purse closures, mermaid motif, papers signed "She Shells," silver lurex aqua damask puff, case signed, case glued mirror, 4" dia. x ⅜", $65.00 – 90.00.

2. Revlon – Plastic, Pressed Powder Compact. Flap-jack, blue case, coin purse closures, femme with big hair lid display, papers signed "Honey Buns," case signed, puff with logo, case glued mirror, 4" dia. x ⅜", Ref.: 1964 Ad., $75.00 – 100.00.

3. Ziegfeld Girl – Plastic, Loose Powder Compact. Flapjack, domed case, reverse mirror lid embossed paper display "Virgo," case signed, puff with logo "Zodiac Girl," case glued mirror, 5" dia. x ⅝", Ref.: 1944 Pat., $65.00 – 90.00.

Chances are good that there were eleven more of this genre.

1
　2
　3

1. Unmarked Pilcher – Lucite, Loose Powder Compact. Super cushion, midnight blue "Venus," square flora lid inset, case glued mirror, puff with legend, see #3 for box, 4½" sq. x ½", $125.00 – 150.00.

See Vol. I – P192 #2 for Pilcher case. This puff has been printed as a souvenir. Case also in mock tortoiseshell.

2. Unmarked – Lucite, Loose Powder Compact. Beveled case, cerise with quatrefoil pierced lid ornament, case glued mirror, 4½" x 4¼" x ¾", $125.00 – 150.00.

3. Venus Lucite Box for #1.

1   2
           3

1. Iva-Mae – Plastic, Loose Powder Compact. Flapjack, purple mottled flat lid case, hand-painted iris design, domed reverse, no case I.D., puff with logo, case glued mirror, 4⅞" dia. x ½", Ref.: Pat. 1943, $225.00 – 250.00.

2. Iva-Mae – Plastic, Loose Powder Compact. Flapjack, domed mock tortoise-shell case, hand-painted maple leaf design, no case I.D., puff with logo, case glued mirror with sticker "Genuine Hand Painting," 5½" dia. x 1", $250.00 – 275.00.

3. Rho-Jan – Plastic, Loose Powder Compact. Flapjack, gray domed case, hand-painted rose lid design, no case I.D., floral puff with logo, case glued mirror, 5" dia. x ¾", $225.00 – 250.00.

Warping on these large cases does not affect the price, if mirror, hinges, etc. are intact.

1   3
2

1. Unmarked – Plastic, Loose Powder Compact. Flapjack, domed ivory case, lid transfer "Atlantic City, N.J." design, bathing femme at seashore, case glued mirror, 5" dia. x ⅜", $250.00 – 275.00.

2. Unmarked – Plastic Loose Powder Compact. Flapjack, domed ivory case, reverse transfer "B.P.O.E.," molded flora on lid, case glued mirror, 5" dia. x ½", $225.00 – 250.00.

B.P.O.E. is not only on the back, it's on upside down. No chance of flashing the emblem while powdering the nose.

3. Unmarked – Lucite, Loose Powder Compact. Flapjack, beveled octagon case, interior mirror reverse publicity print of MGM film star Esther Williams, plastic framed mirror, 4½" oct. x ¾", Rare. (Also in clear Lucite with double lid mirrors, $75.00 – 100.00.)

Why a female star on a woman's compact? This case is mint and original with a well anchored mirror. Photo is not removable nor a later addition.

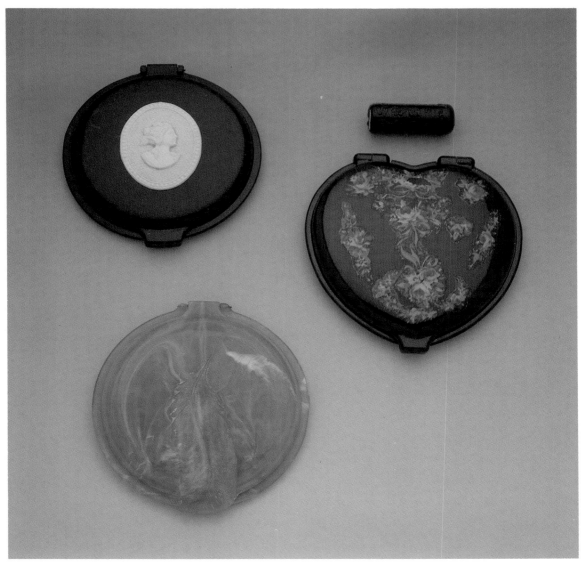

1   3
2   4

1. Lee Products – Ebonite, Loose Powder Compact. Flapjack, domed case, Ivorene faux cameo, papers, case glued mirror, 4¾" dia. x ¾", $225.00 – 250.00.

2. Unmarked – Plastic, Loose Powder Compact. Flapjack, green marbled case with molded plume flange as lid closure, case glued mirror, 4½" dia. x ⅝", $250.00 – 275.00.

Green is a rare color for these big babies.

3. Chen Yu – Plastic Lipstick Tube. Molded faux carved "Black Jade" case, no mechanics, uses spring and taut cord to close cap, paper label, 2" x ¾" dia., Ref.: 1943 Ad., Rare.

A perfect example of W.W. II restrictions on cosmetic items. Wood, cardboard, or plastic lipsticks must have been the ultimate trial of "making do."

4. Unmarked – Ebonite, Loose Powder Compact. Heart, flapjack, domed case, lid flora decals, interior also has decals, case glued mirror, 5" x 5" x ⅝", $275.00 – 300.00.

Fragility of decals set this price.

2

1   3

1. Rho-Jan – Plastic, Loose Powder Compact. Flap-jack, domed mock tortoise-shell case, goldtone lid studs, no case I.D., puff with logo, case glued mirror, 5" dia. x ¾", $175.00 – 225.00.

2. Discus – Plastic, Loose Powder Compact. Flapjack, domed mock tortoise-shell case, no case I.D., puff with logo, case glued mirror, 5" dia. x ¾", $150.00 – 175.00.

3. Vogue Creations – Lucite, Loose Powder Compact. Super, beveled case, silver foil interior sticker "Reflex-ions," case signed "VC," box and puff with logos, double plastic framed mirrors, 4" sq. x ¾", $100.00 – 125.00.

1
2

3
4

1. Mappin & Webb (U.K.) – Tortoise-shell Pendant Vanity. Red leather signed presentation case, gold bands, oval monogram cartouche, braided wrist cord with attached lipstick, latch closure, two interior compartments with hinged lids, no case I.D., framed beveled mirror, marabou puff, 3½" x 2⅜" x ½", tube 2¼" x ½" dia., box 6" x 3¾" x ¾", cord 3¾", complete $650.00 – 750.00.

Mappin & Webb with addresses in London and Paris registered their hallmark in 1899 – 1900. They were using tortoise-shell to enhance cases and small clocks as early as 1907.

2. Unknown (Fr.) – Tortoise-Shell, Loose Powder Compact. Figure eight diamanté lid inlay, case signed "Made in France," case framed beveled mirror, 2⅝" sq. x ½", $150.00 – 175.00.

3. Unmarked – Lucite, Loose Powder Compact. Mock tortoise-shell domed case, sterling femme and dog lid inlay, beveled case glued mirror, 3⅞" dia. x ½", $175.00 – 200.00.

4. Patricia Page Fifth Avenue – Lucite, Loose Powder Compact. Mock tortoise-shell scalloped case, hand-painted flamingo lid display, no case I.D., puff with logo, case glued mirror, 4" x 3¼" x ½", $150.00 – 175.00.

1
2

1. Unmarked (For.) – Tortoise-shell Clutch Carryall.
Coved case, exterior flanges for interior compartments, hinged goldtone framed mirror, comb clip, replacement oval goldtone lipstick, see P199 #1 open, 6¼" x 4" x 1", Rare.
Appears to be handmade.

2. Dorette (U.S.) – Snakeskin Standard Carryall.
Double access, encased green snakeskin, red leather interiors, zipper closures, broad wrist strap, faux ivory suede lined loose powder well, case glued mirror with sticker "Handmade Genuine Snakeskin," case signed, 6" x 3½" x 1¼", strap 3¾", $125.00 – 150.00.
Cardboard cigarette and holder came with the case.

1 Unmarked (For.) – Tortoise-shell Clutch Carryall. See P198 #1 closed for information.

Chapter Five

SHIPS, SOUVENIRS & SETS

Abstract of Ship Log, May 6 – 14, 1959

"...A SHIP IS ALWAYS REFERRED TO AS 'SHE' BECAUSE IT COSTS SO MUCH TO KEEP ONE IN PAINT AND POWDER."
CHESTER W. NIMITZ, 1940

It's hard to imagine in these days of the SST and space stations circling the world that once the "The Only Way To Cross..." from continent to continent was by ship. During the apex of the great liners in the twenties and thirties, the average voyage time from New York to Southampton (U.K.) was five days. The Blue Ribbon prize for breaking this time was hotly sought by the various lines. It was no idle ego award. Speed meant more first class fares such as the big film stars who attracted their own coterie. It was rumored that the *Titanic* was attempting to set a ribbon time when the iceberg was hit.

Crossing the Atlantic was the most active route, with ships leaving New York every day. Each line had pairs of liners. The biggest and the best were the lofty Cunarders and White Stars. Three and four funnels were a mighty image that influenced passengers to such a point that it was not uncommon to have a fake funnel. Each country had its own appeal: the U.K. for space and comfort, Germany for Teutonic massiveness, later for the speed of its ocean greyhounds, and France for elegant chic.

Other routes were just as important to world commerce and ships left ports regularly from Halifax to Liverpool, Vancouver to Australia, and the P & O Liners that were the mail and civil servant carriers to the edges of the British Empire. The U.S. Matson liners had weekly service from San Francisco to Hawaii.

The U.S. did not seriously venture into the Atlantic until after W.W. II, realizing belatedly that as a world power it needed its own ships that could be converted to troop ships in quick order. The S.S. *United States* launched in 1952, was built for speed, and for the first time in 100 years the U.S. gained back the Blue Ribbon; beating the record by ten hours. Although fast, the ship was severely modern and the future troop use was obvious to the more pampered Cunarder and French liner passengers. In 1969, the S.S. *United States* was mothballed by the government at Newport News, VA. She not only missed the gate she also missed the compact market. The liner souvenir compact cases, with a few exceptions, are all of U.K. manufacture.

At the start of W.W. II all commercial traffic ceased and the liners were converted into troop carriers or hospital ships. This was the fate of anything that floated no matter how old, slow, or small. The queens could carry a U.S. Army division and out race the German wolf pack U-boats. Others were converted to armed merchant ships and suffered suicidal loses during convoy duties.

During those halcyon times between the wars, ship travel was more than a trip over water. The call: "Gangways Up!," also unfurled a magic carpet ride. "...Shore life pales beside the brilliance of the hours en voyage." The gift boutiques were the mecca of their country's products and compacts were the ideal souvenir. The only cloud was the world-wide Depression. The quality of the early cases is adequate and the lid depictions are less than artistic. Lapel and locket patch box cases are intermixed and were a more practical buy as they could be adapted to other uses.

The magnificent Butterfly ship souvenir cases are early U.K. maker triumphs by Kwick, Sweet Petals, and Gwenda. A Birmingham, U.K., company, Gwenda was dominant and resumed production in 1948. The parent company, Hussey, Gwenda LTD., ceased operations circa 1963.

The military ship cases (mainly U.K.) may have been given at the ship's launching to dignitaries and officers as commemorative gifts. Intrinsic metal cases might appear in this area, created for the more prestigious patron first launchings.

The major maker of the ship portrait cases was/is Stratton. Again a Birmingham, U.K., company starting production under a parent which eventually became Laughton & Sons Ltd. The Stratnoid line was also added during this pre-war period. In 1938 a German Rowenta designer fled Nazism and joined the vanity case division for a time bringing in new design concepts. All recorded information ceased in 1940 after most of the factories were destroyed by the Luftwaffe. One fact has surfaced — the ship lid portraits were made by a now unknown company other than Stratton.

Collecting these compacts is a step back into history and demands research — hence the Ship Appendix. They tell of good, comic, and tragic times. Each new find is like another voyage and the search begins anew — the struggle for life during the War, the messenger and savior of troops and refugees, the survivor of the passages of the Duke & Duchess of Windsor (with 155 pieces of luggage, valet, maid, secretary, and a pug dog pack), fires, collisions, storms, or to die ignominiously in some scrapyard. They say ships have souls, then maybe some of that spirit still lives on in this tiny fleet.

The souvenirs that complete this chapter again have strong international flavors. Canada is represented in their most famous attraction, Niagara Falls, and a very early souvenir of their infamous attraction, the town of the Dionne quintuplets. Various centennials, expositions, and anniversaries both U.S. and abroad are memory joggers and personal mementos.

Presentation cases, with their studied use of compatible shapes, enamels, and ornamentation to complete their image, were meant to overwhelm the recipient or offer a convenient display of items for a specific occasion or gift. The almost disposable travelettes with their small cargo are gems of graphic art, but timid companions to the Langlois "Train" case. They did serve the same purpose; some weekends were shorter than others.

S. S. POCAHONTAS. AUTOMOBILE AND PASSENGER TRANSPORT BETWEEN CAPE CHARLES AND (LITTLE CREEK)

NORFOLK, VIRGINIA

47798

Postcard — S.S. *Pocahontas*

1. Kwick (U.K.) – White Metal, Pressed Powder Compact. *Esperance Bay*, pearloid domed lid, tortoise-shell inlay, framed mirror, 2" dia. x ½", $75.00 – 100.00.

2. Sweet Petals (U.K.) – White Metal, Loose Powder Compact. R.M.M.S. *Aorangi*, portrait under celluloid, framed mirror, 2" dia. x ¾", $100.00 – 125.00.

3. Unmarked (U.K.) – Goldtone, Loose Powder Lapel Compact. S.S. *Nevasa*, patch box, enameled lid plate, convex mirror, 1½" dia. x ⅜", $125.00 – 150.00.

4. Kwick (U.K.) – White Metal, Pressed Powder Compact. *Highland Patriot*, pearloid domed lid, enameled inlay, framed mirror, 2" dia. x ⅜", $75.00 – 100.00.

5. Unmarked (U.S.) – White Metal, Loose Powder Compact. S.S. *Pocahontas*, portrait under celluloid, metallic mirror, 2" sq. x ½", $150.00 – 175.00.

6. Kwick (U.K.) – White Metal, Loose Powder Compact. H.M.T. *Neuralia*, pearloid domed lid, portrait under celluloid, framed mirror, $100.00 – 125.00.

7. Kwick (U.K.) – White Metal, Pressed Powder Compact. *Berengaria*, pearloid domed lid, tortoise-shell inlay, metallic mirror, 2" dia. x ⅜", $150.00 – 175.00.

8. Unmarked (U.K.) – Goldtone, Pressed Powder Compact. T.S.S. *Cameronia*, pearloid domed lid, portrait under celluloid, framed mirror, 2" dia. x ½", $125.00 – 150.00.

9. Unmarked (U.S.) – White Metal, Loose Powder Locket Compact. *U.S.L.*, patch box, embossed domed lid burgee, convex mirror, 1¾" dia. x ⅜", $75.00 – 100.00.

All named cases are signed.

1	4	7
2	5	8
3	6	9

```
1    3
2    4    6
     5    7
```

1. Stratton (U.K.) – Goldtone, Loose Powder Compact. RMS *Queen Elizabeth 2*, domed scalloped case, enameled lid with silhouette, 3¼" dia. x ½", $50.00 – 65.00.

2. Stratton (U.K.) – Goldtone, Loose Powder Compact. R.M.S. *Queen Elizabeth*, domed flanged case, gold foil lid ground with portrait under plastic, 3" dia. x ⅜", $75.00 – 100.00.
   All Q.E. cases are post W.W. II.

3. Unmarked – Goldtone, Loose Powder Compact. *Queen Mary* life preserver motif with lettering, flanged case, 3¼" dia. x ½", $125.00 – 150.00.

4. Rowenta (For.) – White Metal, Loose Powder Compact. *Queen Mary*, encased domed case portrait, 4" x 2¾" x ¼", $250.00 – 275.00.

Only about two pre-war years of rare German souvenir sales.

5. Stratton (U.K.) – Goldtone, Loose Powder Compact. R.M.S. *Queen Elizabeth*, domed flanged case, lid portrait under plastic, 3½" dia. x ⅝", $125.00 – 150.00.

6. Stratton (U.K.) – Goldtone, Loose Powder Compact. R.M.S. *Queen Mary*, domed flanged case, enameled lid with portrait, 3" dia. x ⅜", $150.00 – 175.00.

7. Stratton (U.K.) – Goldtone, Loose Powder Compact. *Queen Mary*, domed flanged case, gold foil lid ground with portrait under plastic, 3" dia. x ⅜", $75.00 – 100.00.
   All the cases are signed, excluding #3, and all have framed mirrors.

1   4
2   5
3   6

1. Unknown – Sterling, Loose Powder Can Compact. Cosulich line emblem (Italian), case signed: "*Saturnia*," vermeil interior, framed mirror, 1⅞" dia. x ⅝", $125.00 – 150.00.

2. Unknown (U.K.) – White Metal, Loose Powder Compact. H.M.S. *Sussex*, cross-hatch lid, naval cruiser ensignia, 2⅝" oct. x ½", $150.00 – 175.00.

3. Zell Fifth Avenue – Bimetal, Loose Powder Compact. U.S.S. *Soley*, engraved ship silhouette and "Edna" on lid, no case I.D., box and puff with logo, framed mirror, 3⅛" sq. x ¼", $75.00 – 100.00.
   Might have been a presentation gift to "Edna" at the 1944 launch of this destroyer.

4. Pilcher – Silver-plated, Loose Powder Compact. Chameleon, *Merchant Marine*, lid motif of convoy, fighter planes, and eagle, no case I.D., puff with logo, case glued beveled mirror, 2⅞" sq. x ⅜", $100.00 – 125.00.

5. Unknown (U.K.) – White Metal, Loose Powder Compact. Domed case, Royal Navy insignia, framed mirror, 2½" dia. x ⅜", $75.00 – 100.00.

6. Unknown (U.K.) – White Metal, Loose Powder Compact. Saddlebag, H.M.S. *York*, cruiser crest, Art Moderne lid pattern, framed beveled mirror, 2⅝" x 2¼" x ⅜", $150.00 – 175.00.

Postcard – *Caronia*

1. Stratton (U.K.) – Goldtone, Loose Powder Compact. *Caronia*, flanged case, gold foil lid ground, portrait in green under plastic, 3" dia. x ⅜", $125.00 – 150.00.

2. Stratton (U.K.) – Goldtone, Loose Powder Compact. M.V. *Britannic*, flanged case, silver foil lid ground, portrait under plastic, 3" dia. x ⅜", $150.00 – 175.00.

3. Stratton (U.K.) – Goldtone, Loose Powder Compact. S.S. *Empress of Canada*, "princess" case, gold foil lid ground, portrait in white under plastic, beveled mirror, 3" dia. x ⅜", $150.00 – 175.00.

4. Stratton (U.K.) – Goldtone, Loose Powder Compact. R.M.S. *Carinthia*, "regency" case, portrait on gold ground, domed oval framed lid, 3⅜" x 2⅝" x ½", $225.00 – 250.00.

5. Stratton (U.K.) – Goldtone, Loose Powder Compact. R.M.S. *Ivernia*, domed oval flanged case, enameled lid with portrait, 3" dia. x ⅜", $150.00 – 175.00.

6. Stratton (U.K.) – Goldtone, Loose Powder Compact. *Himalaya*, flanged case, gold foil lid ground, portrait in white under plastic, 3" dia. x ⅜", $125.00 – 150.00.

7. Stratton (U.K.) – Goldtone, Loose Powder Compact. R.M.S. *Franconia II*, flanged case, gold foil lid ground, portrait under plastic, 3" dia. x ⅜", $175.00 – 200.00.

8. Stratton (U.K.) – Goldtone, Loose Powder Compact. S.S. *Empress of Scotland*, flanged case, gold foil lid, portrait in white under plastic, 3" dia. x ⅜", $125.00 – 150.00.

All these Strattons are signed and have the "hand/compact" logo, with the exception of #2 which has a powder screen, and all the cases have framed mirrors.

```
1       4       6
2       5       7
3               8
```

Postcard, R.M.S. *Samaria*

1. Unknown (For.) – White Metal, Loose Powder Compact. S.S. *Newfoundland*, butterfly wing lid ground, silhouette under plastic, metallic mirror, 1⅞" sq. x ⅜", $75.00 – 100.00.

2. Unknown (For.) – White Metal, Loose Powder Compact. T.S.S. *Caledonia*, butterfly wing lid ground, silhouette under plastic, metallic mirror, 1⅞" sq. x ⅜", $75.00 – 100.00.

3. Unknown (For.) – White Metal, Loose Powder Compact. R.M.S. *Queen Mary*, butterfly wing lid ground, silhouette under plastic, metallic mirror, 1⅞" sq. x ⅜", $150.00 – 175.00.

4. Gwenda (U.K.) – White Metal, Loose Powder Compact. H.M.T. *Dorsetshire*, domed signed case, butterfly wing lid ground, black enameled border and reverse, white silhouette under plastic, cased metallic mirror, 3¼" dia. x ½", $125.00 – 150.00.

5. Gwenda (U.K.) – White Metal, Loose Powder Compact. *Empress of Australia*, domed signed case, butterfly wing lid ground, black enameled border and reverse, white silhouette under plastic, cased metallic mirror, 3"dia. x ½", $125.00 – 150.00.

6. Unknown (U.K.) – White Metal, Loose Powder Compact. *Warwick Castle*, butterfly wing lid ground, portrait under plastic, double flange closure, framed mirror, signed "Made in England," 3" dia. x ⅜", $100.00 – 125.00.

7. Unknown (For.) –White Metal, Loose Powder Compact. R.M.S. *Carinthia II*, butterfly wing lid ground, white silhouette under plastic, metallic mirror, 1⅞" sq. x ⅜", $75.00 – 100.00.

8. Unknown (For.) – White Metal, Pressed Powder Compact. R.M.S. *Samaria,* octagon step case, butterfly wing lid ground, silhouette under plastic, framed metallic mirror, 2½" oct. x ⅜", $125.00 – 150.00.

9. Unknown (For.) – White Metal, Loose Powder Compact. *Duchess Of Richmond,* butterfly wing lid ground, silhouette under plastic, metallic mirror, 1⅞" sq. x ⅜", $75.00 – 100.00.
The butterfly wing is the Amazonian Blue Morpho.

1 4 7
2 5 8
3 6 9

3
1   4   6
2   5   7

1. Stratton (U.K.) – Goldtone, Convertible Compact.
T.S. *Stefan Batory*, enameled crest "G A L,"(*G*dynia *A*merican *L*ine), case signed, papers, framed mirror, 3" dia. x ½", $75.00 – 100.00.

2. Stratton (U.K.) – Goldtone, Loose Powder Compact. S.S. *America*, lid crest, flanged case, black enameled panels, case signed, framed mirror, 3" dia. x ½", $75.00 – 100.00.

3. Unknown – Goldtone, Loose Powder Vanity Carryall. "Delta Line," double access, enameled lid, portrait, snake chain and exterior lipstick clip, cloth coin purse and comb, case glued mirror, 4" x 3" x 1", chain 4", $175.00 – 200.00.

4. Wadsworth – Goldtone, Loose Powder Compact. Chameleon lid route map of The American President Lines, case signed, framed mirror, 3¼" dia. x ⅜", $75.00 – 100.00.

5. Unknown – Goldtone, Loose Powder Clutch Case. American Export Lines, lid transfer of clipper ship silhouette, cloth coin purse and comb, case glued mirror, unmarked box penciled "August 1960," 4" x 3" x ½", $45.00 – 60.00.
A converted cigarette case with badly fitted interior; might have been a hurry-up job for a ship launch.

6. Stratton (U.K.) – Goldtone, Convertible Compact. *Queen Mary*, see #1 for case information.

7. Stratton (U.K.) – Goldtone, Loose Powder Compact. Blue Star Line crest, domed case, black enameled lid, case signed, framed mirror, 3¼" dia. x ⅜", $65.00 – 90.00.
This model also has a Booth Line lid crest (not shown).

Harper's Bazaar, 1955

1   4
2   5
3   6

1. Unknown (U.K.) – Goldtone, Loose Powder Compact. "Gibraltar/The Rock Ape," flanged case, plastic coated lid inset, case signed "Made in England," framed mirror, 3¼" dia. x ¼", $125.00 – 150.00.
Strong Stratton case design characteristics.

2. Kigu (U.K.) – Goldtone, Loose Powder Compact. Gilt cut-out plastic lid inset, London scenes over black ground, beveled signed case, framed mirror, 2¾" sq. x ⅜", $75.00 – 100.00.

3. Unknown (U.K.) – Pearloid, Loose Powder Compact. Horseshoe, "Channel Islands" legend, zipper closure, black cat on reverse and "Good Luck," paper framed case glued mirror, 3" x 2" x ¾", $45.00 – 60.00.

4. Dorset Fifth Avenue – Goldtone, Loose Powder Compact. Ohio souvenir lid map, no case I.D., puff with logo, case glued mirror, 3" x 3⅛" x ½", $45.00 – 60.00.

5. Kigu (U.K.) – Goldtone, Loose Powder Compact. Domed flanged case, London scenes, case signed, powder door "Darling," Ivorene interior, framed mirror, 3" dia. x ⅜", $75.00 – 100.00.

6. Elgin American – Goldtone, Loose Powder Compact. Chameleon, Canada lid map, case signed, puff with logo, framed mirror, 2¾" sq. x ¼", $50.00 – 65.00.

```
            3
    1       4       6
                    7
    2       5       8
```

1. Unmarked – Goldtone, Pressed Powder Compact.
Black plastic lid plate, "Philadelphia Sesqui-Centennial 1776 – 1926," affixed with rivets, Liberty Bell motif, framed mirror, 2⅝" oval x ⅝", $50.00 – 65.00.

2. Unmarked – White Metal, Pressed Powder Vanity.
Domed case, copper coin lid inset "SesquiCentennial International Exposition, Philadelphia, 1926," top hinged framed mirror, 2" oct. x ⅝", $75.00 – 100.00.

3. Unmarked – Goldtone, Loose Powder Compact.
Marbled plastic lid inset, "Golden Gate Exposition – 1939," medallion, framed mirror, 2¼" sq. x ⅜", $75.00 – 100.00.

4. Unmarked – Goldtone, Loose Powder Vanity.
Encased cream enamel, lid legend "Texas Centennial" (1845 – 1945), coved case with step sides, framed mirror, 4" x 3⅛" x ½", $125.00 – 150.00.

5. Unmarked – Goldtone, Pressed Powder Vanity.
Gray mottled plastic lid plate, affixed with rivets, gilt silhouette "Woolworth Bldg. N.Y.," rhinestones and red tinting, framed mirror, 2½" dia. x ⅝", $125.00 – 150.00.

> *Built in 1913; touted as the world's tallest building at 792.1 feet.*

6. J.E. Mergott – Goldtone, Loose Powder Compact.
Patch box domed case, lid "Pennsylvania Consistory, Pittsburgh, Pa. March 30, 1922," case signed, framed mirror, 2" dia. x ½", $25.00 – 40.00.

7. J.E. Mergott – Goldtone, Loose Powder Compact.
See #6, "Ancient Accepted Scottish Rite, Valley of New Castle, Penna."

8. Unmarked – White Metal, Loose Powder Vanity.
Enameled lid bands, "George Washington, 1732 – 1932" (birthday souvenir), top hinged double metallic mirrors, 2" dia. x ½", $65.00 – 90.00.

1
2
     5
   3
     6
   4
     7

1. Rex Fifth Avenue – Goldtone, Loose Powder Compact. "Niagara Falls," painted lid scene, no case I.D., case glued mirror, 3½" dia. x ⅜", $45.00 – 60.00.

2. Columbia Fifth Avenue – Goldtone, Loose Powder Compact. Flapjack, chameleon, "Niagara Falls," domed flanged case, no case I.D., puff with logo, 3⅞" dia. x ⅜",$65.00 – 80.00.

3. Unmarked – White Metal, Loose Powder Compact. "Souvenir of Canada – Niagara Falls," lid scene under plastic, metallic mirror, 2" sq. x ½", $35.00 – 50.00.

4. Unmarked – White Metal, Loose Powder Glove Vanity. "Niagara Falls," encased gray enamel, hand-painted scene in reverse case, see P74 #4 for Art Nouveau lid, top hinged double metallic mirrors, 1½" sq. x ½", $35.00 – 50.00.

5. Unmarked – Leather, Loose Powder Compact. "Niagara Falls," lid scene, Talon zipper closure, case glued mirror, 3½" dia. x ⅝", $45.00 – 60.00.

6. Unmarked – Celluloid, Pressed Powder Can Compact. Hand lettered lid "Niagara Falls. Canada," maple leaf decal, framed glued mirror, 2½" dia. x ¾", $75.00 – 100.00.

7. Unmarked – Celluloid, Loose Powder Can Compact. Lid transfer of clipper ship silhouette, lettering "Quintuplets Callander Canada," scalloped case, framed affixed mirror, 2½" dia. x ⅜", Rare.
The prices on these two cases are based on survival of the fragile celluloid in mint condition and the homemade aspects; might be one-of-a-kind.

```
              1        5
         2        3        6
              4
```

1. Unmarked – Bakelite, Loose Powder Compact.
Goldtone domed lid frame, "New York World's Fair,"
scene under plastic, black molded case, framed mirror, 2½" dia. x ⅜", $75.00 – 100.00.

**2. Girey – White Metal, Pressed Powder Triple Van-
ity.** Kamra, encased ivory pearloid, exterior lipstick,
lid decal "Century of Progress Chicago 1933," spring
action lid, case signed, framed beveled mirror, 3¼" x
1¾" x ⅜", $125.00 – 150.00.

3.Unmarked – White Metal, Loose Powder Vanity.
Art Deco black enameled lid with "A Century of
Progress Chicago 1933," comet motif, top hinged dou-
ble metallic mirrors, 2" x 1¾" x ½", $150.00 – 175.00.

4. Unmarked – White Metal, Pressed Powder Compact.
Encased red enameled domed case, lid with "Travel and
Transport Building World's Fair Chicago – 1934,"
framed metallic mirror, 2" dia. x ⅜", $75.00 – 100.00.

**5. Mondaine – White Metal, Loose Powder Triple
Vanity.** Art Deco domed red enameled case, exterior
hinged creme rouge lid inset, pierced plate "1934
Chicago" (World's Fair comet & tail logo), no case
I.D., framed mirror, 3¼" dia. x ½", $150.00 – 175.00.
*Three reasons for price: Art Deco, red enameled
cases are not common, and a Mondaine case as a
1934 Fair souvenir.*

**6. Gwenda (U.K.) – White Metal, Loose Powder
Compact.** Coved case, lid with blue foil ground and
plastic cover, transfer scene "New York World's Fair,"
black enameled reverse, case signed, polished interior
lid as mirror, 2¾" x 2" x ¼", $175.00 – 200.00.
*This case must have been one of the last U.K.
exports before the European war storm hit — 1939.*

```
1        5
2    4   6
3        7
```

1. Unknown (U.K.) – Leather, Loose Powder Compact. Horseshoe, faux alligator embossed leather, gilt stamped lid "Festival of Britain 1951," zipper with logo "Lightning," case glued mirror, 3½" x 3¼" x ¾", $65.00 – 80.00.

2. Unknown (U.K.) – White Metal, Pressed Powder Compact. Lid inset under plastic portrait of Edward VIII (or still the Prince of Wales) in a Guards uniform, signed: "Made in England," metallic mirror, 1¾" dia. x ⅜", $100.00 – 125.00.
   Later the Duke of Windsor after abdication; King for only nine months in 1936.

3. Beautibox (U.K.) – White Metal, Loose Powder Compact. Domed enameled case, blue silk tassel, lid affixed plate of Queen Mary and King George V, 25th Jubilee commemoration — May 6, 1935, case signed, puff with logo, framed metallic mirror, 3¼" x 2¾" x ⅜", $200.00 – 250.00.

4. Vovan (U.K.) – Bimetal, Loose Powder Compact. Flapjack, "E II 1953" lid medallion (coronation issue for Queen Elizabeth II), enameled border of Tudor rose wreathing, case signed and "Made in England," framed mirror, 3¾" dia. x ⅜", $175.00 – 200.00.

5. Unknown (U.K.) – Goldtone, Loose Powder Compact. Tinted "Tower Bridge, London" photograph lid inset under plastic (Stratton clone), flanged case signed "Made in England," framed mirror, 3¼" dia. x ½", $50.00 – 65.00.

6. Unknown (U.K.) – White Metal, Loose Powder Compact. Domed enameled case "Union Jack" lid colors, blue reverse, pewter lid medallion "Coronation.King George.And.Queen Elizabeth. 1937," framed mirror, 2¼" sq. x ½", $150.00 – 175.00.

7. Stratton (U.K.) – Goldtone, Loose Powder Compact. Domed flanged case, metallic finish, coronation crown transfer, case signed, framed mirror, 3" dia. x ⅜", $75.00 – 100.00.

1
2   4   5
3   6

1. Volupté – Goldtone, Convertible Compact. Chameleon, "Cub Scouts Den Mother – BSA" activity lid display, case signed, puff with logo, papers, case glued beveled mirror, 2¾" dia. x ½", $125.00 – 150.00.

2. Elgin American – Goldtone, Loose Powder Vanity. Watch case, enameled top and reverse, lid legend "College of Mount St. Joseph on the Ohio, Cincinnati, Ohio," with crest and motto, deep chased sides, signed creme rouge tray "Elgina," no case I.D., lunette puff with logo, case framed mirror, 2" dia. x ½", $150.00 – 175.00.

3. Parker Pen "Wadsworth" (Can.) – Goldtone, Loose Powder Compact. "Boy Scouts" lid medallion chased border, case signed and "Made in Canada," puff with logo, case glued mirror, 3" sq. x ⅜", $150.00 – 175.00.

The parentheses are a part of this logo.

4. Unmarked – Goldtone, Loose Powder Compact. Heart, blue lid enamel, "U.S. Capitol Washington D.C." disk, framed mirror, 2⅛" x ½", $50.00 – 65.00.

5. Unmarked – Goldtone, Loose Powder Compact. Red cloisonné heart with Boy Scout motto and crest ("Life Scout Award"), black silk tassel, framed beveled mirror, 2¼" sq. x ⅜", $150.00 – 175.00.

6. Bailey, Banks & Biddle Co. – Goldtone, Loose Powder Compact. Lid portrait "1950 Ring Dance" (U.S. Naval Academy), no case I.D., pouch with U.S.N.A. crest, date, and logo, case glued beveled mirror, 3" sq. x ⅜", Rare.

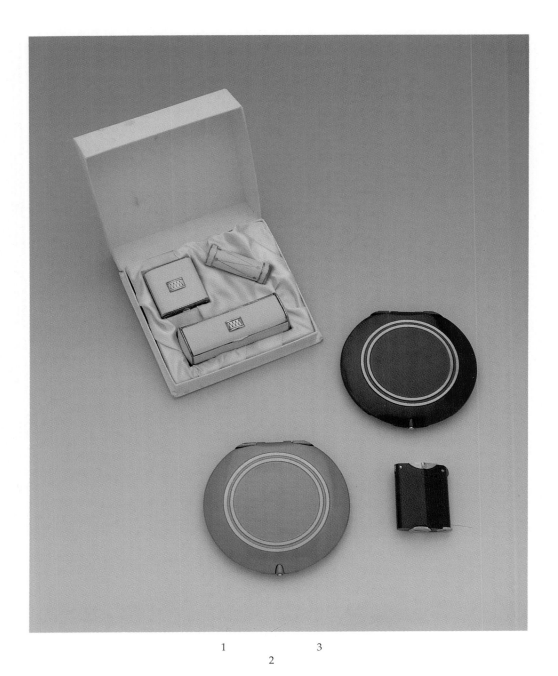

1
      3
2

1. Charbert – Goldtone Presentation Set. "Drumbeat," encased ivory enamel, lid affixed drum motif, three pieces, pressed powder compact, case signed, puff with logo, framed mirror 1½" sq. x ⅜", lipstick tube 1¾" x ⅝" dia., cigarette case, no case I.D., 3⅛" x 1⅛" sq., box 4¾" x 4¼" x 1¼", Ref.: 1937 Ad., complete $150.00 – 175.00.

2. Warner of California – Aluminum, Loose Powder Compact. Flapjack, "Jealousy Green," see #3 for information.

3. Warner of California – Aluminum, Loose Powder Compact. Flapjack and cigarette lighter "Soul Mates," cast cases, anodized finishes, molded lid circles, case and puff signed, case framed mirror, 4" dia. x ⅝", lighter, no I.D., 1⅞" x 1½" x ⅝", Ref.: 1946 Ad., set $175.00 – 200.00, flapjack only $75.00 – 100.00.

Legend has it that these cases were made from W.W.II B-17 Flying Fortresses which were scrapped for their metals after the war. Matching lighters are very rare.

Movieland, 1946

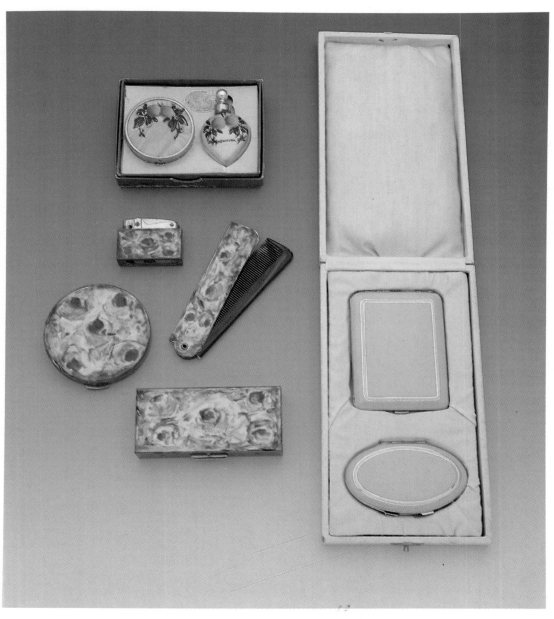

1
2   3

1. Arrow Studios – White Metal and Glass, Boxed Set. Souvenir "St. Augustine, Fla.," oranges and blossoms motif, compact with pressed powder, mottled plastic lid inset, no I.D., puff with "Anco" and arrow, framed mirror, 2" dia. x ½", pearlized coated perfume flacon and mercury glass dauber, 2¼" x ½"; cardboard box, gold foil I.D. sticker "Hand Painted by Arrow Studios," 4" x 3⅛" x ¾", complete: $75.00 – 100.00.

2. SFCO – Goldtone, Hand-painted Four Piece Set. "Roses," compact with loose powder, case glued mir-

ror with I.D. sticker, 2¾" dia. x ⅜", cigarette case, no I.D., 3⅝" x 1¾" x ¾", comb case, white enameled reverse, I.D. sticker, 4¼" x 1", lighter, I.D. sticker and "Lester, Japan," 1¾" x 1¼" x ½", set $50.00 – 65.00.

3. Rowenta (For.) – White Metal, Presentation Set. Encased pink enamel pieces, faux leather box, padded silk interior, compact with loose powder, case signed, framed mirror, 3" oval x 1¾" x ¼", cigarette case, no case I.D., 3¼" x 2⅜" x ¼", box 7½" x 4" x 1", complete $125.00 – 150.00.

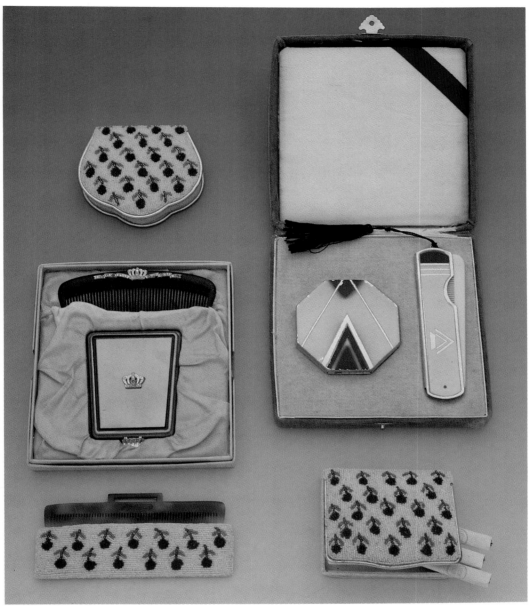

1
2
3

4
5

1. Henri Bendel (Fr.) – Beaded, Three-piece Set. Encased handworked beaded items, cherry motif, rolled goldtone lid edging, compact, saddlebag, white kid leather interior, loose powder, case glued mirror, 3¼" x 3¾" x ⅝", Ref.: 1951 Ad., set $175.00 – 225.00, see #3 – comb, #5 – cigarette case.

2. Girey – Goldtone, Presentation Set. Goldtone compact, lid affixed crown bijou, loose powder, no case I.D., puff and box with logo, 2¾" x 2¼" x ⅜", comb, Bakelite, affixed crown and ribbons, 3¾" x 1¼", box 5⅛" x 4¾" x ⅝", set $75.00 – 100.00.

3. Henri Bendel (Fr.) – Beaded, Cased, Tortoise-shell Comb. Silk lined, 4⅜" x 1¼", see #1 for information.

4. Unknown (For.) – White Metal, Presentation Set. Yellow enameled lids, Art Moderne air-brush motif; compact with loose powder, framed mirror, 2½" oct. x ⅜", comb case with silk tassel, hinged ivorene comb, no I.D., mauve velvet jeweler's box, padded silk lid, formed velvet base, 5" sq. x 1", complete $150.00 – 200.00.

5. Henri Bendel (Fr.) – Beaded, Cigarette Case. Padded top, 3" x 2½" x ¾", see #1 for information. Standard cigarettes just fit. (This case could be used as a compact — has a mirror, but no powder screen.)

The Bendels are negotiable as individual pieces.

McCall's, 1928

1
2

1. Coty – White Metal, Presentation Set. Compact with pressed powder, case signed, puff with logo, papers, metallic mirror, 1⅞" sq. x ⅜", cased glass perfume, signed, label "Emeraude," 2½" x 1⅝" oval x ¾", lipstick tube, blue enameled banding, signed, 2" x ⅝" dia., blue faux shagreen papered box, fitted blue velvet base, signed, 5½" x 4¾" x 1¼", Ref.: 1929 Ad., complete set $275.00 – 350.00.

2. Weisner of Miami – Goldtone, Three-piece Set. All items with plastic pearl mountings, faceted rhinestones and pierced filigree plates, lipstick only I.D., pouches with logo, compact 2¾" dia. x 1", case glued mirror, cigarette case 3⅝" x 1⅝" x 1", lipstick 2½" x 1" dia., Ref.: 1953 Ad. (var.), complete $200.00 – 250.00.

LADIES' HOME JOURNAL

December, 1936

It is le Père Noël advising

a Lesson from the French in the Giving of Gifts

It is le Père Noël, the Santa Claus of France, speaking... We men do not clutch the head and search for gifts in frenzy when it comes to the season of the joyous Noël. But no! Because we know that from the cradle it is natural for the ladies to be concerned with their beauty... and that the loveliest ladies of our belle patrie are devoted to Evening in Paris.

So do as we do if you would delight the ladies at Noël... give to them *all* sets of Evening in Paris... For yes, there are in all twenty different sets, costing from a little one dollar and ten cents all the way up to twenty dollars for the set de luxe, the gift glorious for the loveliest lady you know.

At your favorite drug or department store

De luxe bottle of Evening in Paris Perfume. **$10.00**

Triple Vanity—Rouge, Lipstick and Face Powder. . **$2.75**

Evening in Paris Purse Flacon of Perfume, Face Powder, Rouge and Talcum Powder. **$2.95**

Evening in Paris Perfume, Toilet Water, Face Powder, Talcum Powder, Single Loose Vanity and Lipstick. **$10.00**

Evening in Paris Perfume, Toilet Water, Face Powder, Talcum Powder, Single Loose Vanity and Lipstick. . **$7.75**

Evening in Paris Perfume in silver and blue gift box. . . **$1.10**

Evening in Paris Perfume, Face Powder, Lipstick, Single Loose Vanity and Talcum Powder in a gift box of mirror-like silver. **$4.95**

Evening in Paris Purse Flacon of Perfume and Single Compact. **$1.75**

Evening in Paris Perfume and Face Powder in a luxurious box. **$2.25**

Evening in Paris Perfume in special bottle with atomizer. . . **$1.65**

Evening in Paris BOURJOIS

Ladies' Home Journal, 1936

```
1        4        6
2        5        7
   3              8
```

Bourjois advertised their Evening in Paris extensively; all these items were probably parts of presentation sets.

1. Powder Box. Plastic, script logo, 3½" dia. x 1¼", $15.00 – 25.00.

2. Powder Box. Cardboard, 2⅛" sq. x ⅝", lipstick, plastic 2" x ⅝", Ref.: 1943 Ad., set $35.00 – 50.00.

3. Compact. Bakelite and aluminum, loose powder, blue case signed, metallic mirror, 2¾" sq. x ½", Ref.: 1938 Ad., $65.00 – 80.00.

4. Powder Box (U.K.). Cardboard, Eiffel Tower motif, 2⅜" dia. x ⅝", $25.00 – 40.00.

5. Rouge Box. Cardboard, loose rouge, signed box and puff. 1¾" dia. x ½", Ref.: 1936 Ad., $20.00 – 35.00.

6. Compact. Plastic, flora lid silhouette, no case I.D., puff with logo, case glued mirror, 3¼" x 2½" x ½", $35.00 – 50.00.

7. Display Box Star. Cardboard, Ref.: 1934 Ad., N.F.S.

8. Compact. Lucite, pressed powder, lid star motif, case and puff signed, papers, case glued mirror, 2¾" dia. x ⅝", $50.00 – 65.00.

```
1          5
2          6
3     4    7
           8
```

All these pieces are hallmarked Sterling, but other than the lipstick box information on a Firenze (Florence) Italian silversmith, U. Bellini, there is no identification. The encased hand-chased rococo design with niello accents, is obviously similar, exempting only #8 (plain reverse) so unknown but Italian.

1. Compact. Loose powder, case glued beveled mirror, 2¾" sq. x ⅜", $175.00 – 200.00.

2. Pendant Combination Case. Pressed powder, link wrist chain 6½", beveled case, two coin holders, framed mirror, 3" x 2½" x ⅝", $150.00 – 175.00.

3. Boxed Combination Pill Box and Lipstick. Spring action lid with cabochon malachite lipstick slide as catch, framed mirror and polished mirror on lipstick side, 2⅛" x ¾" sq., with box $50.00 – 65.00.

4. See #3 for information, a red variation on lid stone (several other variations), $45.00 – 50.00.

5. Compact. Loose powder, case framed mirror, 3⅛" sq. x ⅜", $225.00 – 250.00.

6. Cased Comb. Tortoise-shell capped with silver, 4" x 1", $35.00 – 50.00.

7. Pill Box. 1½" x 1¼" x ½", $25.00 – 40.00.

8. Compact. Attached snake link chain necklace, loose powder, framed mirror, 2¾" dia. x ¼", $150.00 – 175.00.
This case has an unknown maker's mark. The chain is crudely soldered on. A homemade conversion attempt?

Life, 1927

1

2   3

1. Hampden – Cardboard Travelette. "Going Places," pseudo luggage with travel decals, brown silk ribbon handles, four items including face powder, foundation boxed stick, rouge stick, wood lipstick, 7¼" x 5¼" x 1½", $175.00 – 225.00.

The lipstick has a "United Nations for Victory" decal.

2. Richard Hudnut – Cardboard Travelette. "Three Flowers," box with modes of transportation, four items including tubes of face creams, glass perfume

flacon, face powder, papers, 4⅜" x 3⅛" x 1", $150.00 – 200.00.

3. Melba – Cardboard Travelette. "Fleurs," automobile and chauffeur scene, seven items including powder tin, four tubes of various face creams, glass perfume flacon, powder packet, 5¼" x 4" x 1", $200.00 – 250.00.

Mint with all the pieces for these prices, otherwise negotiable.

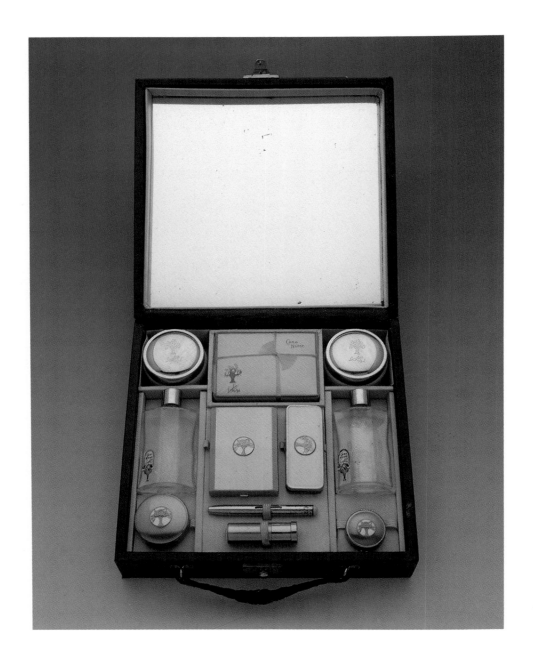

1. Langlois – Faux Black Leather Make-Up Train Case. Braided leather handle, latch closure with no key, full lid mirror, eleven items all signed or have paper stickers "Cara Nome," compact, loose powder, puff with logo, and framed mirror; pressed rouge with puff with logo and framed mirror; creme rouge case with framed mirror; mascara case with brush, embossed logo, and metallic mirror; lipstick retractable brush; lipstick; powder box; two metal capped jars, two metal capped bottles, set 8⅜" x 8⅛" x 1⅞", $350.00 – 400.00.

Unlike other cases by Richard Hudnut or Marie Earle, this has no tray that lifts out for storage of ancillary items; no room for non-Langlois products.

Chapter Six

NOVELTIES & WHIMSIES

Artist signed

"...THE MOST AMUSING GADGET FROM PARIS IS THE POWDER WINDMILL. IT IS MADE JUST LIKE A WINDMILL WITH FOUR SHADES OF POWDER WHICH YOU DROP INTO THE LITTLE WINDOW OF THE MILL... WIND THE HANDLE UNTIL MIXED TO THE SHADE THAT MATCHES YOUR COMPLEXION AT THE MOMENT."

HARPER'S BAZAAR, 1935

After the novelty of well designed compacts and vanity cases began to pale, the next logical progression was gadgetry. Some of the items in this chapter may flirt with the gadget sobriquet, and it does seem that with the above quote the phenomena was universal. Humor in design is acceptable within good taste and can be charming whimsy; gadgetry, however, tends to sometimes make the fool. Most novelties gravitate to their own sphere and are hard workers who serve a particular purpose.

Some cases started out as well meaning and became an inadvertent joke, i.e. the cases that tried to produce light. Hence they are novelties not gadgets. The designers failed to consider the adverse nature of portable batteries and light bulbs and their side effects other than a desired tiny ray of light. Very few women need to put on makeup in total darkness or require a portable light to do so. These cases don't or shouldn't work, since all the lighting apparatus must be removed to protect the case from battery acid corrosion.

Some cases are a dichotomy: a serious novelty. The cookie compacts were originally working advertising cases. Now they are an important historical link in the evolution of compacts. The dated 1902 Blue Danube case is here and cherished as all antecedents are. The various puff and chamois powder rag carriers should also be considered more than a novelty. They were ideas that failed, but if the attempt had not been made the later carriers may never have reached the design heights of the Ostertag carryall.

The other working novelties — that worked — are still clever and owe no apologies. These include cases with music boxes, interior photo frames, mirror cleaners, piggy banks, clothes brushes, time pieces, billfolds and coin purses with a nearby compact, and the initial cases that can be adjusted as initials change.

The true novelty cases of birds with real feathers, domestic butterflies and their exotic jungle cousins, dried flowers and grasses are tiny hand-crafted works of art and should be treated as such — very carefully. The cartoon case may now have a dated joke or incident, but it is still, in its category, a colorful collectible novelty.

There are good examples shown of the international sense of humor such as the oversize watch fobs, "daters" with time reminders both in English and French, and the charming envelope cases with their genuine postage stamps. The miniature luggage, or valises, come in different patterns, some serious replicas, others with their flash of travel labels that manage to sneak in an advertisement or two for the price of the case. They could be converted to business and visiting card cases without too much disruption.

In several instances the novelty and whimsy cases overlap. The ball cases with dice and games in their domed lids are novelties, but the ball shape takes a trip into the whimsy category. This definition applies to the minuscule walnut cases that are pure whimsy but served a purpose as carriers for perfume flacons, thimbles, dress pins, and a photo frame.

A major overlap occurs with the jewelry items that served as costume ornamentation and compact or vanity cases. The lockets, dress clips, and bracelets may be considered working whimsies. The French bangle bracelet deserves a place all its on for the ultimate blend of engineering, design, and style into a useful ornament. All the cosmetics in the bracelet were used, so it did not reside in pristine idleness as a fanciful objet d'art.

The furniture whimsies mix U.S. and U.K. designs and the pianos stand on sturdier legs. They are gems of construction and imagination. The player piano is a remarkable union of a music box and compact. The music could have been more appropriate; maybe *Rule Britannia* rather than *The Third Man Theme*.

The other furniture items were a large puzzle: the mini cedar chests. The logical first step had been contact with the maker, The Pilliod Cabinet Co., Swanton, Ohio — still in business — but again too late, nothing was gained by persistent inquiry. However, there was enough material to study including logo stickers, advertisements, and even a dated message in pencil on the bottom of one of the boxes. The Pilliod boxes are different yet similar to the McGraw boxes from McGraw, N.Y. The interior fittings were the same, but the box shapes are different. There is a box available with only bridge item fittings such as fancy pencils, table markers, tally cards, etc. — no cosmetic items.

Another question about the supposed slot for combs was answered. The existing slot proved to be too shallow and narrow. It was later found to be a shim gap to secure the interior contents for shipping or handling. A trade ad identified the Reich-Ash company as the case wholesalers for the metal cosmetic items to both cabinet companies. The Bakelite fittings supplier is as yet unidentified.

These chests were always meant to be a boudoir whimsy for jewelry, other cosmetics, love letters, diaries (the cases do have a lock and key), and other precious keepsakes once they were emptied of their original disposable contents. The sooner the better on some of the gifts — cedar flavored chocolates must surely be a whimsy's whimsy.

```
        1       3           6
    2           4           7
                5
```

1. Cruver Mfg. Co. – Tin, Loose Powder Can. Cookie, encased lithographed scenes White House, Washington, D.C and The Capitol, Washington, D.C., 2¼" dia. x ½", $65.00 – 80.00.

2. Parisian Novelty Co. – Tin, Loose Powder Can. Cookie, encased lithographed advertising, 2¼" dia. x ⅜", Ref.: Pat. 11/2/15, $75.00 – 100.00.

3. Unknown (For.) – Tin, Powder "Rag" Can. Lithographed paper lid inset Spanish femme, rose paper interior, no mirror, 2" dia. x ¾", $50.00 – 65.00.

Powder rags were another name for chamois cloths used for removing facial perspiration after an active dance.

4. Parisian Novelty Co. – Tin, Loose Powder Can. Cookie, encased matte finish, lithographed femme lid motif and legend "Compliments of Madison & Kedzie State Bank" (Chicago, ILL.), 2¼" dia. x ⅜", $75.00 – 100.00.

5. Unknown – Tin, Loose Powder Can. Cookie, "Blue Danube Vanity Box" legend on back of interior lid, inset metallic mirror, Persian case motif (reverse and lid interior shown), 2" dia. x ⅝", Ref.: April 15, 1902 Pat., designer Ella Lichenstein, N.Y., Rare.

Collection's earliest documented case.

6. Cruver Mfg. Co. – Tin, Loose Powder Can. Cookie, encased lithographed scenes Pennsylvania State Memorial, Gettysburg, PA, and "House in Which Jennie Wade Was Shot, Gettysburg, Pa.," 2" dia. x ⅜", $65.00 – 80.00.

"Only civilian killed at battle side...stray bullet through two wood doors...."

7. Parisian Novelty Co. – Tin, Loose Powder Can. Cookie, encased lithographed femme lid motif, advertising on reverse (shown), 2¼" dia. x ⅜", $75.00 – 100.00.

All cases have framed metallic mirrors and are signed (except #3). Parisian Novelty cases may be signed "PNCO."

```
           3
   1       4       6
   2       5       7
```

1. Rion (Bra.) – White Metal, Pressed Powder Compact. Silhouette tropical beach scene, butterfly wing ground, plastic cover, "Rio," paper "Brasil – J. Eisenstadler" and tax stamp "400 Reis," case signed, framed mirror, 2⅛" dia. x ½", $65.00 – 80.00.

2. Unmarked – "Nickle Silver" [sic], Loose Powder Pendant Vanity. Lid inset feathered bird on milkweed ground and dried flora, plastic cover, mesh wrist band, side hinged metallic backed mirror, 2" dia. x ⅝", chain 5", Ref.: 1927 Ad., $75.00 – 90.00.

3. Coty (Fr.) – White Metal, Pressed Powder Compact. Color enhanced femme silhouette, butterfly wing ground, plastic domed cover, case I.D. "Paris, France," puff with logo, papers in French, metallic mirror, 1⅞" sq. x ½", $125.00 – 150.00.

4. Unknown (Fr.) – Goldtone, Loose Powder Compact. Glass domed lid, feathered bird duo, green moiré ground, only case I.D. "France," case glued beveled mirror, 2¾" dia. x ¾", $250.00 – 300.00.

5. Gwenda (U.K.) – White Metal, Loose Powder Compact. Domed case, black enameled reverse, multicolored accented Kingfisher silhouette, butterfly wing ground, plastic cover, case signed, polished lid reverse mirror, 3" dia. x ⅜", $125.00 – 150.00.

6. Coty (Fr.) – Goldtone, Pressed Powder Compact. Domed lid inset, silhouette view of Sugarloaf Mountain, Rio, butterfly wing ground, plastic cover, case signed "Paris," puff with logo, framed mirror, 2" dia. x ½", $100.00 – 125.00.

7. Unmarked – "Nickle Silver" [sic], Loose Powder Pendant Vanity. Lid inset true butterfly over milkweed and straw flowers, plastic cover, mesh wrist band, side hinged metal backed framed mirror, 2¼" x 2⅛" x ½", chain 4½", $75.00 – 90.00.
All these cases contain natural materials as stated.

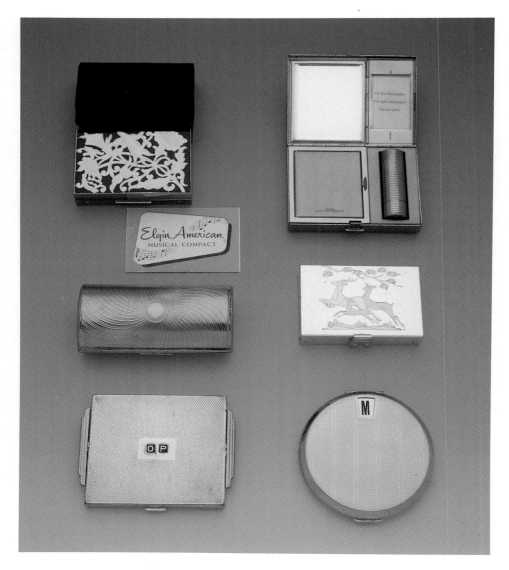

```
1    4
2    5
3    6
```

1. Elgin American – Goldtone, Loose Powder Compact. Music box playing *Anniversary Waltz* black enameled lid, faille slip case, box and case signed, puff with logo, papers shown, case glued mirror, 2⅞" x 1⅞" x ¾", Ref.: 1953 Ad., $100.00 – 125.00.

2. Kigu (U.K.) – Goldtone, Loose Powder Baton Compact. Music box, plays ?, embossed comet and tail lid motif, case signed, framed beveled mirror, 3½" oval x 1⅛", $125.00 – 150.00.

> *Unusual for KIGU engineering — there is no access to either domed area; mirror is not hinged to act as a cigarette lid compartment.*

3. AGME (Sw.) – Goldtone, Loose Powder Compact. Side bars contract to change lid window initials, case signed, framed broad beveled mirror, 3⅜" x 2⅝" x ⅜", $75.00 – 100.00.

4. AGME (Sw.) – Bimetal, Loose Powder Vanity. Portrait, silvertone inlay lid panels, no detail, hinged interior ⅓ lid frame, papers, framed beveled ⅔ mirror, goldtone case, signed, lipstick no I.D., 3¼" x 2⅜" x ⅝", $75.00 – 90.00.

5. Elgin American (Jp.) – Bimetal, Loose Powder Compact. Music box plays *Brahm's Waltz*, goldtone lid leaping gazelles overlay, silvertone slip case over goldtone interior, lyre closure, case and pouch signed, puff with logo, stamped "Japan" below exterior hinge, case glued mirror, 2¾" x 1¾" x ⅝", $50.00 – 65.00.

> *In 1963 E.A. moved their complete operation to Japan. This is an authentic E.A. case.*

6. Stratton (U.K.) – Goldtone, Loose Powder Compact. Lid initial window, case signed, puff, box, and pouch with logo, framed mirror, 3" dia. x ⅜", Ref.: 1956 Ad., $50.00 – 65.00.

```
          2    5
   1      3    6
          4
```

1. Clearview Box – See #3.

2. Dunhill – Goldtone, Loose Powder Compact. "Clearview" mirror powder wiper, encased green snakeskin, case signed, framed beveled mirror, 2¾" sq. x ⅝", Ref.: 1938 Ad., $125.00 – 150.00.

3. Clearview – Sterling, Loose Powder Compact. Box shown (see #1), mirror powder wiper, beveled lid, sculpted peacock, case and box signed, puff with logo, framed broad mirror, 2¾" sq. x ½", $175.00 – 200.00.
This device seems to have begun with the German Rowenta 1930s foreign Pat.s, then the word "Clearview" became somewhat generic.

4. Stratton (U.K.) – Goldtone, Loose Powder Compact. "Miraclean" mirror powder wiper, black enamel banded lid, case signed, puff with mirror, framed mirror, 3" x 2⅛" x ⅜", Ref.: 1953 Ad., $100.00 – 125.00.

5. Unknown (Aus.) – Bakelite and White Metal, Loose Powder Compact. "Turnabout" mirror powder control, pivot mirror frame, chamois with ribbon, Austrian Pat., magnified metallic mirror backing, 3¼" x 2⅜" x ½", $150.00 – 200.00.

6. Maquet (Fr.) – Leather, Loose Powder Compact. "Whisker" exterior clothes brush, base slide-out mirror, folded lid, white kid leather liner, goldtone clip closure, box and case signed, marabou puff, 2⅝" x 2¾" x ⅝", $225.00 – 250.00.

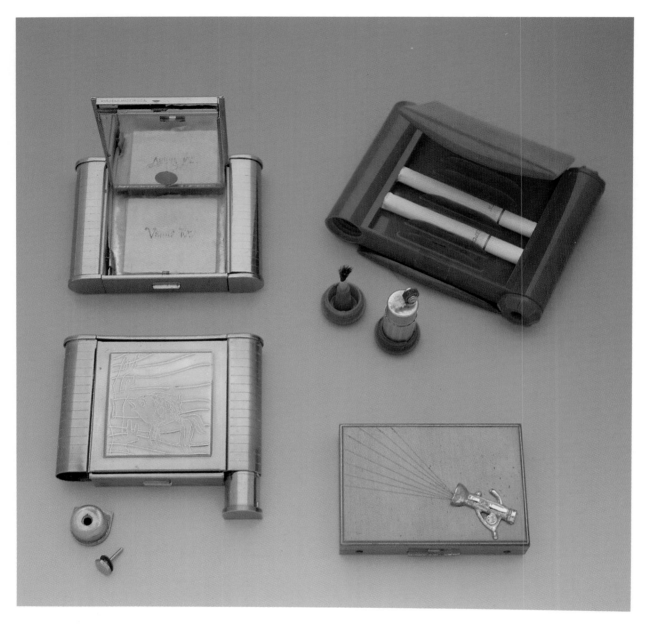

1   3
2   4

1. Spotlite Corp. – Goldtone, Loose Powder Combination Vanity. "Venus-Ray," see #2 closed.

2. Spotlite Corp. – Goldtone, Loose Powder Combination Vanity. "Venus-Ray," aquatic embossed lid, exterior lipstick tube in right compartment, left contains battery for interior mirror light and metallic perfume flask with screw top and dauber (acts as battery base), case signed, puff with logo, framed mirror, 3½" x 2⅝" x ⅝", perfume ⅝" dia. x ½", Ref.: 1947 Ad., see #1 open, $125.00 – 150.00.

Also has cross work and diagonal squares lid designs.

3. Revell's Glamour Kit – Plastic, Loose Powder Combination Case. Double access, mottled plastic,

cigarette compartment, right exterior tube contains lipstick brush (?) and lighter, left contains bulb, battery and push button, case signed, puff with logo, 4½" x 3½" x 1", $175.00 – 200.00.

Also has black model, see Volume 1 – P167 #6 closed.

4. Zell – Goldtone, Loose Powder Combination Compact. "First Nighter," detachable interior flashlight case, lid affixed silvertone flashlight and wishbone, no case I.D., puff with logo, papers, case glued mirror, 3¼" x 2¼" x ¾", $75.00 – 100.00.

A true gimmick: loose powder and batteries? And then there is that wishbone on the lid?

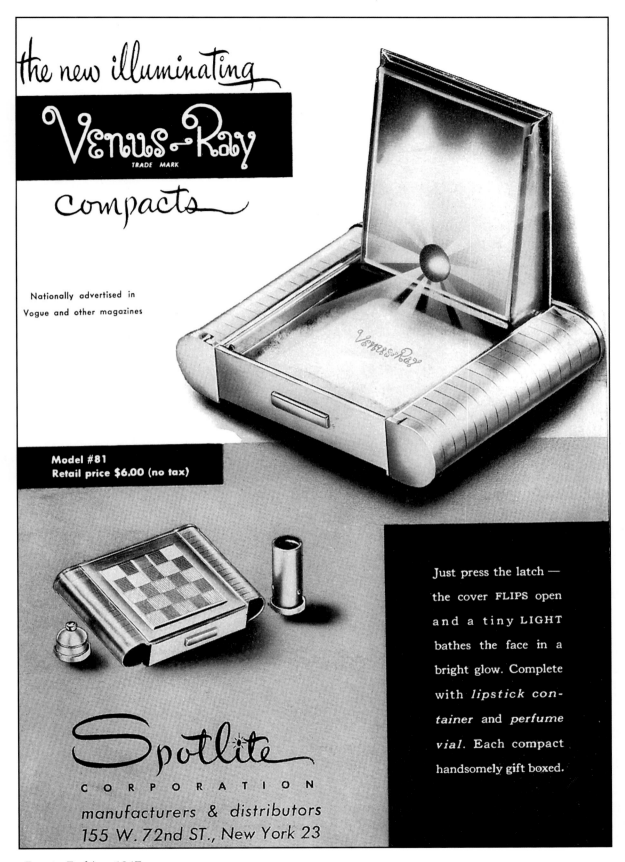

the new illuminating

Venus-Ray
TRADE MARK

compacts

Nationally advertised in
Vogue and other magazines

Model #81
Retail price $6.00 (no tax)

Just press the latch —
the cover FLIPS open
and a tiny LIGHT
bathes the face in a
bright glow. Complete
with *lipstick con-*
tainer and *perfume*
vial. Each compact
handsomely gift boxed.

Spotlite
C O R P O R A T I O N
manufacturers & distributors
155 W. 72nd ST., New York 23

Beauty Fashion, 1947

```
1    4    6
2    5    7
3    8
```

1. Unknown (U.K.) – Goldtone, Loose Powder Compact. Envelope, encased enamel, issued cancelled stamp with King George VI profile, flap outline on reverse, framed beveled mirror, 3⅛" x 2⅝" x ¼", $150.00 – 175.00.

2. Unknown (Aus.) – White Metal, Loose Powder Compact. Envelope, encased enamel, faux wax seal in reverse flap, no design on top, framed beveled mirror, 3" x 2⅜" x ⅜" (with seal intact), $175.00 – 200.00.

3. Elgin American – Goldtone, Loose Powder Compact. Chameleon, lid thermometer and femme sport activities, case and puff signed, case glued mirror, 2¾" sq. x ⅜", $100.00 – 125.00.

4. Unknown (Fr.) – Goldtone, Loose Powder Compact. Plastic domed lid thermometer, center rosette, Fahrenheit degrees, framed beveled mirror, 3⅜" dia. x ¾", $150.00 – 175.00.

5. Rendezvous (Ger.) – Goldtone, Loose Powder Compact. Flapjack, lid display of clock and pointer with movable hands, social caricatures, no case I.D., box with information, framed mirror, 4" dia. ⅜", $150.00 – 175.00.

6. Unknown (U.K.) – Goldtone, Loose Powder Compact. Envelope, encased enamel, issued cancelled stamp of King George VI profile, "London, 1939," flap outline on reverse, framed beveled mirror, 3⅝" x 3⅛" x ¼", $200.00 – 250.00.

7. Unmarked – Goldtone, Loose Powder Compact. Envelope, encased green leather with goldtone rim, faux stamp and cancellation "New York, U.S.A. 1939" (a World's Fair souvenir?), flap outline on reverse, framed mirror, 2¾" x 2" x ⅜", $75.00 – 100.00.

8. Unknown (Fr.) – Goldtone, Loose Powder Compact. "Mon Rendezvous," lid display Bakelite indicator and timer discs, femme social activities, domed plastic cover, "Made in France," framed beveled mirror, 3⅜" x 2¾" x ½", $200.00 – 225.00.

1 2
3 5
4

1. Liberty of London (U.K.) – Goldtone, Loose Powder Compact. Domed case, lid decals of mythical figures and center clock, legend "No minute gone ever comes back again, take heed and see ye nothing do in vain," reverse lettering "The Liberty Clock," framed mirror, 3¼" dia. x ½", $75.00 – 100.00.

Liberty's London Department Store has a mechanical clock on the Tudor side of the building off Oxford St. The box legend says "St. George he fought for England a dragon he did slay above the clock at Liberty He strikes the chimes each day. Oh lady here's a pretty thing that show him in the act, for beauty and St. George we think you'll cherish this compact."

2. Wadsworth – Bimetal, Loose Powder Compact. Silvertone lid overlay, incised outline of bank building clock, goldtone case signed, puff with logo, case glued beveled mirror, 3" sq. x ⅜", $65.00 – 80.00.

3. Illinois Watch Case Co. – Goldtone, Loose Powder Combination Compact. Fotopak, enameled banded lid, inset watch "Weldwood," case signed "I.W.C.Co.," puff with logo, framed metallic hinged mirror, portrait pocket on mirror reverse with plastic protector, 2" sq. x ⅞", $125.00 – 150.00.

4. Rho-Jan – Goldtone, Loose Powder Compact. Super, red metallic lid finish, cut-out clock face, rotating hands, no case I.D., puff with logo, case glued mirror, 3½" sq. x ⅜", $125.00 – 150.00.

5. Illinois Watch Case Co. – Goldtone, Loose Powder Compact. Chameleon, domed lid motif of Marshall Field's Department Store (Chicago) logo, watch inset "Rockford/Swiss" movement, case signed, pouch "Elgin American," 3⅜" dia. x ½" (with clock ⅝"), $100.00 – 125.00.

1
2

4
5

3

1. Cara Mia – Goldtone, Loose Powder Compact. Timer, red metallic lid finish, embossed numerals, rotating pointers, framed interior and reverse mirrors, case signed, 3¼" dia. x ⅜", $75.00 – 100.00.

2. Zell Fifth Avenue – Goldtone, Loose Powder Compact. Pocket watch, silk wrist cord and tassel, enameled lid with photo locket, no case I.D., puff with logo, case glued mirror, 2½" dia. x ⅜", $50.00 – 75.00.

3. Stratton (U.K.) – Goldtone, Loose Powder Compact. Pocket watch with suede fob handle and ring, enameled transfer lid, pouch and case signed, puff with logo, case glued mirror, 2¾" dia. x ½" (strap: 4½"), Ref.: 1952 Ad., $125.00 – 150.00.

4. Wadsworth – Goldtone, Loose Powder Compact. Railroad watch case, applied lid dial, antique train engine reverse design, no case I.D., puff with logo, case glued mirror, 2¾" dia. x ½" (w/ring 1"), $125.00 – 150.00.

5. Unknown (Fr.) – Silver-plated, Loose Powder Compact. Pocket watch, silk fob and tassel, domed lid inset of abstract blown blue and silver glass, signed "Made in France," framed mirror, 2½" dia. x ½", $150.00 – 200.00.

1	4
2	5
3	6

1. Kigu (U.K.) – Goldtone, Loose Powder Compact. Valise, bark-like case finish and luggage straps, handle opener, case signed and "Bon Voyage," framed mirror, 3¼" x 2½" x ½", $100.00 – 125.00.

2. Mascot/ASB (U.K.) – Goldtone, Loose Powder Compact. Valise, case B.O.A.C. decals, handle opener, no case I.D., puff with logo, framed mirror, 3" x 2⅛" x ½" (w/handle 2½"), $150.00 – 175.00.
British Overseas Air Corp. decals are very fragile so the price is high.

3. Mascot/ASB (U.K.) – Goldtone, Loose Powder Compact. Valise, lid embossed international cities, see #2 for case information, but $75.00 – 100.00.

4. Unknown (For.) – Cloth, Loose Powder Compact. Hat box, lid leather strap, snap closure, leather labels Paris, Berlin, London, case glued mirror, 3" x 3⅛" x ⅝", Ref.: penciled date – 5/38, $125.00 – 150.00.
Case is upside down because labels are right side up or....

5. Mascot/ASB (U.K.) – Goldtone, Loose Powder Compact. Valise, lid embossed flap and lock, see #3 for price and information.

6. Riviera – Faux Alligator, Loose Powder Compact. Valise, encased leather handle, goldtone clasp, kid interior, case signed, case glued beveled mirror, 3¼" x 2¾" x ¾", $100.00 – 125.00.
Author's BOAC luggage tag added — NFS.

Liberty magazine, 1943

```
1    3    6
2    4    7
     5
```

1. Unmarked – Goldtone, Loose Powder Compact. Domed, encased green and gold metallic finish, marching tin soldier lid motif, framed mirror, 2" dia. x ⅜", $45.00 – 60.00.

2. Unknown (U.K.) – Goldtone, Loose Powder Compact. Lid plastic inset, soda parlor scene and duo in silhouette, case signed "Made in Great Britain," framed mirror, 3" dia. x ⅝", $40.00 – 55.00.

3. Unmarked – White Metal, Loose Powder Compact. Encased enamel, transfer lid design sailors dancing a jig, case glued mirror, 2⅜" sq. x ½", $30.00 – 45.00.

4. Rex Fifth Avenue – Goldtone, Loose Powder Compact. Super, enameled lid "Bicycle Built For Two," artist signed "Laura Jean Allen," no case I.D., puff with logo, case glued mirror, 3¾" sq. x ½", $75.00 – 90.00.

5. Piccadilly (U.K.) – Goldtone, Loose Powder Compact. Lid transfer scene "Mary Had a Little Lamb," case signed, case glued beveled mirror, 3⅛" x 2½" x ⅜", $65.00 – 80.00.

6. Unmarked – Goldtone, Pressed Powder Compact. Enameled lid with painted Flapper dancing the Charleston, framed mirror, 2" dia. x ⅜", $30.00 – 45.00.

7. Unmarked – White Metal and Leather, Loose Powder Compact. Lid enamel snow scene, femme skier transfer, black leather reverse, case framed mirror, 2¾" dia. x ⅜", $35.00 – 50.00.

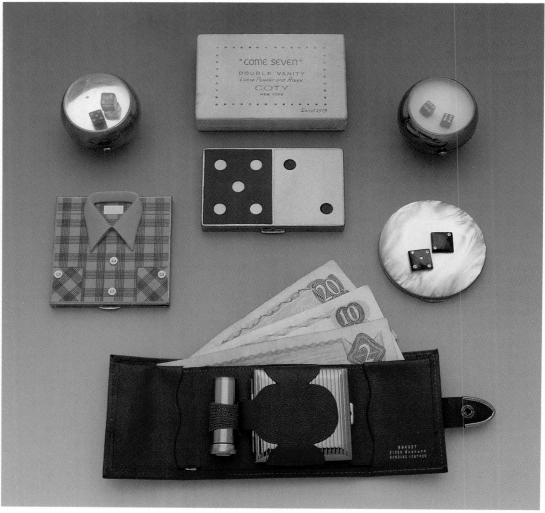

1   3   6
2   4   7
        5

1. Henriette – Goldtone, Loose Powder Novelty Compact. Ball, dice on mirror ground, plastic dome, interior inscription "Arabian – Ohio's Smartest Supper Club – Columbus, Ohio," no case I.D., box with logo, framed mirror, 2" x 2", Ref.: 1941 city directory, $200.00 – 250.00.

2. Wadsworth – Goldtone, Loose Powder Novelty Compact. Lid plaid shirt transfer, buttons flat, affixed collar, case signed, puff with logo, case glued mirror, 3" sq. x ⅜" (collar + ¼"), $225.00 – 250.00.

3. Coty – "Come Seven" box, 4" x 2¾" x ¾", see #4.

4. Coty – Goldtone, Loose Powder Novelty Vanity. "Come Seven" black and white enameled lid dice, recessed dots, everything signed, case glued beveled mirror, papers, 3¾" x 2¼" x ½", Ref.: 1942 Ad., model #1905, complete $250.00 – 275.00.

5. Dorset Fifth Avenue – Goldtone and Leather, Loose Powder Novelty Set. Red billfold 4" x 3⅛" x ⅞", signed cushion compact with ribbed case, no I.D., puff with logo, framed mirror 2¼" sq. x ½", lipstick, with no I.D., 1⅞" x ¾", $75.00 – 100.00.

He lost his shirt at the dice tables, she took her Bingo winnings home.

6. Wadsworth – Goldtone, Loose Powder Novelty Compact. Ball, dice on ivory ground, plastic dome, Ivorene interior, no case I.D. (see Vol. I P235 #1), 2" x 2", $175.00 – 200.00.

7. Marhill – Goldtone, Loose Powder Novelty Compact. Plastic mottled lid plate, affixed rhinestone accented dice, no case I.D., gold foil I.D. sticker, case glued mirror, 2¾" dia. x ½", $75.00 – 100.00.

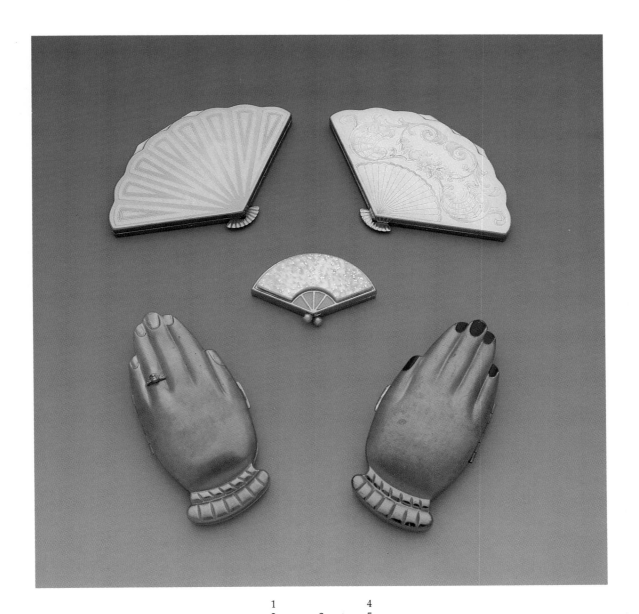

1
2   3   4
                   5

1. Henriette – Bimetal, Loose Powder Compact. Fan, silvertone lid overlay as outlined sticks, glossy goldtone interior, no case I.D., puff with logo, framed mirror, 4¾" x 3" x ⅜", $125.00 – 150.00.

2. Volupté – Goldtone, Loose Powder Compact. Engagement ring hand, molded signed case, puff with logo, framed mirror, 4⅝" x 2" x ¾", Ref.: 1947 Ad., $225.00 – 250.00.

3. Unknown (Jp.) – Goldtone, Loose Powder Compact. Fan, Lucite spangled lid plate, champlevé enamel , faux pearl capped coin purse closure, signed, case glued mirror, 2½" x 1½" x ⅜", $25.00 – 40.00.

4. Wadsworth – Bimetal, Loose Powder Compact. Fan, silvertone lid rococo overlay, goldtone interior, case signed, puff with logo, framed mirror, 4¾" x 3" x ⅜", Ref.: 1947 Ad., $125.00 – 150.00.

The similarity between the Wadsworth & Henriette cases is not cloning. Henriette was The New York division of The Wadsworth Watch Case Co. of Dayton, KY. This design sharing occurs in other cases. The Wadsworth's are usually signed.

5. Volupté – Goldtone, Loose Powder Compact. Manicured hand, see #2 for information and price.

The nail manicure is on both sides of the hand.

1	3	6
2	4	7
	5	

1. Evans – White Metal, Pressed Powder Locket Vanity. "Opera Vanity," enameled lid, leaping gazelle, S link 26" neck chain, side hinged metallic mirror, no case I.D., 1⅞" dia. x ⅜", Ref.: 1932 Cat., $150.00 – 175.00.

2. Unmarked – Bimetal, Pressed Powder Locket Compact. White metal lid, affixed Art Nouveau helmeted heAd., goldtone reverse and oval link 24" neck chain, framed mirror, 1½" dia. x ¼", $75.00 – 100.00.

3. Unmarked – White Metal, Loose Powder Compact. Dress clip, domed diamanté pavé lid, polished interior lid mirror, 1⅝" dia. x ⅜", Ref.: 1932 Pat., $150.00 – 200.00.

4/3/32 patent designed by Elisha A. Phinney, N. Attleboro, Mass., issued to "GE. H. Fuller & Son Co., Pawtucket, R.I."

4. Unmarked – Goldtone, Pressed Powder Locket Compact. Domed flanged octagon lid, cloisonné femme portrait, black enameled framing, oval link 26"

neck chain, filigree enameled link clasp, locket, 1⅞ oct., compact 1⅝" dia. x ⅜", $250.00 – 300.00.

5. Unknown (For.) – Silver-plated, Loose Powder Lapel Compact. Patch box, lid cartouche engraved "Bruselles" [sic], crimped framed mirror, gold lapel pin, 1½" dia. x ½", $175.00 – 200.00.

Lapel pin can be removed for neck chain; might be a W.W.I souvenir from Belgium.

6. Unmarked – White Metal, Pressed Powder Locket Vanity. Cloisonné lid, flapper length (36") neck chain, pink, rose, green, faux tourmaline enameled chain links, top hinged double metallic mirrors, 1½" sq. x ½", $150.00 – 175.00.

7. Unmarked – Goldtone, Pressed Powder Locket Compact. Collet mounted oval onyx lid ornament with pearl, case affixed metallic mirror, 1¾" oval x ⅜", $65.00 – 80.00.

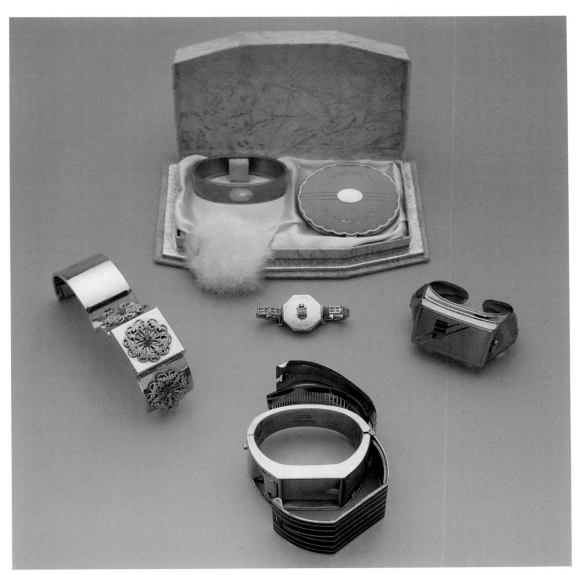

1   2

       3   5

       4

1. Unmarked – Goldtone, Loose Powder Bangle Compact. Filigree lid bijoux with faux amethyst, framed mirror, 2½" x 2½" x 1¼" x ⅜", $175.00 – 200.00.

2. Unmarked – Goldtone, Presentation Set. Lavender enameled bangle and vanity, oval center cartouche, incised accents, domed loose powder vanity, side hinged double metallic mirrors, 2¾" x 2¼" x ⅜", bracelet 2½" x 2¼" x ⅝", box 7¼" x 4½" x 1½", complete $225.00 – 250.00.

See Vol. I – P230 #1 for similarity to Pitman & Keeler Set.

3. Modette – White Gold Filled, Pressed Powder Bracelet Compact. Octagon lid with crest, pierced fili-gree expansion bracelet, case signed, framed mirror, 5" dia. x 1" oct. x ¼", $175.00 – 200.00.

4. Zama (Fr.) – Goldtone, Loose Powder Bangle Vanity. Black enameled case, goldtone horizontal line accents, side hinged lids, pressed rouge, oval lipstick, case glued square mirror over center powder compartment, reverse clip for curved tortoise-shell comb, everything signed and "Paris, 1938," 2¾" x 2¼" x 1⅜", tapered back x ¾", $400.00 – 450.00.

5. Kotler & Koppet – Goldtone, Loose Powder Bangle Compact. Chameleon lid motif, side lid hinge, no case I.D., puff with logo "K&K," case glued mirror, 2¾" x 2¼" x 1½", $175.00 – 200.00.

```
1        3        6
2        4        7
         5
```

1. Unmarked – White Metal, Pendant Compact. U.S. Army campaign hat, link chain, finger ring, hinged crown, convex base mirror, lid storage, 2½" dia. x 1¼", chain 4¼", see P249 #1 open, $175.00 – 200.00.

2. Hattie Carnegie – White Metal, Pressed Powder Compact. Napoleon medallion, case signed, framed mirror, 1¾" dia. x ½", see P249 #5, $75.00 – 100.00.

3. Elgin American – White Metal, Art Moderne Automobile Accessory. Three part carrier, rigid handle pressed powder compact, no case I.D., framed mirror (see Vol. I P118 #1), 2½" dia. x ½", match box sleeve 2¼" x 1⅝" x ⅜", cigarette box holder same dimensions, carrier 6" x 3¼" (center) x 2½" x 1", signed "Elgin Vanity," gray velvet interior (reverse mounting holes), complete, Rare.

4. David M. Zell – White Metal, Loose Powder Compact. Piggy bank, coin slot and removable reverse panel, paper instructions, case signed and motto "Insure and Smile," framed mirror, key, 2" dia. x ¾", see P249 #2 reverse, $150.00 – 175.00.

5. Unmarked – Walnut Shell, Novelty Compact. Hand carved, center threading, no mirror, see #1 for similar example of a nose dabber and P249 #4 open, 1½" x 1⅛", with marabou puff $125.00 – 150.00.

6. Unmarked – Wood and Goldtone, Pressed Powder Novelty Set. Sewing kit, goldtone thimble top, red painted wood body, removable center bobbin with spools and needle case, bottom capped compact, exterior metallic framed mirror, felt puff, 2¾" x 1" dia., see P249 #3 open, complete $150.00 – 175.00.

7. Unmarked – Silver-plated, Faux Walnut Shell Novelty Set. Right side has hinged goldtone encased glass perfume flacon with cork pin cushion liner, left side has hinged framed portrait and convex mirror, marabou puff, top ring, 1¾" x 1½", see P249 #7 open, $225.00 – 250.00.

```
1     3     5
2     4     6
            7
```

1. Unmarked – White Metal, Pendant Compact. U.S. Army campaign hat, link chain with finger ring, see P248 #1 closed.

Since there is no powder well, the case was probably a nose dabber carrier with either a puff or chamois.

2. David M. Zell – White Metal, Loose Powder Compact. Piggy bank, reverse, See P248 #4 lid.

3. Unknown (For.) – Plastic, Loose Powder Pendant Compact. Castanet shaped case, cat face of oval rhinestones, coral silk rope carrier, no case I.D., case glued mirror, 4" x 3" x ¾", $250.00 – 275.00.

4. Unmarked – Walnut Shell Novelty Compact. Hand carved, nose dabber case, See P248 #5 closed.

5. Hattie Carnegie – White Metal, Pressed Powder Compact. Napoleon medallion, eagle reverse motif, see P248 #2 lid.

6. Unmarked – Silver-plated, Faux Walnut Shell Set. See P248 #7 closed.

7. Unmarked – Wood and Goldtone, Novelty Set. Sewing kit and compact, see P248 #6 closed.

```
            1           4
            2       3   5
```

1. Volupté – Goldtone, Loose Powder Carryall.
"Chatelaine," double access, mesh wrist band, ivory enameled interior center compartment, pressed rouge with lid, case signed, puff with logo, bottom hinged double metallic mirrors, 3¾" x 2¾" x ⅞" (slopes to 2" at top), band 6", Ref.: 1938 Ad., $225.00 – 250.00.

2. Volupté – Goldtone, Loose Powder Pendant Vanity. "Lucky Purse," double access, link wrist chain, pressed rouge compartment under exterior flap, case signed, puff with logo, framed mirror, 2¾" x 3½" x ½", chain 6", Ref.: 1948 Ad., $100.00 – 125.00.

3. La Mode – Goldtone, Loose Powder Pendant Vanity. Padlock, rigid handle, vertical lid banding, side

hinged heart-shaped double metallic mirrors, no case I.D., puff with logo, chased sides, 2⅜" heart x ½" (3" with loop), $150.00 – 175.00.

4. Volupté – Goldtone, Loose Powder Carryall.
"Chatelaine," black enameled chevron case with center cartouche, see #1 for information, $250.00 – 300.00.

5. Volupté – Goldtone, Loose Powder Pendant Compact. "Lucky Purse," faux lid flap, rhinestone teardrop motif, see #2 for information, $75.00 – 100.00.

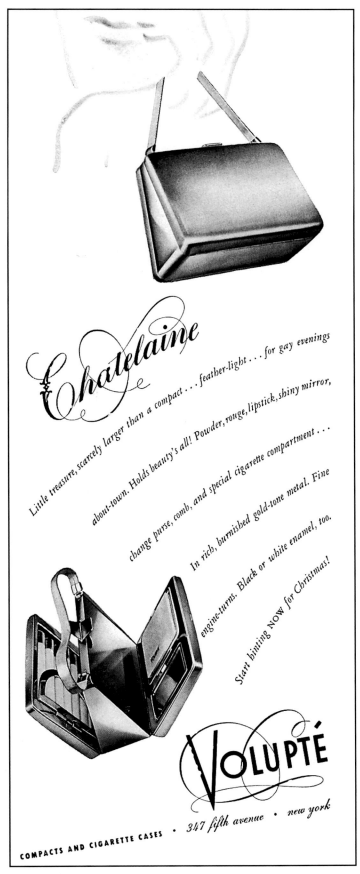

Chatelaine

Little treasure, scarcely larger than a compact . . . feather-light . . . for gay evenings about-town. Holds beauty's all! Powder, rouge, lipstick, shiny mirror, change purse, comb, and special cigarette compartment . . . In rich, burnished gold-tone metal. Fine engine-turns. Black or white enamel, too. Start hinting NOW for Christmas!

Volupté

COMPACTS AND CIGARETTE CASES · 347 *fifth avenue* · *new york*

Harper's Bazaar, 1938

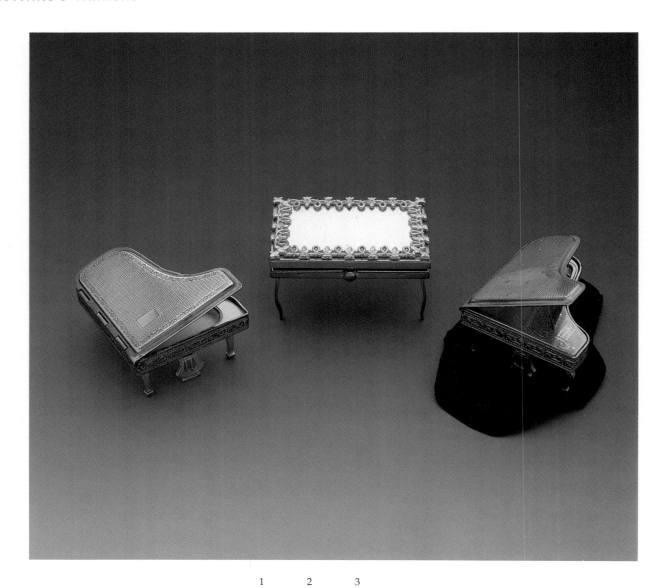

1   2   3

1. Pygmalion – Goldtone, Loose Powder Whimsy Compact. "Grand Piano," folding Sheraton legs, lyre pedal rest, lid monogram cartouche, chased sides, case signed, puff with logo, case glued mirror, 2¾" x 3⅜" (at keyboard) x 1⅜", $300.00 – 350.00.

2. Wadsworth – Goldtone, Loose Powder Whimsy Compact. "Vanity Table," folding bowed legs, looped lid framing with crowns and fleur de lis, metallic plateau mirror, case signed, puff with logo, case glued mirror, 3" x 2⅛" x 1", Ref.: 1950 Ad., $225.00 – 250.00.

3. Pygmalion – Goldtone, Loose Powder Music Box Whimsy Compact. "Grand Piano," folding cabriole legs, lyre pedal rest, sunrays, and stars lid motif, music clef interior motif, case signed, puff with logo, case glued mirror, shaped black faille pouch, 2¾" x 2⅜" etc., $450.00 – 500.00.
Plays The Third Man Theme.

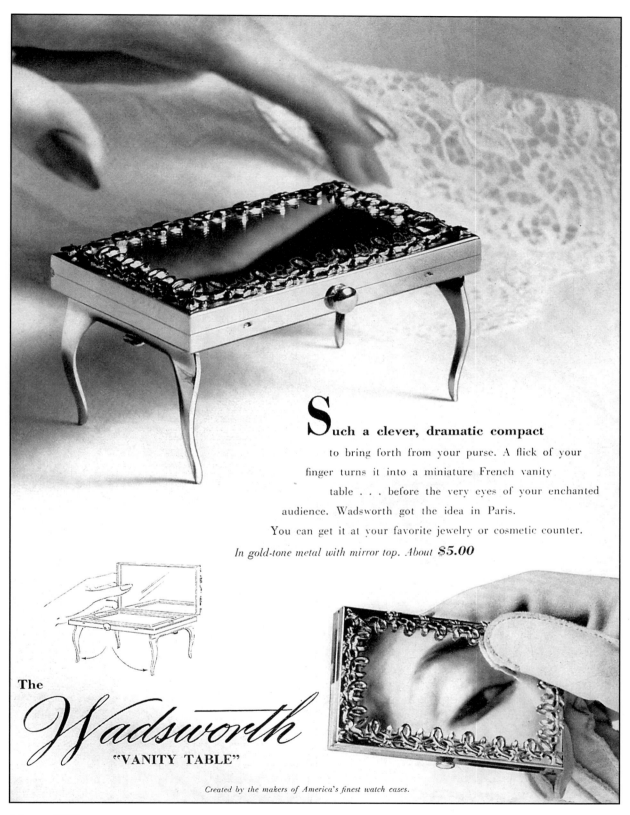

Such a clever, dramatic compact
to bring forth from your purse. A flick of your
finger turns it into a miniature French vanity
table . . . before the very eyes of your enchanted
audience. Wadsworth got the idea in Paris.
You can get it at your favorite jewelry or cosmetic counter.
In gold-tone metal with mirror top. About **$5.00**

The

Wadsworth

"VANITY TABLE"

Created by the makers of America's finest watch cases.

Vogue, 1950

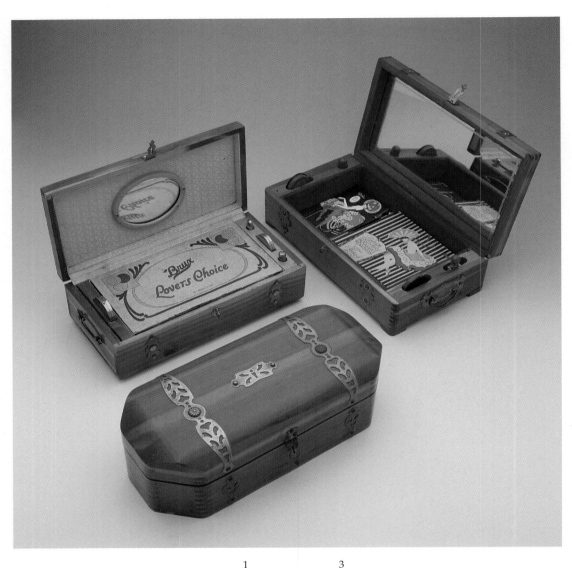

1
          3
   2

1. Pilliod Cabinet Co. "Art Boxes." Cedar, brass straps, handles and key latch, padded pink damask lining, pink painted oval affixed mirror, *"Brux* Lovers Choice" candy box insert, red and gold foil reverse logo sticker, goldtone fittings of pressed powder gold-tone compact, engine-turned case banding, no case I.D., framed mirror, 2" dia. x ⅜", rouge case, 1⅝' x ⅜", oval lipstick tube, 2", glass perfume falcon, capped with dauber, 2¾" x ⅜" sq. (no comb – the slot was formed by a shim used to secure the candy box and contain the compact slot), 12" x 6" x 4", Ref.: inscription – "Dec. 25, '21," see P235 #1 closed and fittings, complete $375.00 – 450.00.

2. McGraw "Treasure Chest." See P255 #3 open.

3. Pilliod Cabinet Co. "Art Boxes." Cedar, brass straps, handles and key latch, box glued red velvet lining, full case framed mirror, Gibson Bridge accessories, reverse incised logo, red/black Bakelite fittings of two screw top cases — pressed powder and rouge, puffs, no mirrors, no case I.D., 1¾" dia. x ½", molded glass perfume flask, 2" x 1¼" x ⅜", red enameled metallic lipstick, 1⅝" x ½" dia., box 13" x 7" x 4", see P255 #2 closed and fittings, complete $300.00 – 350.00.

This Pilliod box also came with stationery and was used as prizes for bridge tournaments.

1   3
          2

1. Pilliod "Art Boxes." Cedar, see P254 #1 open.

2. Pilliod "Art Boxes." Cedar, see P254 #3 open.

3. McGraw Box Co. "Treasure Chest." Cedar, brass strops and key latch, beveled chest, no handles or feet, padded blue faille lining, full case framed mirror, reverse incised logo, similar fittings as Pilliod #1, case design more detailed, embossed honeycomb reverses, also same shim gap for interior objects, 13½" x 6" x 4¼", see P254 #2 closed, complete $350.00 – 400.00.

Author's guess at what these boxes might have been used for after the initial gift was removed. The contents of this box are vintage family wedding items including silk/lace handkerchief, garters, original wedding ring and box. NFS.

All the goldtone cases are in a 1928 trade magazine; wholesale manufacturer is Reich-Ash Corp. N.Y.

Chapter Seven

POWDER BOXES & BEAUTY EPHEMERA

Vogue, 1945   Artist : Salvador Dali

"...THE PEACH-LIKE FINISH GIVEN TO THE SKIN BY FACE POWDERS IS OBTAINED BEST BY THE USE OF RICE STARCH...POTATO STARCH SHOULD BE AVOIDED. COMPLETE DISSIPATION ON THE SKIN IN A SHORT TIME IS VERY NOTICEABLE IN THOSE POWDERS WITH A LARGE AMOUNT OF TALCUM."

AMERICAN PERFUMER, 1928

Old issues of the *American Perfumer* trade magazine provides a revealing look at what went into a powder box besides powder. The numerous wholesale companies offered their specialities by featuring their most successful clients in the ads.

The issues also feature short histories of those companies that have achieved longevity, essays on the "Royal Name Influence" and how it affected American marketing, and the lure of exotic products, usually from the Orient.

A.A. Vantine of New York began importing Oriental products in 1854, right behind Admiral Dewey's 1853 U.S. fleet landing in Japan. Vantine's opened Yokohama offices in 1895, as the world went manic over Eastern products. Similar to the 1922 King Tut mania, anything that hinted of the romance of the East (which by now had included everything east of Gibraltar) such as Arabian nights, sheiks, and Peking's Forbidden City, Vantine's supplied. At first their persona was the geisha girl, particularly in perfumes, but later the famous Buddha at Kamakura, Japan, became the symbol of Vantine's, giving them the nickname of the "Buddha Company."

In 1911, for the first time, they presented their face powder in a glass Buddha jar. Emptied of powder and filled with sand it could then be used as a door stop! The Jafleur perfume was also premiered. Packaging was everything with all types of ornamentation to reinforce the Oriental mood including the scent of rose bud potpourri under gold lace on box lids, the sparkle of the Peking glass beads, the Buddha figure as a lid handle, the use of porcelain creme jars, and the hand-covered fabric boxes. Ads occured as late as 1924.

In the U.S. was J.A. Pozzoni Pharmacal Co. of St. Louis, MO, who claimed to have invented his powder and who registered his trademark of JAP in 1874. Pozzoni later expanded to New York and Chicago. The 1910 ad of his complexion powder states 1906 compliance with the U.S. Pure Food and Drug Act, "...relieves all pimples, freckles and discolorations and makes the skin delicate." Compliance appears to have been a bit lax. His gimmick was the use of sterile wooden boxes with detailed instructions on the proper chamois and powder application (or else no cure?).

Another company that did fancy handwork in boxes was R. Newman of N.Y. distributing the Fansimo Line. A March 1921 ad stated of "Flowers in the Garden" ornamental boxes covered in damask and silk, "You can let us cover your old boxes or odd shaped...and they can be sold as novelties." The ad depicts boxes with silk rose buds, ribbon ruching, and lace. Early recycling?

The magnificent Lazell Perfumer line of "As The Petals Fall" is featured in 1919 ads by two companies — Improved Mailing Case Co., N.Y. (who made the cardboard powder boxes), and the American Can Co., N.Y. (who made the can compacts). The American Stopper Co. Brooklyn, N.Y., in 1912 was a lithographer who specialized in the design and finish on powder tin boxes; "Surfine Riz Poudre" can is featured. E.N. Rowell Co. Batavia, N.Y., in 1928, displayed one of their prized client's products, the powder box with the multicolored Nylotis peacock logo.

Stanley Mfg. Co. of Dayton, Ohio, specialized in metal seals and labels. A Rieger's gold embossed foil seal is obvious in their 1920 ad. Some companies were more prolific and the Modern Cigarette Box Co., Brooklyn, N.Y., did silk and satin presentation boxes for holiday gift sets that included perfume, and face and rouge powders. Their prize customer was Kerkoff's "Djer-Kiss." Presentation boxes were a feature of F.N. Burt Co., Buffalo, N.Y., featuring, in 1935, such fancy work as tassels and other coordinating design effects to complement the vanity case.

The beauty ephemera is a new category to this volume. These inexpensive novelties were mainly for fun, were rarely practical, and except for the elegant French pli, were made to be disposable. The Jacqueline Cochran gift pouch does take the weekender travelette in another direction and makes it purse portable. Also the lipstick/perfume wands, if closed securely, made for a handy accessory, as did the lipstick carriers with their own mirror.

From the oddity to the rarity, the bon ton groupings in this chapter must be the boudoir sets and accessories. The powder puff wands are lacking their dresser powder jars, but these jars were usually not part of the elaborate dresser set with more items than a hope chest. The paired wands are of mixed lineage and are more inventive and amusing than a clump of feathers on a sterling stick. The Bakelite wand hints at other surprises in this genre.

The silver-plated Art Deco "Beauty Make-Up Boxes" appear as items in wholesale gift catalogs, circa 1928 – 1938, with a wide choice of style, finish, and dimension. This may have lengthened its popularity. They all came with generic rouge and powder patens and plain satin backed puffs. There might have been some choice between the second tube containing either an eyebrow crayon or solid perfume. Alas, there is no artist's mark on the splendid figures.

The Quaker Silver Co. three-piece set is tres chic. The workmanship is Art Deco and gracefully functional. Easily refillable, containing all the essential beauty items, it surely was a splendid gift of love for milady's boudoir.

1

2

3

4

5

1. Fallis, Inc. – Peter Pan Powder Box. "Opal Hue Beauty Powder," encased black silk, paper decals, lid tassel, peach silk interior, 4⅛" x 3⅛" x 2⅝", tassel 4", $50.00 – 65.00.

2. Jarvaise – Narcisse Ea Nuit. "Brunette," silk padded lid, 4" x 3⅛" x 1⅝", $35.00 – 50.00.

3. Langlois – Shari. "Rachelle-dark," encased chinois-erie patterned silk, 2¾" oct. x 1½", Ref.: 1931 Ad., $40.00 – 55.00.

4. Langlois – Shari. "Naturelle," see #3 for information, 3" oct. x 2⅛", $50.00 – 65.00.

5. Richard Hudnut – Deauville. "Naturelle," silk box, lid portrait of femme at dressing table, 3⅝" x 3½" x 1½", $40.00 – 55.00.

2   4

1   3

1. Tokalon (Fr.) – Petalia. "Ocre," femme mask, 2⅝" dia. x 1¼", $250.00 – 300.00.

2. Schiaparelli – Radiance. Silk lid art signed "Salvador Dali, 1944," 5" heart, 4¾" x 2", Ref.: Ad., $475.00 – 600.00.

3. Langlois – Duska. "Naturalle," Art Deco lid art with 1925 Paris Exposition Lalique Fountain variation, 4¼" x 3" oval x ½", Ref.: 1930 Ad., $125.00 – 150.00.

4. Tokolan (Fr.) – Pero. "Rachel," male mask, 2⅜" dia. x ¾", $150.00 – 175.00.

1   4
2   5
3   6

1. Dabrooks'. "White," padded silk lid cartouche, 3" sq. x 1½", $25.00 – 35.00.

2. Melba – Melbaline. "Flesh," papers shown, 3¼" sq. x 1", $35.00 – 50.00.

3. Marjolet. "Flesh," 3¼" x 2½" x 1½", $25.00 – 35.00.

4. American Products Co. – Zanol. 3" sq. x 1⅝", $25.00 – 35.00.

   Reverse information, "...apply the powder with a chamois, rubbing it on evenly...."

5. Colgate & Co. – Florient. "Flowers of the Orient," "Flesh," 3" octagon x 1½", Ref.: 1920 Ad., $35.00 – 45.00.

6. Nelson – Garden Court. "Natural," 3" sq. x 1½", Ref.: 1919 Ad., $45.00 – 60.00.

Florient
Flowers of the Orient

An attractive miniature
box of Florient Talc will be
sent upon request if you
mention *Life*.

*A*T Christmas, the daintiest offering, Florient (Flowers of the
Orient) is chosen in Perfume, Toilet Water, Talc Powder, Face
Powder and Soap. Florient expresses by its fragrance the thought-
ful consideration you wish conveyed by your gift.

This delightful perfume was preferred by a jury of discriminating
women, in an impartial International Perfume Test.

The Florient Gift Box, lined, and decorated in the Florient design,
contains a bottle of Perfume, a bottle of Toilet Water, Face Powder
and Soap, all fragrant with "Flowers of the Orient." A difference
in the boxes affords a range of prices from $5.00 to $12.00.

COLGATE & CO.   *Est. 1806*   NEW YORK

Life, 1920

Artist signed: WDT

1	4
2	5
3	6

1. L.T. Piver (Fr.) – Le Trefle Incarnat. "Naturelle," 3½" oct. x 2⅞" x 1¾", Ref.: 1923 Ad., $75.00 – 100.00.

2. Maison Violet (Fr.) – Ambre Royal. "Naturelle," 3¾" x 3" x 1½", Ref.: 1921 Ad., $65.00 – 90.00.

3. Talcum Puff Co. – Corylopsis. "Air–Float," "Flesh," 3" dia. x 1", $50.00 – 65.00.

4. United States Cosmetic Co. – La Florita. 3¼" dia. x 2⅛", $50.00 – 65.00.

5. A. Bourjois & Cie (Fr.) – Dora. "Rachel," 3" dia. x 1¾", $40.00 – 55.00.

6. Harmony of Boston – Violet Dulce. 3" sq. x 1⅜", $35.00 – 50.00.

1   4
2   5
3   6

1. A. Bourjois & Cie (Fr.) – Manon Lescaut. "Naturelle," 3¼" dia. x ½", Ref.: 1924 Ad., $50.00 – 65.00.

2. Harmony of Boston – Alma-Zada. "White," 3¼" dia. x 1⅝", $65.00 – 80.00.

3. Golden Peacock. "Brunette," 3⅜" x 2⅝" x 1", $30.00 – 45.00.

4. Salon Palmer – Gardenglo. "Brunette," 3⅛" dia. x 2", $50.00 – 65.00.

5. Lazell Perfumers – As The Petals. "Flesh," 3⅛" dia. x 2", Ref.: 1920 Ad., $75.00 – 90.00.

6. Font (Sp.) – Gatita. "Rachel," 2⅜" dia. x ¾", $50.00 – 75.00.

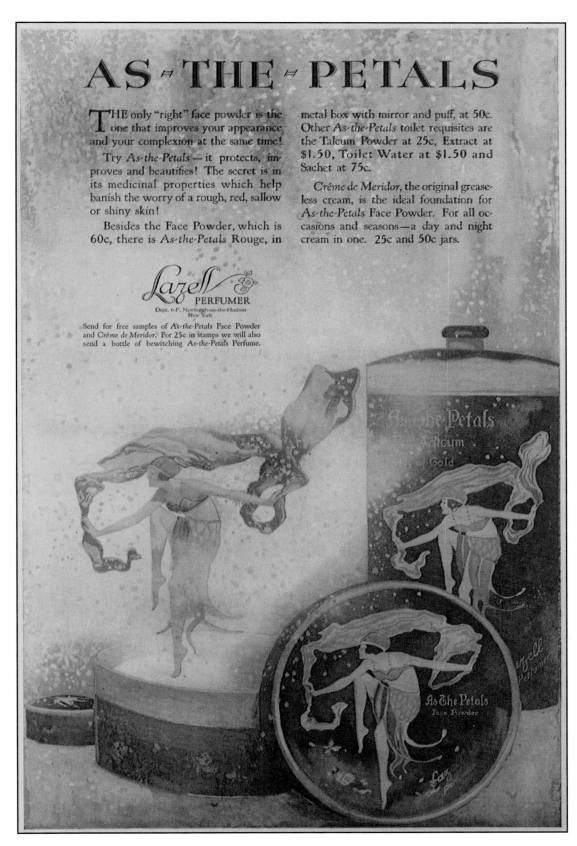

Ladies' Home Journal, 1920

1   4
2   5
3   6

1. The Vege-Lene Co. – Mokusei of Japan. "Flesh," 3" sq. x 1½", $25.00 – 40.00.

2. Armand Co. – Symphonie. "Perfumed with Gracious Peridore," 3" sq. x 1⅛", $25.00 – 40.00.

3. Moziak Co. "Flesh," 3¼" x 2¼" x 1⅜", $25.00 – 40.00.

4. Linda Lee. "Rachel #2," 3⅜" sq. x 1½", Ref.: 1944 Ad., $20.00 – 25.00.

5. Chamberlain. "Flesh" (English and Spanish information), 3⅛" dia. x 1⅝", $20.00 – 25.00.

6. C.H. Stuart & Co. – La Fleur. "White," 3¼" x 2½" x 1½", $35.00 – 50.00.

1	4
2	5
3	6

1. La Cipria Orientale (It.). "Ocre," 3⅝" dia. x 1⅛", $75.00 – 100.00.

2. Overton-Hygienic Co. – High Brown. "Olivetone," 2½" sq. x 1⅛", Ref.: 1944 T.M., $20.00 – 25.00.

3. Snow White Products Co. – Snow White. "Topaz Tan," 2¾" dia. x 1⅛", $20.00 – 25.00.

4. American Products Co. – Dream Girl. 3½" x 2¾" x 1¾", $35.00 – 50.00.
This is the shipping box. Powder box is similar to

P266 #6 Stuart, but in red. Also has Zanol logo and credit Lorenz Perfumer. (?)

5. Cheatham Chemical Co. – Polly Peachtree. "High Brown," 3" sq. x 1½", $25.00 – 35.00.

6. Crystal Laboratories – Outdoor Girl. "Flesh," 2¼" dia. x 1¼", $25.00 – 35.00.
Many of the American face powders were made as a side line by chemical laboratories, emphasizing the healing aspects rather than the vanity imaging.

```
1     3
2     4
      5
```

1. Grivaud Parfumeur (Mx.) – Te Quiero. "Surian," 3½" dia. x 1¼", complete $45.00 – 60.00.

2. Health-O-Quality Co. – Enticement. "Flesh," 2⅞" dia. x 1¾", $25.00 – 40.00.

3. De Lite Chemical Co. – De Lite. "Flesh," 3⅛" dia. x 1⅝", $20.00 – 25.00.
   The paper is handmade with a different pattern on each box.

4. Lazell Perfumer – De Meridor. "Flesh," 2¾" dia. x 1½", $35.00 – 50.00.

5. Del-Reska – Twilight Glow. "White," 3" sq. x 1¼", $20.00 – 25.00.

1
2   5
          3   6
     4

1. The Palmolive Co. – Fanchon. "Flesh," 2⅞" dia. x 1½", $25.00 – 35.00.

   "New style container adopted January, 1926...."

2. Maison Jeurelle – Seventeen. "Naturelle," 3" dia. x 1½", Ref.: 1930 Ad., $35.00 – 50.00.

3. Para Ti Corp. – Tuya. "Caracas Medium," 3¼" dia. x 1⅝", $35.00 – 50.00.

4. Health-O – Tre'Lis. "Brunette," 3⅜" x 2⅝" x 1⅞", $25.00 – 35.00.

5. P. Giraud (Fr.) – Rodoll. "Ocre," 2⅞" dia. x 1¾", $35.00 – 50.00.

6. Andrew Jergens Co. – Ben Hur. "Brunette," 2¾" dia. x ⅞", $35.00 – 50.00.

```
        1           5
      2       4       6
        3           7
```

1. Lady Esther – Lady Esther. "Tawny Rachel," 3" oct. x 1½", $25.00 – 35.00.

2. Lady Esther – Lady Esther. "Brunette," 3¼" dia. x 1½", Ref.: 1944 Ad., $25.00 – 35.00.

3. Lady Esther – Lady Esther. "Brunette," 3⅛" dia. x 1", $20.00 – 25.00.
  Northcliff Laboratories on #3 reverse.

4. William A. Woodbury Corp. "Flesh," 2½" oct. x 1⅜", $25.00 – 35.00.

5. The Andrew Jergens Co. – Woodbury's. "Flesh," 3" dia. x 1⅞", $50.00 – 65.00.
  "Not genuine without John H. Woodbury – dermatologist head and signature."

6. John H. Woodbury Inc. – Woodbury's. "Radiant," 2¼" sq. x ⅝", $15.00 – 25.00 (sample packet enclosed).

7. John H. Woodbury Inc. – Woodbury. "Tropic Tan," 2¼" sq. x ⅝", $25.00 – 35.00 (MGM 1945 star brochure, Lana Turner shown).

```
1    4
2    5
3    6
```

1. Carrel, Ltd. – Leon Laraine, Flotex. "Rachel #1," 3⅛" dia. x ⅝", $25.00 – 35.00.

2. Corlon, N.Y. – Jaciel Poudre. "Medium," 2¾" dia. x 1½", $35.00 – 50.00.

3. Boots (U.K.) – Devonshire Violets. "Peche," 2½" dia. x ¾", $35.00 – 45.00.

4. Varva – Nonchalant. "Rachel #3," 3" dia. x 2⅝",

Ref.: 1943 Ad., $25.00 – 35.00 (top contains six powder pads, bottom has powder).

5. Renaud (Fr.) – Sweet Pea. "Naturelle," 2⅞" dia. x 1¾", complete $65.00 – 80.00 (glass perfume flacon has gold foil label).

6. Elizabeth Post – Elizabeth Post. "Brunette," 2½" dia. x 1", $20.00 – 25.00.

Beauty Fashions, 1946

1
2   3   5
    4   6

1. Schiaparelli (Fr.) – Shocking. "15 Schiap," 3¼" dia. x 1⅛", complete $75.00 – 100.00.

2. Charles of the Ritz – 2½" oct. x 1¼", $25.00 – 35.00.

3. Tattoo – "Nude," 2" dia. x 1", $25.00 – 35.00.

4. Varva – Follow Me (Suivez Moi). 2" x 1½" x 1⅛", Ref.: 1944 Ad., $35.00 – 50.00.

5. Golden Petals. 3" dia. x 1", $65.00 – 80.00.

6. Helen English, Inc. – First Love. "Natural," 3¼" dia. x ¾", $30.00 – 45.00.

1
2
6
3
7
4 5

1. Charles of the Ritz. "Hand Blended," 4¼" dia. x 2¼", $35.00 – 50.00.

2. Guerlain (Fr.) – Shalimar. "Rachel," 3¼" dia. x 1⅝", $50.00 – 65.00 (introduced in 1926).

3. Countess Exine Cie. "Rachel," 2½" sq. x ¾", papers: 1942, $25.00 – 40.00.

4. Princess Pat Inc. "Ochre," 2¼" x 1¾" x 1", Ref.: 1930 Ad., $25.00 – 40.00.

5. Harriet Hubbard Ayer – Ayeristocrat. "Theatrical Powder," 1¾" dia. x ⅝" Ref.: 1927 Cat., $25.00 – 35.00.

6. Alexandra Markoff – Countess Isserlyn. "Velvet Pink," 3⅞" dia. x 1½", Ref.: 1968 Ad., $45.00 – 60.00.
Box reverse has Anatole Robbins, Inc. as distributor.

7. Harriet Hubbard Ayer – Ayerstocrat. "Roseayer" (bad logo pun!), 3½" dia. x 1⅜", $20.00 – 25.00.

1
2
4
5
3

1. Bourjois – Springtime in Paris. "Rachel," 3 dia. x 1⅜", Ref.: 1933 Ad., $30.00 – 45.00.

2. Clary King. 2½" sq. x ⅜", $20.00 – 30.00.

3. C.H. Stuart & Co. – Quest? "Day & Evening Powder" (two interior boxes), 5¾" x 2¼" x 1⅛", $45.00 – 60.00.

4. Derny Perfumeur (Ca.) – 3 Secrets (Beauty, Charm & Romance). "Naturelle," 2¾" sq. x 1⅝", $35.00 – 50.00.

5. Myrurgia (Sp.) – Maderas de Oriente. "Rachel Suave" (outer box with logo), reverse has veiled femme, 3⅛" dia. x 1¼", $75.00 – 100.00.

1
2
5
3
6
4

1. American Can Co. – Beautebox. Canco logo, lithograph on tin, 4" dia. x 1⅝", $45.00 – 60.00.
Fourth in a 1922 artist-signed series by Henry Clive of silent film star Betty Compson. Reference: 1922 article. Some debate on series count of ten or eleven.

2. Lyric. Brass with embossed lid logo, 2⅞" dia. x 1⅝", $35.00 – 50.00.

3. A.A. Vantine Ltd. – Embassy. "Rachelle," aluminum with enameled lid and logo, information on reverse, 2½" dia. x 1½", $25.00 – 40.00.

4. Contouré. Brass with impressed lid logo, 2¼" dia. x ¾", $25.00 – 40.00.

5. California Perfume Co. – Vernafleur. Brass with Art Deco lithographed case, 3" dia. x 1¼", $65.00 – 80.00.

6. Talcum Puff Co. – Fleur de Glorie. Brass with embossed nymph logo, 2½" dia. x ½", $35.00 – 50.00.

1
2   3   5
     4   6

1. Cia Industrial (Mx.) – Conga. "Rachel #2," embossed copper top with logo, 3½" dia. x 1⅛", $65.00 – 75.00.

2. Vantine – American Way. "Rose Rachel," see #3.

3. Vantine – American Way. "Rose Rachel," enameled metal top with affixed star, see #2 reverse information, 2½" dia. x 1¾", $50.00 – 65.00.

4. D'Amour Poudre. "Flesh," celluloid flanged boudoir box with removable logo lid sticker, 4⅜" x 2¾" x 1¼", $45.00 – 60.00.

5. Carlton Cosmetics – Carlton. "Brunette," enameled aluminum top with logo and side column motif, 2¾ dia. x 1⅝", $40.00 – 55.00.

6. Vantine – Zanadu. "Peach," enameled metal top with logo, "...powdered milk base...," 2⅜" dia. x ¾", $45.00 – 60.00.

1   4
2   5
3

1. Roger & Gallet (Fr.) – Poudre de Ritz/Anthea.
Packaging box, see #2.

2. Roger & Gallet (Fr.) – Poudre de Ritz/Anthea.
"Natural" heliotropo (scent), Spanish reverse information, agent "A. Reuff Y Cia, Mexico," see #1 for packaging box, 3" sq. x 1¼", complete $75.00 – 100.00.

**3. Roger & Gallet (N.Y.) – Fleurs d'Amour, Pressed
Powder Can.** "Pink Champagne," fleece and suede
puff with logo, interior mirror, Lalique (No "R."), on
lid, orange tint, reverse square cartouche with silver
foil sticker, 3" dia. x ⅝", $175.00 – 200.00.

**4. Roger et Gallet (Fr.) – Fleurs d'Amour, Pressed
Powder Can.** "Poudre Blanche," chamois topped
fleece puff with ribboned logo, Lalique (No "R.") on
lid, terra-cotta matte champlevé case highlight
accents, reverse stamped "Paris," 3" dia. x ⅞", $250.00
– 275.00.

5. Roger et Gallet (Fr.) – Fleurs d'Amour. "Poudre
Naturelle," hand chased lid, faint yellow gold accents,
"R. Lalique" on reverse, 3" dia. x 1⅛", $300.00 – 350.00.
*The #3, 4, 5, cases are aluminum. The #5 birds vary
slightly in detail with more decisive tooling.*

Theatre, 1924

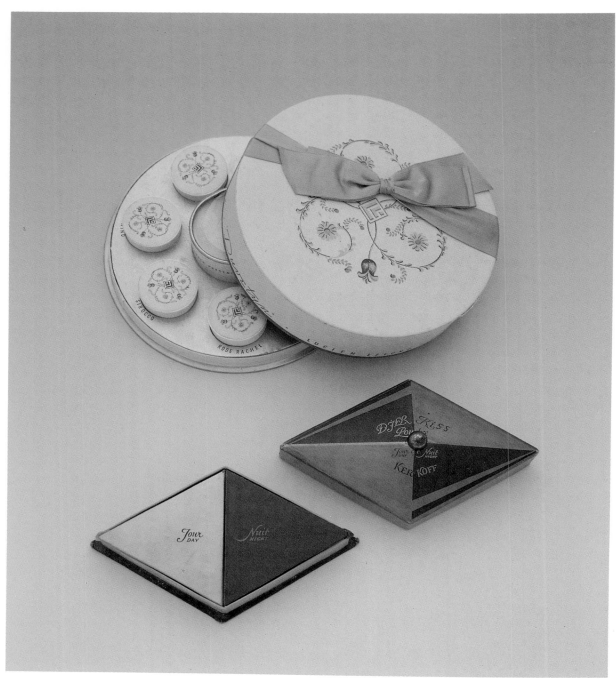

1
2

1. Lucien LeLong – Duvetyn, Powder Presentation – Guest Powder Set. Seven shades of powder, center well with multicolor cotton pads, 6¾" dia. x 1⅝", minis 1½" dia., Ref.: 1935 Ad., complete $60.00 – 75.00.

2. Kerkoff – Djer-Kiss. "Jour et Nuit" (Day & Night), beveled lid, brass knob opener, interior center hinge, "brunette skin," 6¼" x 3¾" x ¾", $50.00 – 65.00.

Richard Hudnut Folding Cardboard Advertising Fan — 7¼" x 14", N.D. $75.00 – 100.00.

```
        1           7
        2      4    8
        3      5    9
               6
```

1. Vantine's – Jafleur Boudoir Set. Three tiered boxes hand covered in soutache and black silk, gold thread dangle cords with blue Peking beads, carved ivory Buddha on top as cord anchor and logo symbol, first tier has pressed rouge, second pressed powder, third porcelain cold creme jar, puffs with logo, and jar stickers, Ref.: 1922 Ad., 3¼" dia. x 3¼" (Buddha + 1"), see P283 #4 open, Rare.

2. Colgate & Co. – Cashmere Bouquet. "Flesh," 2½" dia. x ½", $10.00 – 15.00.

3. A. Bourjois & Cie – Ashes of Roses. "Brunette," 1½" dia. x 1", $15.00 – 20.00.

4. Ste Brocard et Cie (Fr.) – Duvet Mervielle. "Naturelle," 1¾" x 1⅝" x 1½", $65.00 – 80.00.

5. Maubert (Fr.) – Louisette. "Violette," 1¾" sq. x ⅞", $35.00 – 50.00.

6. Lorency–Palanca (Fr.) – Nymphea. 1¾" sq. x 1", $25.00 – 35.00.

7. Vantine's – Potpourri, Pressed Powder Box. "Flesh," dried rose buds under net, Peking beads threaded on crossed lid cords, gold lace bands on gold foil box, puff with logo, See P283 #5 packaging box, 3¼" dia. x 1¾", $75.00 – 100.00.

8. National Toilet Co. – Nadinola. "Natural," 2" dia. x ⅞", $20.00 – 35.00.

9. Freeman's – Veloutine. "Flesh," 1¾" dia. x ¾", $15.00 – 20.00.

1   4   5

2   6

3   7

1. Dorin (Fr.) – Rouge Blondine #1259. 1¾" dia. x 1", Ref.: 1921 Ad., $20.00 – 25.00.

2. Dorin (Fr.) – Ziska. 1⅜" dia. x ½", Ref.: 1898 date, $25.00 – 35.00.

3. Pond's Extract Co. – "Cheeks." "Dry Rouge," "Rascal Red," 1⅝" dia. x ½", $10.00 – 15.00.

4. Vantine's – Jafleur Boudoir Set. Three-tiered boxes, see P282 #1 closed, for information.

5. Vantine's – Potpourri. Pressed powder box, packaging box with stickers, see P282 #7.

6. Harmelle–Salarnier (Fr.) – Poudre de Beaute. 2¼" dia. x 1¼", $25.00 – 35.00.

7. Pritchard & Constance (U.K.) – Amami. "Flesh," "By Appointment to the Queen of the Belgians," "...Famous powder supplied to the theatrical profession from our London Haymarket Store" (interior paper), 1⅝" dia. x 1", $35.00 – 50.00.

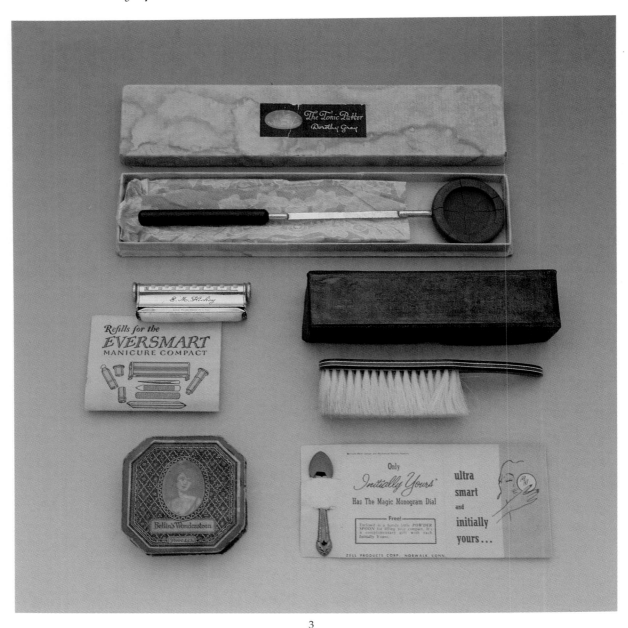

3

1   4

2   5

1. The Wahl Co. – Eversmart Manicure Compact. Boxed with papers, this is *not* a compact. The word is used in the usual meaning of "...arranged neatly in a small space." The loose powder capsule contains nail whitener which was popular in the twenties. This case is dated 1924. Value as a collectible is approximately $50.00 – 65.00.

2. Bellin's Wonderstoen Co. Paten with a pressed rouge looking powder, facial depilatory, this is *not* a face powder or rouge item, 2¾" sq. x ⅝", $15.00.

3. Dorothy Gray – Tonic Patter. Rubberized disk affixed to chrome shaft and Bakelite signed handle, 9⅝" x 2" x ½", Ref.: 1923 Pat., $125.00 – 150.00.

4. Max Factor's Society – Face Powder Brush. Layered Bakelite handle, natural bristles, 5¾" x 1½" x 1½", Ref.: 1932 Ad., $35.00 – 50.00.

5. Zell Products Co. – Powder Spoon. Was to have been with "Initially Yours" compact, Re: Vol. I, P237 #2, but was mislaid, and is not priced separately.

All these items are either presented to correct common errors in compact and powder box collecting, or are just parts of the strange history of women's cosmetics.

Woodbury Cardboard Advertising Fan — 8⅛" x 11⅛", N.D. $65.00 – 75.00.

Helena Rubinstein brochure, 1933

1. A. & F. Pears (U.K.) – Pears' Fuller's Earth. Double access, "for use as dusting powder...upper...use with puff...lower compartment...," white, wad of wool fleece as puff, 2¾" dia. x 2⅝", $50.00 – 65.00.

2. J.A. Pozzoni – Pozzoni's Jap Pressed Rouge. "Medium," 1¾" dia. x ¾", Ref.: 1916 "New Style," see #4.
JAP are the company initials.

3. Chamois Cloth (Powder Rag). 3½" x 2¾", see #4.

4. J.A. Pozzoni – Pozzoni's "Boodle" Box. Carton contains brass embossed oval powder case, 3¾" x 3" x 2", Ref.: 1912 Pat., and 1910 Ad., see #2 rouge, #3 chamois, #8 powder box, complete set $275.00 – 300.00.
The brass case was used by Gibson Card Co. in their 1996 calendar (June) as an example of male Victorian items (?). The sturdy case with its snug lid was probably used by both sexes for everything but bait...no air holes.

5. H.W. Goodnow – Cardboard Wall Sandpaper Match Scratcher. "Dr. Ferguson's Lily Whites (?) & Powders" shield shaped advertisement, 5" x 3½", $35.00 – 50.00.
Usually hung in kitchens of non-electified houses for oil lamps, stoves, etc.

6 & 7. Luxor Powder Containers. 1⅝" dia. x 1½", see #9.

8. J.A. Pozzoni – Wood, Complexion Powder Box. "Flesh," Ref.: JAP T.M. 1874, 2½" dia. x 1½", see #2.

9. Luxor Powder Blender – Tin Canister Set. Lid with logo, interior pierced screen, 4¾" x 2½" dia., Ref.: 1930. #6 & 7 examples of powder shades for blending "Azure" and "Blanc" – instruction papers list five. Complete $250.00 – 275.00.

1   3   5
2   4   6

1. Unmarked – Glass Beaded Kit Bag. "Pansy," duo pocket carrier, silk lined with black moiré backed mirror, chamois lined with chamois powder cloth, 3¾" x 3½", $100.00 – 125.00.

This was not meant to hold powder, chamois was used as a perspiration remover.

2. Unknown (Fr.) – Suede and Silk Loose Rouge. Stitched pocket with lid watercolor design, signed, no mirror, removable rouge silk pouch (used as a patter) with duplicate suede lid design, draw strings, pocket 3" dia., pouch 2⅛" dia., $75.00 – 100.00.

Back to the drawing board on this, loose rouge everywhere.

3. Diamond Powder Puff Co. – Vinyl. "Com-Pat Puff," pouch with puff, center tin revolving powder access, velour puff backing, no mirror, papers shown, pouch 3¼" sq., $65.00 – 80.00.

4. Odette (Fr.) – Faille, Fold-over Powder Pouch. Hand-applied chameleon glass beaded lid bucolic scene, goldtone rim clamps, ivory moiré interior snap flap pocket for chamois, beveled suede framed affixed horseshoe mirror, 4¼" x 3¼" x 1", $125.00 – 150.00.

5. California Perfume Co. – Cardboard, Boudoir Vanity Set. Saddlebag, paper encased box and framed mirror, lid foil seal with logo and "Daphne," pressed powder and rouge, 3⅝" x 2⅜" x ⅝", Ref.: 1915 Cat., $125.00 – 150.00.

6. Elmo – Navy Moire, Fold-over Powder Pouch. Saddlebag, ivory suede lining, snap flap powder pocket, kid framed beveled affixed round mirror, double velour puff with blue string loop, signed, 2½" x ½", Ref.: 1928 Pat., $45.00 – 60.00.

Interior powder pocket has a mesh backing; puff slides in behind it to absorb powder. Puff is a tight fit and huffs powder with some energy on release.

Roystone
Advertising
Coupon — N.D.

1   3
   2

1. Herbert Roystone Co. – La-May. "Poudre L'Amé," band box motif, "brunette," ⅛" dia. x 2", Ref.: 1927, enclosed and displayed papers, $35.00 – 50.00.

Reverse box information "Five Thousand Dollars is offered if found to contain white lead or rice powder."

2. See papers: "German Silver Watch Case Vanity." Domed compact (no rouge), lid logo, case signed

"L'Amé," framed mirror, 2" dia. x ½", $65.00 – 80.00.

3. La May-Sport – Tin Compact. Lithographed lid logo scene, reverse with sale information, papers, pierced tin powder screen, framed mirror, see Vol. I, P229, 2½" dia. x ½", $40.00 – 60.00.

Pond's brochure, 1941

1. "Lehcaresor" (U.K.) – Papier Poudre. Powder papers tablet, design on both sides, scent card enclosed "Rose," 3" x 2⅛" x ¼", $45.00 – 60.00 (with card).

2. Johnson & Johnson – Beauty Spots. Packet, "One Hundred Assorted," 3" x 1⅞", $3.00 – 5.00.

3. Lamkin (U.K.) – Bakelite, Powder Puff Carrier. Lamb's wool brush, access chain, top unscrews, case signed, 2¾" x 1" dia., Ref.: 1937 Pat., $65.00 – 80.00.

4. Powderette Corp/Chicago. – Plastic, yellow, loose powder purse carrier, green button tap-it dispenser, 4" x ¾" dia., $25.00 – 35.00.

5. Luxor – White Metal, Powderette. Loose powder purse carrier, 3" x ½" dia., $25.00 – 35.00.

6. Colt – "Purse Makeup Kit." Bakelite, black and white fillable four section threaded tube, no case I.D. (see #13 open), 2⅜" x ⅞" dia., $35.00 – 50.00.

7. R. & B. (Fr.) – Bakelite Pli. Red cord, bead, and woven silk tassel, lid powder dispenser, feather duster, signed on base, 3¼" x ¾" dia., Rare.

8. Marlene – Powderette. Red enameled metallic tube, loose powder dispenser, 1" x ⅝" dia., $10.00 – 15.00.

9. Princess Pat – "Vaniteen." Powderette, goldtone, loose powder dispenser, lidded creme rouge in base, case signed, 2¼" x ⅝", Ref.: 1940 Ad., $35.00 – 50.00.

10. Molinard (Fr.) – "Houppette." Pli (powderette), boxed, black Bakelite, diamanté enhanced case, everything signed, papers, feather duster, threaded top and bottom, extended 3⅜" x ¾" dia., $150.00 – 175.00.

11. Molinard (Fr.) – "Houppette." Pli (powderette), mock tortoise-shell, see #10, $100.00 – 125.00.

12. Jacqueline Cochran – "Purse Make-Up Kit." Silk damask pouch contains stack tube with loose powder dispenser in base, foundation creme, cleansing salve, creme rouge, solid perfume, signed "Wings to Beauty," 3½" x ⅞" dia., "Skin Lotion" glass bottle, mirror, lucite comb, ivory plastic spatula, everything signed, pouch 4" x 3½", Ref.: 1940 Ad. ("Bag of Tricks"), complete $125.00 – 150.00.

13. Colt – "Purse Make-Up Kit." Bakelite, fillable five section threaded tube, case signed, 3¼" x ⅞" dia. (see #6 closed), $50.00 – 65.00.

1		6		10
2		7		11
3			8	12
4	5		9	13

```
1        4        7
2        5        8
3        6        9
```

1. Fracy – White Metal, Allumettes. "Matchbook Lip Sticks," "For Thy Lips," boxed, mint, vertical lid bands, triangular hinge ring for chain, monogram cartouche, boxed, case signed, framed oval mirror, 2¼" x 1¾" (shown open), Ref.: 1926 Pat., complete $65.00 – 80.00.

2. Unknown – Cloth Guest Towel. Red with script embroidery "Lipstick," 12½" x 9", $50.00 – 75.00.

3. Rejuvia Beauty Labs – Goldtone Lipsticks. "Flame-Glo," king 3¼", purse 2¼", sample ⅝", all 1" dia., $5.00 – 7.50.

4. Richard Hudnut, DuBarry. Matchbook lipstick blotting tissues, sample lipstick attached with clear tape, "The Lipstick that kisses and never tells," 3" x 1⅞" x ¼", $15.00 – 20.00.

5. Revlon/Kleenex. Matchbook, lipstick blotting tissues, "Indelible Creme," 3" x 1⅞" x ¼", Ref.: 1936 Pat., $10.00 – 15.00.

6. Fracy Allumettes. "Matchbook Lip Sticks," "Perfumed with Fracy Passionata," 2½" x 2", Ref.: 1926 Pat., $35.00 – 50.00.
"Each stick may be used several times...for the cheeks, eyes, ears, etc." (Not a refill for #1.)

7. Kleenex – Aluminum. Art Deco lipstick tissue case, see #8 closed for information.

8. Kleenex – Aluminum. Art Deco femme scribed lid motif, cased lipstick tissue packet, "For Your Handbag," case signed, 3¼" x 2" x ¼", see #7 open, $35.00 – 50.00.

9. Unknown – "Fleure Bouquet." Perfumed lipstick tissues, "For Your Handbag," 2½" sq. x ½", Ref.: 1938 T.M., $15.00 – 20.00.

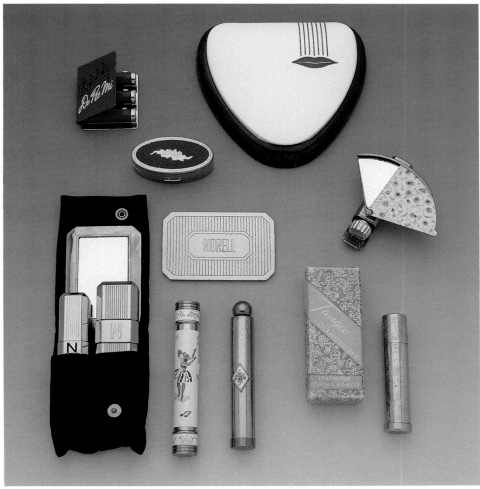

```
1        3        7
2        4
         5   6        8
                      9
```

1. Unknown – White Metal, Lipstick Carrier. Book, red enameled exterior, musical lid motif "Do Re Mi," polished mirror interior, three-hinged lipstick tubes "Derby Red," "Watermelon," "Night Club," 1⅞" x 1⅝" x ½", tubes 1½" x ⅜"dia., $25.00 – 40.00.

2. Norell – Goldtone, Purse Kit. Three-piece set including mirror 3⅛" x 2⅛" x ⅛" (see #4 reverse), lipstick ¾" sq. x 3", and perfume atomizer 3⅛" x 1⅛" x ⅞" (Norell Perfume), black faux suede pocketed pouch, everything signed, 3¾" x 2¾" x 1¼", complete $50.00 – 65.00.

3. Max Factor – Goldtone, Lipstick Case. "Hi Society," black enameled top, lid flora, tube with paper label "Once Upon a Red," oval case signed and "Container Made in England," case glued mirror, beveled tube 2" x ⅝", case 2¼" x 1¼", Ref.: 1958 Ad., $25.00 – 40.00.

4. Norell Mirror – Reverse, see #2.

5. Lehn & Fink Corp. – Goldtone, Tussy Purse Set. Enameled tube, multicolor harlequin figures, lipstick

with paper label, metal encased glass perfume vial, both signed "Optimiste," 3⅞" x ¾" dia., Ref.: 1948 Ad., $35.00 – 50.00.

6. Unmarked – Goldtone, Purse Set. Case affixed cloisonné plaque, ball topped encased glass perfume vial, lipstick tube, 4" x ⅝" dia., $25.00 – 40.00.

7. Geo. W. Luft Co. – Plastic, Boudoir Case. Signed "Tangee," red, white, and blue, intaglio lid motif, lipstick, rouge, and powder interior wells for loose cosmetic containers, 4⅞" x 5⅛" x ¾", Ref.: 1941 Pat., $65.00 – 80.00.

8. Stratton – Goldtone, "Fan Lipstick Mirror." Enameled fan with transfer flora, glued mirror, lipstick case, base signed "Hand" logo, 2½" x 2¼", Ref.: 1955 Ad., $25.00 – 40.00.

9. Geo. W. Luft Co. – Goldtone, Purse Set. "Tangee," boxed case scribed flora, fillable perfume atomizer, lipstick "Gay–Red," 3¼" x ¾" dia., $50.00 – 65.00.

1. Avon – Powder Sampler. "Heavenlight," nine tins on cardboard artist's palette, 10" x 7½", everything signed, tins 1¾" dia. x ¼", $135.00 – 150.00.

American Perfumer, 1919

1	5		10
2	6		11
3	7	9	12
4	8		13

Brochure — N.D.

1. Carrel – White Metal. Domed case, Art Deco lid motif, signed "L'Peggie," framed signed mirror, 1½" dia. x ½", $15.00 – 25.00.

2. Armand Duval – White Metal. Domed case, lid signed "Valencia D'Amour," and logo, framed mirror, 1½" dia. x ½", $25.00 – 35.00.

3. Gordon Gordon – Goldtone. Lid peacock motif and logo, signed "Mem'ry," framed mirror, 1½" dia. x ¾", $25.00 – 35.00.

4. Tiffany Perfumers (Can.) – Goldtone. Domed lid with logo, framed mirror, 1⅝" dia. x ½", $25.00 – 35.00.

5. Darnée – Goldtone. Domed oval case, lid signature "Colleen Moore," case signed, framed mirror, Ref.: 1924, $35.00 – 50.00.
   Silent film star of the twenties, "Sally" and "So Big."

6. House of Westmore – Goldtone. Aqua base enamel, intaglio lid logo, case metallic mirror, 1½" dia. x ⅜", $10.00 – 15.00.

7. Margaret Rose (U.K.) – Goldtone. Faux cameo lid bijou, case signed (case gutted for other use), 1½" dia. x ⅝", $10.00 – 15.00.

8. Doucette – White Metal. Decagon flanged case, signed, convex attached mirror, 1⅜" x ¼", $15.00 – 25.00.

9. Marinello – Goldtone. Domed rectangular case, embossed "Lucky Elephants," signed, framed mirror, Ref.: 1915 Ad., 1¾" x 1¼" x ½", $25.00 – 35.00.

10. Woodworth – White Metal. "Karess," blue tinted embossed lid, signed, framed mirror, 1½" dia. x ⅜", $25.00 – 35.00.

11. Bourjois – White Metal. "Fiancée," pink tinted intaglio lid logo, signed, framed mirror, 1½" dia. x ⅜", $25.00 – 35.00.

12. Princess Pat – Goldtone. Embossed lid logo, signed, framed mirror, 1½" dia. x ½", $20.00 – 30.00.

13. Boncilla – Goldtone. Lid script logo, framed mirror, 1½" dia. x ½", Ref.: 1922 Ad., $25.00 – 35.00.
   All these cases are for pressed or creme rouge. The early twenties oval lipsticks are signed and valued at whatever the dealer and buyer agree to.

Brochure — N.D.

1. Fuller Brush Co. – Goldtone. Flora transfer lid motif, signed "Debutante," embossed rouge, framed mirror, 1½" dia. x ½", $10.00 – 15.00.

2. Jacqueline Cochran – Goldtone. Stylized plane prop in motion lid motif, "Wings to Beauty," case signed, framed mirror, 1½" sq. x ⅜", Ref.: 1941 Ad., $25.00 – 35.00.

3. Reich-Ash Co. – Goldtone. "Ash's Deere Brand," domed lid bands and champlevé enamel, case signed, framed mirror, 1½" dia. x ⅜", $25.00 – 35.00.

4. Richard Hudnut – Goldtone. Enameled lid, bas-relief sunburst, signed "Gemey," framed metallic mirror, 1⅝" dia. x ⅜", Ref.: 1936 Ad., $20.00 – 25.00.

5. Fascination – Goldtone. Script logo, lid plaque, molded metallic mirror, 1½" dia. x ½", $15.00 – 20.00.

6. Charles of the Ritz – Goldtone. Encased enamel, lid with pink vertical bands, case signed, framed mirror, 1¾" dia. x ⅜", $20.00 – 25.00.

7. Dorothy Gray – Goldtone. "Swash Buckle," case signed, framed mirror (see Vol. I P32/#5 for compact), 1½" sq. x ⅜", Ref.: 1947 Ad., $35.00 – 50.00.

8. Darnée Perfumers – Goldtone. Beveled case, plastic Oriental scene lid inset, signed "Lola Montez," framed mirror, 1½" oct. x ⅜", $25.00 – 35.00.

9. Coty – Goldtone. Champlevé red enameled lid, flora and logo, framed metallic mirror, 1½" dia. x ⅜", $20.00 – 25.00.

10. Mary Pickford – Goldtone. Encased enamel, "Mary Pickford," profile and signature logo, framed mirror, 1⅝" dia. x ½", $25.00 – 35.00.
   Mary's long curls were clipped in 1928.

11. Lucien LeLong – Goldtone. Banded lid with signed logo "Petite Baguette," framed mirror, 1½" sq. x ⅜", $25.00 – 35.00.

12. Bourjois – White Metal. Encased blue enameled lid with logo, case signed "Evening in Paris," framed metallic mirror, 1¾" dia. x ⅜", $20.00 – 25.00.

13. Harriet Hubbard Ayer – Goldtone. Plaid enameled lid, case signed "Luxuria," papers, framed mirror, 1⅝" dia. x ⅜", Ref.: 1951 Ad., $25.00 – 35.00.
   The only exception to these rouge cases is #8. It's blue creme eye shadow. (Too pretty to leave out.)

```
              5        9
    1              6        10
    2              7        11
         3         8        12
         4                  13
```

```
1     4
  2     5      9
  3     6     10
     7   8    11
```

1. Chen Yu – Cardboard. Sample box, lid logo, reverse sticker, no puff, no mirror, signed "Cloud Silk," 1⅝" dia. x ⅜", base 2¼" sq., Ref.: 1945 Ad., $25.00 – 40.00.

2. Dermetics – Goldtone. Post Deco gazelle logo, domed case signed, framed metallic mirror, 1⅝" dia. x ½", Ref.: 1949 Ad., $25.00 – 35.00.

3. Armand – Goldtone. Red enamel, femme lid logo, case signed, framed metallic mirror, 1½" dia. x ⅜", $15.00 – 25.00.

4. Houbigant (Fr.) – Plastic and Cardboard. Duo dresser set, mock tortoise-shell pressed powder case and mottled green rouge case, goldtone basket logos, ivory velvet puffs and papers, no mirrors, box signed "Quelques Fleurs" (cases are not removable), 1¾" dia. x ⅜", box 4¾" x 2½" x 1", $65.00 – 80.00.

5. Valdour – Plastic. Black and white case with faux cameo lid image of Don Juan, case signed, no mirror, 2" dia. x ⅜", $25.00 – 35.00.

6. Langlois – Plastic. Blue case, basket logo, ruffled flanged base, signed "Cara Nome," case glued mirror, 2" dia. x ⅝", $10.00 – 15.00.

7. Coty – Goldtone. Black faux lacquer lid, chinoiserie motif, "New East Indian Box," case signed, framed mirror, 1¾" dia. x ⅜", Ref.: 1925 Ad., $35.00 – 50.00.

8. Marly – Goldtone. Black enameled lid with logo, signed "Swagger," framed metallic mirror, 1⅝" dia. x ⅜", $15.00 – 20.00.

9. Don Juan – Plastic and Cardboard. Sample, molded lid logo (no mention of Valdour), 1⅜" dia. x ⅜", card 3" x 2½", $10.00 – 15.00.

10. Bonne Bell – Goldtone. Domed lid, Paris scene, case signed, framed mirror, 1¾" dia. x ½", $15.00 – 25.00.

11. Bonne Bell – Plastic. Flanged case, gilt stamped lid logo, scalloped base, reverse signed, 1½" dia. x ½", $10.00 – 15.00.

Luzier's automatic roll-top lipstick, $5.00.

1	5	8
2	6	9
3	7	10
4		11
		12

1. Melba – Powder Tin. Sample, "Fleurs," 1¼" dia. x ¾", Ref.: 1926 Ad., $15.00 – 20.00.

2. Luxor – Powder Tin. Sample, "Encharma," 2" oval x 1⅝" x ¼", $15.00 – 20.00.

3. Freeman's – Powder Tin. Sample, 1¼" x ⅞" x ⅝", $10.00 – 15.00.

4. Richard Hudnut – "Deauville." Pressed powder refill box (no puff), 2" dia. x ¼", $25.00 – 35.00.

5. Allied Drug Products Co. – Rouge Tin. Sample, "Southern Girl," 1¼" dia. x ¼", $5.00 – 10.00.

6. Vani Pufs – Refill Puffs. 4" dia., $5.00 – 10.00.

7. Elgin American – Pressed Powder Refill #1294. Boxed, puff, paten, and brochure order form, 3" x 2¾" x ⅜", $15.00 – 20.00.

8. Transogram Co. – Red Powder Tin. Sample, "Gold Medal," 1¼" dia. x ¼", $5.00 – 10.00.

9. Gwenda (U.K.) – Powder Tin. Lid script logo, 1⅝" dia. x ⅜", $10.00 – 15.00.

10. Colgate & Co. – Powder Tin. Sample, lid logo "Cashmere Bouquet," 1½" dia. x ½", $10.00 – 15.00.

11. Potter & Moore (U.K.) – Pressed Powder Refill. "Mitcham Lavender," puff, papers, embossed powder logo, 2⅛" dia. x ½", $25.00 – 35.00.

12. Norida – "Compacte Refill & Puff Set." "Fleur Sauvage," boxed, papers, pressed powder paten, 2¼" sq. x ⅜", $20.00 – 25.00.

1
2
3

4
5

1. Unknown – Craft Kit Set. Celluloid baby "Renwall" #8, 3" length, movable arms and legs, feet with toes, molded brown bangs and white diaper, blue eyes (one crossed!), crocheted bonnet, affixed skirt and doily to peach velour puff, 4" dia., molded sign on dolly back, she sits up and secured enough to act as puff handle, $45.00 – 60.00.

2. Dermetics – Boxed Gift Set. "Powder & Puff," four puffs with molded powder, 2" dia., handkerchief 7" sq., $35.00 – 50.00.

3. Lid to #5 - Hand-painted poppies.

4. Askin's – Advertising Puff Packet. Powder and rouge puffs with coupon ("Askin's Credit Clothing Stores" used gimmicky promotions in the thirties), $3.00 – 5.00.

5. Unmarked – Boxed Duo Gift Set. Hand-painted poppies on box, linen handkerchief and taffeta puff pocket, box 5⅜" x 3⅞" x ¾", complete $25.00 – 35.00.

1   3   5
  2   4

1. Unmarked – Boudoir Face Powder Puff Wand. Mirror reverse, see #3 for puff mate and owl scene.

2. Unmarked – "Wand." Pink velour puff with yellow silk appliqué, lace, faux pearls, and silk ribbon wrapped stick (Vol. 1, P280 #1), 3" dia. x 6", $75.00 – 100.00.

3. Unmarked – "Wand." Ivory velour puff with silk screened owl scene on silk, blue rhinestone eyes, border ruching, 4¼" dia. x 6", see #1 for mirror mate, pair $150.00 – 175.00.

4. Unmarked – "Wand." Duo set, pink oval velour puff with silk appliquéd hand-worked flora, border ruching (mirror mate not shown), 4¼" oval x 3" x 6", pair $125.00 – 150.00.

5. Unmarked – "Wand." Green velour puff with Pearloid backing and scalloped stick, Art Deco femme transfer, 3" dia. x 11", Rare.

1
2

1. Quaker Silver Co. – "1001 Dresser Set." Gold washed molded base metal, Art Deco paneled flora case, design, beveled borders three pieces including perfume, black glass topped bottle, glass lined and glass dauber, 6½", footed casket vanity case, hinged interior tray, duo pressed rouge shades, oval lipstick tube, loose powder well, marabou puff, 3¾" x 2⅝" x

4", atomizer, ivory silk crocheted bulb and tubing cover, 7", all pieces signed, complete $375.00 – 450.00.

2. Fostoria Glass Co. – Glass Boudoir Set. Stenciled lid femme silhouette, tray with wells for two lipstick tubes, rouge and loose powder, fleur-de-lis handle, 6½" x 6¼" x 2", $125.00 – 150.00.

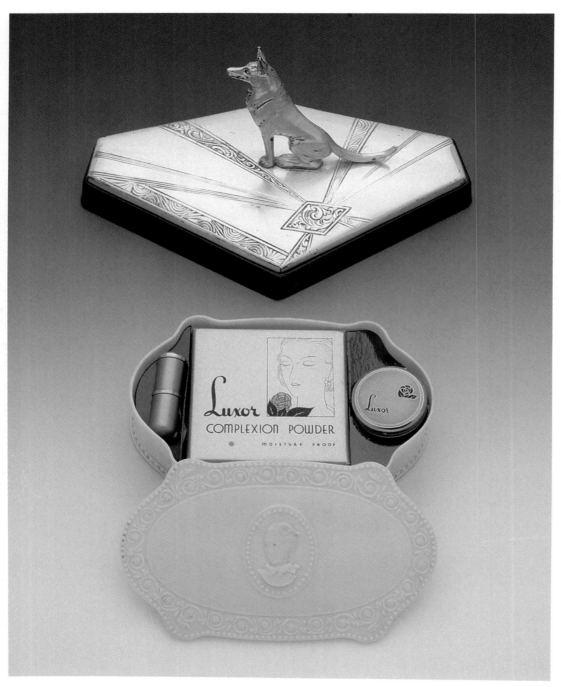

1
2

1. Weidlich Bros. – Silver-plated Lid, "889 – Beauty Box." Alert German shepherd dog affixed to Art Moderne domed lid display, Fostoria Glass Co. "Black Onyx" glass base, fitted with pink double velour puff, 3½" dia., pressed rouge paten and wells for lipstick and "eyebrow crayon," lid signed "W.B. mfg. co.," 9" x 5¼" x 5½", Ref.: 1932 Cat., $150.00 – 175.00.

2. Luxor – Molded Ivory Bakelite, Boudoir Vanity Box. Scalloped case, domed lid, femme in high relief, flora border, 6¼" x 3¾" x ½", three pieces including powder box, 3¼" x 1⅜", green metallic finish on lipstick, 1⅞", and rouge compact, framed mirror, 1½" dia. x ½", Ref.: 1934 papers, complete $125.00 – 150.00.

2

1   3

1. Weidlich Bros. – Silver-plated Case, #696-2 – Beauty Box." Standing rabbit lid ornament with erect ears, open, see #3 closed.

2. Weidlich Bros. – Silver-plated Lid, "684 – Beauty Box." Art Deco standing gold plated draped femme nude, domed lid Art Moderne display; Fostoria Glass Co. "Black Onyx" glass base, fitted with pink double velour puff, 3½" dia., pressed rouge paten and wells for lipstick and "eyebrow pencil," lid signed

"W.B.mfg. co." (same base as clear Fostoria, P306 #2), 6½" x 6¼" x 2", nude 5", Ref.: 1931 Cat., $425.00 – 475.00.

3. Weidlich Bros. – Silver-plated Case, "696-11 – Beauty Box." Dancing couple lid ornament, fitted pressed powder and rouge, lipstick and eyebrow crayon tubes, signed "W.B.mfg. co.," see #1 open, 3" dia. x 3¾", Ref.: 1938 Cat., $150.00 – 175.00.

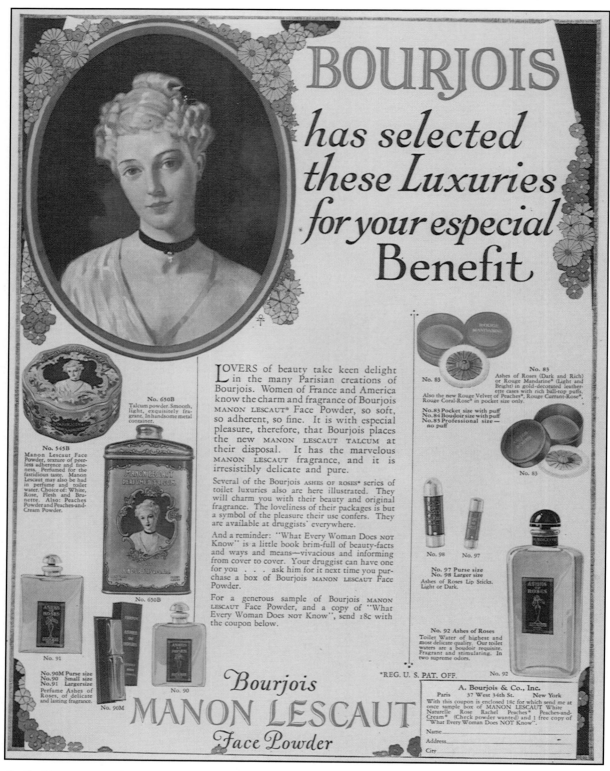

Ladies' Home Journal, 1924

MELBA

Smoothest Powder in the World

An artificial cyclone whirls Melba face powder into fineness like mist. Such tiny particles seem really to merge into the most delicate skin. The genteel bloom of Melba comes as from within—the effect is irresistible—the source is quite invisible. Only the private Melba air-floating process creates face powders so infinitely smooth.

Other exclusive Melba methods give all the other Melba preparations distinctive excellence. Each Melba aid to loveliness assures the purity, fragrance, and benefits which have won the confidence of millions. Because they are so widely appreciated, the luxury of using Melba toiletries is not extravagant, you will find.

MELBA FACE POWDERS. FLEURS · LOV'ME · BOUQUET
MELBA PREPARATIONS EMBRACE EVERYTHING YOU NEED
TO MAKE YOUR BEAUTY MORE BEWITCHING
MELBA CO., CHICAGO · NEW YORK · PARIS

McCall's, 1926

Harper's Bazaar, 1918

Ladies' Home Journal, 1919

MAGNETISME!

This day she is irresistible!

HE has no words to describe the strangely elusive charm which sets *her* apart from all other women ... Hers is the unfathomable, captivating allure of sheer femininity. He thrills to a new fascination ... an irresistible enchantment ... to the subtle, lingering fragrance which surrounds her. Tender, poignant, bewitching ... is that haunting *magnétisme*.

✦ ✦ ✦

The divine Parfum Djer-Kiss—with its subtle magnetism—is the creation of that master *parfumeur*, Monsieur Kerkoff of Paris. Gloriously feminine—delightfully seductive—this same exquisite *parfum* pervades each smart Djer-Kiss toiletry ... the Face Powder ... the Parfum ... the Sachet ... the Rouge ... the Lipstick. One matchless, harmonizing fragrance .... *Magnétique!*

ALFRED H. SMITH CO., *Sole Importers*

PARIS · NEW YORK · CHICAGO · MONTREAL · LOS ANGELES

Djer-Kiss

KERKOFF-PARIS

Parfum Djer-Kiss—irresistibly alluring...the parfum of magnetism!

Djer-Kiss Face Poudre —petal-smooth...the same alluring fragrance.

Djer-Kiss Sachet—utterly lovely ...fragranced with Parfum Djer-Kiss.

New! Djer-Kiss Vanity Moderne. For loose powder and rouge. Smartly Parisian ... a stunning accessory. Only $2.50

Ladies' Home Journal, 1929

Artist signed

F.R. ARNOLD & CO. N.Y.
ORDER AS
SOLE IMPORTERS

Without exception, my genuine Dorin preparations, made especially for the women of America, have this label on the bottom of every box. Only Rouges and Poudres that bear the name F. R. Arnold & Co., New York, in addition to my own label, are genuinely guaranteed by me.

Signed

Dorin

Paris, 26ième mars, 1921

"She always looks so individual—so herself"

Learn the Parisian secret of emphasizing your own style of Beauty.— your own true coloring

"NO matter where you see her, she is the centre of attraction. And it is not because she is unusually beautiful—it is just that she seems to have a style of her own."

That is the secret. Simply by accentuating your individuality, your own coloring, you can be distinctive, so that you are not overshadowed when in a group.

Emphasize your own individuality

The French woman has learned nature's secret of charm—that one's skin must have two colors, perfectly harmonized to be attractive. Knowing, too, how subtly nature has blended the coloring of the skin, the hair, the eyes, she chooses with the utmost care the powder and rouge that blend best with her natural coloring. They must be unobtrusive and still bring out the lights in her hair and her eyes, making her always a distinct type.

Study your own coloring

It is quite natural that the study of skin colorings—of skin textures—has reached its zenith in the century-famed *ateliers* of Dorin of Paris—in the heart of France. There, powders and rouges—of exquisite softness and refinement—have been evolved with exact tints for the many types of blondes and brunettes—for the "indefinite" type (the brune-blonde)—for the Titian beauty.

These powders and rouges have become so well known by American women—and so much in demand—that they can now be secured in the better drug stores and department stores throughout the states.

There are 10 distinctive rouges and 8 shades of *poudres*, each supplied in 6 sizes from the large bureau size (3 in.) to the smallest vanity size (¾ in.). Also a complete line of facial preparations such as eyebrow crayons, lip pomades, etc.

There has been prepared for American women an illustrated booklet, "What Is Your Coloring?" showing exactly which shade of rouge and powder should be used with each type of coloring. Send for it and find your style. Then you will be sure you are using harmonizing tints.

For 25c. in stamps or coin, this booklet, together with two miniature *compactes* (La Dorine *Poudre* and Dorin's Rouge), will be mailed you. Tell us the color of your eyes, hair and skin so that we can select the exact shades for you.

Or for 10c., the booklet and two packets—one of face powder and one of rouge—*en poudre* (loose powder form) will be sent you. Remember to send description of your coloring.

Address your letter to F. R. ARNOLD & CO., Sole Importers, 5 West Twenty-Second Street, New York.

1258

ROUGE FRAISIA DORIN PARIS

Look for this label on the bottom of every box.

ROUGE BRUNETTE DORIN PARIS

1249

F.R. ARNOLD & CO. N.Y.
ORDER AS
SOLE IMPORTERS

DORIN OF PARIS

Poudres Compactes (La Dorine)-Rouges Compactes

RED. U.S. PAT. OFF.

To be genuine, Dorin Rouges and Poudres made for the U.S.A. must also bear the name F. R. ARNOLD & CO.

Theatre Magazine, 1921

Motion Picture, 1944

FOR PERFECT MAKE-UP

Cosmetics

by **AVON**

It's so easy to achieve a perfect make-up with Avon cosmetics. Here is a finely textured powder, in two weights with 8 becoming shades for each weight,—a powder that fluffs on evenly, naturally—yet clings for hours. Here is a rouge that applies smoothly,—sleekly fading out at the edges like a natural blush . . . lipstick that harmonizes with the subtle over-tints of your complexion . . . mascara that frames the eyes delicately, enchantingly.

You can be sure of the purity and quality of Avon cosmetics. They have been tested and approved by Good Housekeeping Bureau. And their prices are an agreeable surprise.

For 51 years Avon toiletries and perfumes have been sold only through carefully selected Avon Representatives, in the comfort of your own home and under an absolute, money back guarantee.

There is an Avon Representative living in your community. She has many lovely things to show you. Welcome her the next time she calls. Avon Products—The California Perfume Co., 114 Fifth Ave., N.Y.C.

Avon Face Powder comes in two weights and 8 shades,—78¢ a box. The Avon Representative will help you select the correct weight and shade. Avon Single Compact—$1.25. Double Compact—$1.75. Lipstick—52¢. Mascara—$1.04. Rouge Compact—52¢. Cream Rouge—78¢.

Good Housekeeping, 1937 Artist signed

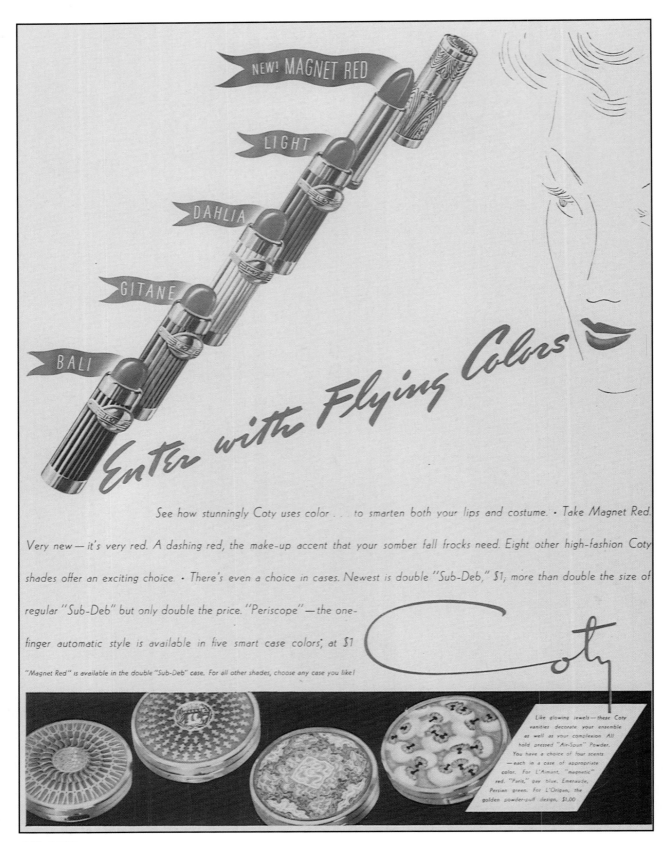

NEW! MAGNET RED

LIGHT

DAHLIA

GITANE

BALI

Enter with Flying Colors

See how stunningly Coty uses color . . . to smarten both your lips and costume. • Take Magnet Red. Very new — it's very red. A dashing red, the make-up accent that your somber fall frocks need. Eight other high-fashion Coty shades offer an exciting choice. • There's even a choice in cases. Newest is double "Sub-Deb," $1; more than double the size of regular "Sub-Deb" but only double the price. "Periscope" — the one-finger automatic style is available in five smart case colors; at $1

"Magnet Red" is available in the double "Sub-Deb" case. For all other shades, choose any case you like!

Coty

Like glowing jewels — these Coty vanities decorate your ensemble as well as your complexion. All hold pressed "Air-Spun" Powder. You have a choice of four scents — each in a case of appropriate color. For L'Aimant, "magnetic" red. "Paris," gay blue. Emeraude, Persian green. For L'Origan, the golden powder-puff design, $1.00

Life, 1939

CHEN YU creates striking new color-beauty for lips!

Utterly, entirely, completely new colors your heart will lose its mind to. Read about them . . . GOLDEN MAUVE . . . a new Chinese red touched with both blue and gold . . . POWDER BLUE FUCHSIA—a totally new version of bluey-red . . . DRAGON'S BLOOD RUBY—the first real deep red of conquest . . . EXOTIC PINK—a brilliant red-pink-red you've never seen before, and FLAME SWEPT RED—a heavenly holocaust for your lips! And each is wrapped in CHEN YU's terrific reputation for super-lasting staying power. This fantastic new lipstick in a clever automatic case faithfully resembling a carved ivory treasure piece, is now the "talk" at the smarter stores . . . $1. Associated Distributors, Sole U. S. Distributors, Chicago.

lipstick **CHEN YU**
made in U.S.A.

Harper's Bazaar, 1943

"I'm a helpless prisoner!"

says MYRNA LOY

"I'm caught! . . . in a spun-silk web! I'm held . . . in a star-dust rapture! I'm captive to a lilting mood! But I love my captor . . . I'll never escape. For this mood that's captured me is Youth itself . . . a mood which stole from a perfume bottle and entered my heart . . . surrounded my soul . . . and I surrendered! See, here's the bottle . . . there's the name—Seventeen —but wait! Not a breath of it—unless YOU want to be carried away—too!"

Seventeen

Seventeen . . . not a perfume alone
but a whole ensemble of gay toiletries!

The ensemble idea is smart in toilet accessories, too! . . . so Seventeen's gay and lightsome fragrance has been breathed into each of these essentials: *Powders* . . . a face powder, bath powder and talcum . . . all charmingly packaged, all exquisitely soft, all faintly scented with *Seventeen* . . . a *Compact*, the smartest you've ever seen, in gleaming black . . . a *Sachet*, the subtlest way to perfume lingerie . . . *Brillantines*, one solid, one liquid, to restrain straying locks and leave a fragrance that's ever so elusive.

Ladies' Home Journal, 1930

Life, 1946

Ladies' Home Journal, 1947

Ladies' Home Journal, 1945

How to Make Up Your Lips to Last
8 Hours or More

9 A. M.—*You apply when you go out*   5 P. M.—*Eight hours later—lovely red lips!*

New 8-hour lip coloring discovered in Paris by Edna Wallace Hopper. Formulated on entirely new principle. Waterproof .... Wearproof .... Indelible .... Ends constant "making-up."

EDNA WALLACE HOPPER, famous stage beauty, discovered it in Paris. A lip color that banishes all the smearing and fleeting life of present ways in make-up. An utterly new kind of lipstick.

She sent it to Hollywood, and it swept through the studios like a storm. Old-time lipsticks were discarded overnight.

Now—Kissproof, the world's largest makers of lipsticks, has obtained the formula from Miss Hopper, and offers its amazing results to you. A totally New type, different from any other you have ever tried ... *Kissproof or any other kind.*

You put it on before you go out. Then forget about it. Six hours, eight hours later your lips are still naturally lovely!

No more constant making-up. No more fuss and bother. Do you wonder that women are flocking to its use?

Utterly NEW Principle

It is different in formula and result from any previously known lipstick. It does what no other lipstick does or has ever done ... *actually seems to last indefinitely.*

That's because the color pigment it embodies has never before been used in a lipstick. It holds where others smear.

Then, too, it is a true, NATURAL color. Thus it ends that artificial smirk women have tried for years to overcome. A color that glorifies the lips to pulse-quickening loveliness—trust the *French* for that!

What to Ask For

To obtain, ask for the NEW Kissproof Indelible Lipstick (or Lip and Cheek Rouge). AND—remember it is NOT the "same" as any other lipstick known. Don't believe that just because you have tried Kissproof before—that you have tried this one. You haven't; this is ENTIRELY NEW.

Edna Wallace Hopper paid $2.50 for the original in Paris. Owing to tremendous demand the price is much less in this country. Two forms at all toilet counters—lipstick—lip and cheek rouge. Remember—Kissproof gives you imported lipstick quality without imported prices. Money cannot buy a finer lipstick.

NEW *Kissproof*
Indelible LIPSTICK

The New Movie Magazine, 1932

TANGEE
Nature's loveliest color...

Lips of Tangee...elusive blush-rose, akin to Nature's own glow of youth and health Natural color . . . smartest vogue of today . . . subtle individuality . . . this is the gift of Tangee to every woman, blonde, brunette or titian.

Quite unlike other lipsticks, Tangee changes color as you put it on . . . to the blush-rose of youth and beauty . . . and blends with each individual complexion. Truly a marvel in make-up!

The exact shade depends upon your own complexion and upon how much you apply. Tangee leaves no trace of grease or pigment . . . nothing except a lovely glow — so beautiful, so natural that it seems a part of your own lips . . . and as permanent as the day is long.

Ask for TANGEE, *and be sure you see the name* TANGEE.

Tangee Lipstick in gunmetal case. $1.00; in gold and black enamel, $2.50. Based on the same marvelous color principle . . . Tangee Rouge Compact, 75¢ . . . Tangee Crème Rouge, $1.00. The new Tangee Powder, blended to match the natural skin tones, $1.00. Tangee Night Cream, for cleansing and nourishing, $1.00. Tangee Day Cream, to protect the skin and as a base for powder, $1.00. The new Tangee Cosmetic, for beautifying lashes, brows and tinting the hair, $1.00. All prices 25¢ more in Canada. The Geo. W. Luft Co., 417 5th Ave., N.Y.

Vogue, 1930

"MAGNET RED" inspires LILLY DACHÉ

When Mme. Daché saw the brilliant

Coty make-up success, "Magnet Red",

she created a thrill

of a hat in the same ringing red.

"Magnet Red" took its inspiration

from Coty's romantic

Perfume, L'Aimant, The Magnet.

Coty Magnet Red "Pochette," (above) . . . a smart zipper-purse with a magnet "charm." In it "Sub-Deb" Lipstick, and "Air-Spun" Rouge, both in "Magnet Red," also "Air-Spun" Vanity. $2.95.

Harper's Bazaar, 1940

There's more
than one
hat that will
"do things"
for you

...but only one *face powder*
will do the most for your beauty

. . . the one that's made-to-order exclusively for you . . . hand-blended right
before your eyes . . . for your very own skintone and its needs . . .
to brighten or subdue, as the case may be . . . but always to make the
most of your own natural loveliness . . . because it's

made-to-order face powder by

Charles of the Ritz

$2, $3 the box (Introductory Size $1) plus tax.

Vogue, 1951

Vogue, 1951

ROYAL CHRISTMAS

To greet your favorite peeresses with long-to-be-cherished memories of this ceremonial Christmas. The perfume of the year, Yardley's "Bond Street," in original, royally emblazoned packings. In appealing gift sizes; priced from $2.50 to $13.50 or with other "Bond Street" baubles, at finer stores. Yardley & Co., Ltd., New York; London; Paris; Toronto.

"BOND STREET" CASE OF PERFUME, POWDER, COMPACT AND LIPSTICK. $11.25

"BOND STREET" COMPACT, BOXED. $3.50

YARDLEY'S *Bond Street*

McCall's, 1958

MAX FACTOR has a gift for making lips beautiful— Hi-Society in dazzling new designs for Christmas

give HI-SOCIETY...case, mirror and lipstick, all-in-one

Choose (if you can) from these beautiful new HI-SOCIETY case designs...each complete with lipstick refill.

A. BLACK AND GOLDEN WREATH DESIGN,
smart enamel finish $3.50

B. GOLDEN SWIRL,
graceful pattern on gleaming gold-tone $2.50

C. GOLDEN CLASSIC WHITE DESIGN,
etched on lustrous gold-tone $3.50

D. GOLDEN SUNBURST,
with shimmering gold-tone finish . . . $2.50

E. CLASSIC SILVER AND WHITE,
elegantly silver-plated $4.50

F. MOTHER-OF-PEARL DESIGN,
richly inlaid $4.50

G. MODERN FLORENTINE DESIGN,
set with a glittering gem $3.50

H. CHIC TORTOISE-TONE or
POLISHED EBONY-TONE $1.50

I. GOLDEN FLORAL,
etched on a glowing golden finish . . . $2.50

MAX FACTOR...master of make-up artistry for 50 years.

Harper's Bazaar, 1937

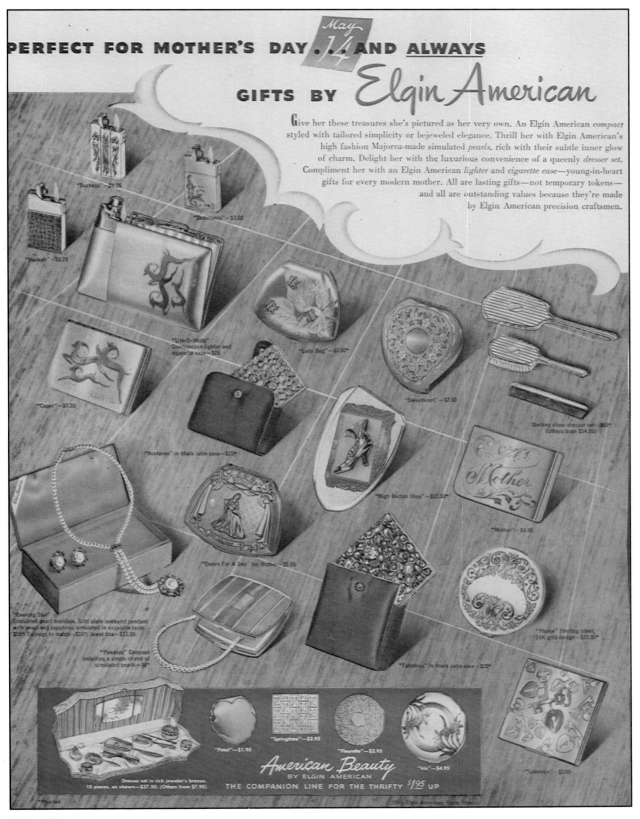

Life, 1950

Vogue, 1945

Appendix

SHIPS & PASSENGER LINERS

This is an attempt to identify and furnish information on the ships presented in these volumes. However, after consulting over two dozen reference books and other sources of ship statistics, it became apparent that consensus does not exist among many of the authors. Also, the liner class initials are not used since some of the ships changed status several times. The final word, therefore, is that this information is not the final word. Any offered documented final words will be considered.

CODE:
AMV – Armed Merchant Vessel
H – Hospital Ship
LA – Launched
LU – Laid Up
P – Passage or Route
R – Recommissioned or Repaired
SC – Scrapped
SO – Sold
SU – Sunk
T – Troop ship

Note: Abbreviated dating follows American sequence: month/day/year.

America (II) – Stratton
United States Lines & U.S. Merchant Marine Flag Ship, 1940 to 1952
LA: 8/31/39 by Eleanor Roosevelt
P: Carribean & California cruises because of European war
T: 1941/1946 as **U.S.S. West Point** – 5,000 troops a turn
R: 11/14/46
SO: 8/28/64 – Greek Flag – *Australis*
   1980 – *America, Italis, Noga*
   1984 – *Alferdoss*
LU: 1992 – Greece
Note: Sister ship – S.S. United States with an unusual design feature: a dummy fore funnel.

Aorangi (II) – Sweet Petals
Union Steamship Lines of New Zealand – 1924 – 1931
Canada–Australasian Lines – 1931 – 1953
LA: 1924 (first motorship to carry first class passengers)
P: Sidney to Vancouver
T: 1940
R: 8/48 – Sidney
SC: 5/53
Note: Carried enough fuel oil for round trip, Sidney to Vancouver with stops at Fiji and Honolulu.

Berengaria – Kwick
Cunard Lines
LA: 5/23/12 by Kaiser Wilhelm II as *Imperator*, Ballin Lines (Ger.)
P: Hamburg to New York
LU: 1914 – 1919 – World War I
T: 5/4/19 – Commandeered by U.S. as **S.S. Imperator** (returned 28,000 American troops in 3½ turns)
R: U.S. release to Cunard 4/16/21 – Renamed *Berengaria*
P: Southampton to New York
R: 3/2/38 – New York pier fire
LU: Southampton
SC: 7/23/46
Note: Third funnel a dummy.

Britannic III – Stratton
White Star Lines
LA: 6/30
P: Southampton to New York
R: 5/10/34 – To Cunard Flag
T: 8/29/39 – Luftwaffe and U-boat damage
R: 5/22/48
SC: 11/25/60 – Liverpool
Note: Last ship to sail Atlantic route under White Star Flag; fore funnel a dummy for wireless room.

Caledonia (IV) – Unmarked
Anchor Lines (U.K.)
LA: 1925
P: Glasgow to New York and winter cruises
AMV: 9/39 – H.M.S. *Scotstoun*
SU: U-boat .25 west of Northern Ireland
Note: Middle funnel a dummy.

Cameronia (II) – Unmarked
Anchor Lines (U.K.)
LA: 5/11/21
P: Liverpool to New York
T: 1/41 – Action off Algeria
R: 9/48 – Australian Immigration Service
T: 1953 – *Empire Clyde* (Korean action)
SC: 1958

Carinthia (II) – Unmarked
Cunard Lines
LA: 1925
P: Liverpool to New York and world cruise, 1933
AMV: 1939
SU: U-Boat .46 off Uster, Ireland
Note: Sister ship – Franconia II.

Carinthia (III) – Stratton
Cunard Lines
LA: 6/27/56
P: Liverpool to Montreal
R: 1966 – winter cruiser, painted white
SO: 1/68 – Italian Sitmar Lines:
   Fairland 1968 – 1971
   Fairsea 1971 – 1988
SO: 1988 – P&O Lines as *Fair Princess*.

Caronia (II) – Stratton
Cunard Lines
LA: 12/48
P: Southampton to New York and world cruiser
R: 11/18/67 – last voyage as a Cunarder
SO: 1968 – Universal Lines (GK.) as *Columbia* & *Caribia*
SC: 4/74 – rammed a pier at Guam after earlier colliding with a lighthouse in Yokohama harbor.
Note: Had three shades of green paint, nicknamed "The Green Goddess." A N.Y. woman passenger resided aboard for 15 years at a cost of £8,000,000 in fares. Was the world's largest single funnel liner. Funnel acted as a balky mainsail and caused mule-like steering problems.

Constitution – Elgin American
American Export Lines
LA: 9/16/50
P: New York to Mediterranean ports of call
R: 3/1/59 – collision in New York Harbor with tug, painted white for cruising
SO: 3/74 – Atlantic Far East Lines as *Oceanic Constitution*.
LU: 1980
Note: Used by Grace Kelly to carry her 66 member wedding party to Monaco in April 1956.

Dorsetshire – Gwenda
Bibby Lines (U.K.)
LA: 1920
P: Belfast to Africa and Australia
T: 1939, Australia to Africa
P: postwar immigration service to Australia
SC: 1954
Note: Only two-masted Bibby liner and motor ship.

Duchess of Richmond – Unmarked
Canadian Pacific Steamship Lines
LA: 6/28
P: Liverpool to Halifax
T: 12/39 – 1946
R: 7/16/47 – *Empress of Canada*
1/25/53 – fire at Liverpool, total loss
SC: 9/1/54

Empress of Australia – Gwenda
Canadian Pacific Steamship Lines
LA: 1913 – *The Tirpitz* – Hamburg American Lines
P: Hamburg to South America
R: 7/21 – commandeered by Can Pac and renamed
P: 7/24 – Pacific Route
5/27 – Southampton to Quebec
5/39 – Royal Family passage to Canada
T: 1939
SC: 1952

Empress of Canada (II) – Stratton
Canadian Pacific Steamship Lines
LA: 5/10/60
P: Liverpool to Montreal
R: 12/68 – repainted in new colors
P: 11/27/69 –first from Southampton
LU: 11/23/71
SO: 1/72 – Carnival Lines as *Mardi Gras*,
Carribean cruiser

Empress of Scotland (II) – Stratton
Canadian Pacific Steamship Lines
LA: 12/17/29 – *Empress of Japan*
P: Liverpool to Quebec City
8/30 – Trans-Pacific service
T: 1939 – 1944 – American and British troops to Africa
R: 10/42 – renamed
P: 1948 – Liverpool to Quebec City
11/51 – Princess Elizabeth and Prince Philip on
Canadian tour
R: 5/52 – masts shortened by 40' for Montreal passage
SO: 7/58 – Hamburg American Lines renamed as
Hanseatic
R: 9/7/66 – caught fire at New York Pier
SC: 10/66

Esperance Bay – Kwick
Aberdeen and Commonwealth Lines (U.K.)
LA: 1922
P: London to Australia via Suez Canal
SC: 1955
Note: This is the prime example of conflicting information. In 1936 the company decided to switch names among its fleet. If this case is pre-1936 (which it seems to be) it may have been originally the **Hobson's Bay** *or* **Hobson Bay**, *or the other way around. Also the name* **Arawa** *appears obliquely in several references during this time.*

Franconia (II) – Stratton
Cunard Lines
LA: 6/23
P: Liverpool to New York and annual world cruise
T: 9/30/39 – 1946, carried 149,000 troops
6/16/40 – hit by Luftwaffe off Brittany
2/13/45 – Churchill Yalta headquarters
R: 8/48
P: 6/49 – Liverpool to Quebec
SC: 12/18/56

Franconia (III) – Stratton
Cunard Lines
LA: 12/14/54 – *Ivernia* (II)
P: 7/1/55 – Greenock to Montreal
R: 6/63 – renamed
P: 7/63 – Rotterdam to Montreal
R: 2/67 – painted white as a winter cruiser
P: New York to Bermuda
P: 11/70 – last run for Cunard
LU: 1971 – 1972
SO: 8/73 – to Black Sea Steamship Co. (USSR)
R: 1973 – renamed *Feodor Shalyapin*
P: Southampton to Australia
T: 6/80 – Cuban Troops to Middle East via Suez Canal
LU: Currently inactive
Note: Sister ship **Carmania II.**

Highland Patriot – Kwick
Nelson Lines (U.K.)
LA: 12/10/31
P: London to Buenos Aires
SO: 8/4/32 – to Royal Mail Lines Ltd.
SU: 1/10/40 – torpedoed, Atlantic Ocean

Himalaya – Stratton
P & O Lines (U.K.)
LA: 10/5/48
P: London to Sidney via Suez Canal
R: 1958 – world cruiser
SC: 11/28/74

Idaho – Unmarked
U.S. Navy
LA: 6/30/17 Battleship – "New Mexico Class"
P: 5/41 – left Pearl Harbor for N. Atlantic convoy duty
with *Mississippi* & *Yorktown*
6/44 – Pacific Fleet duty
4/45 – Okinawa Invasion duty
8/27/45 – Tokyo Bay with *Missouri* for W.W.II peace
signing
LU: 7/3/46
SC: 11/24/47

Ivernia (II) – Stratton
Cunard Lines
LA: 12/14/54
P: Greenock to Montreal
R: 6/63 – renamed *Franconia* (III) and painted white
for winter cruising

Neuralia – Kwick
British India Steam Navigation Co.
LA: 1912
P. England to Calcutta
SU: 5/1/45 – mined off Southern Italy
Note: Sister Ship **Nevasa.**

Nevasa – Unmarked Locket
British India Steam Navigation Co.
LA: 12/12/12
P: England to Calcutta
H: W.W. I hospital ship
P: resumed
W.W. II information lacking
SC: 1948
Note: Locket shows line flag. Largest liner of this flag to date (1912); sister ship **Neuralia.**

Newfoundland (I) – Gwenda
Furness Warren Lines (U.S.) or Warren Line (U.K.)
LA: 1925
P: Liverpool to Boston, Mass.
H: no dates
SU: 9/13/43 – with Red Cross flag bombed off Salerno
by Luftwaffe with heavy loss of life

Pocahontas – Unmarked
Virginia Ferry Corp (U.S.)
No Dates: in service between Cape Charles and Nor-
folk. VA. (See postcard.)

Queen Elizabeth – Various Cases
Cunard Lines
LA: 2/40 by then reigning Queen Elizabeth
P: no pre-war passenger passage, entered New York
Harbor in camouflage paint to be refitted
T: 11/3/40 to 3/6/46 – ferried 811,324 troops (2,000 a
turn)
R: 10/15/46 – returned to Southampton/New York
passage with 907 crossings eventually
2/63 – New York to Bermuda cruising
SO: 4/5/68 – to the City of Lauderdale, Fla.
LU: 1968 – mid 1970
SO: 8/70 – to Orient Overseas Line (Hong Kong)
R: docked in Hong Kong Harbor and renamed *Seawise University*
SC: 1/9/72 – caught fire with total loss
Note: Largest Cunarder afloat.

Queen Elizabeth 2 – Stratton
  Cunard Lines
  LA: 4/69 by Queen Elizabeth II
  P: Southampton to New York
  1/10/75 – first world cruise
  T: 5/3/82 – Gray paint for Falklands – 3,200 troops
  R: various
  P: still in service as world cruiser
Note: Only passenger liner with a non-Roman numeral in name. Might have been a carry-over from the pre-launch designation of "Q4" (missing a queen here). The ship has gained — almost officially — the nickname of "QE2."

Queen Mary – Various Cases
  Cunard White Star LTD.
  LA: 9/26/34 by Her Majesty Queen Mary
  P: Southampton to New York
  LU: 1939 – New York Harbor for safety
  T: 5/5/40 to 9/46 – carried 810,000 troops (whole division) and post W.W. II War brides and families
  P: 10/2/42 – Rammed and sunk escort British cruiser H.M.S. *Curacao* with minor damage to Q.M.
  R: Refit at Clydebank
  P: 7/31/47 – resumed crossings
  SO: 10/67 – City of Long Beach, CA, and permanently berthed
  SO: 11/80 – Wrather Port Corp. as a convention center
Note: Last three-funnel passenger liner and first Cunard White Star. Since Cunarder names traditionally ended in "ia" and White Star had "ic", a break with both lines was made and King George V approved the new tradition. It almost became the Q.M. III since two other Q.M. ships were on the British Registry, but national pride prevailed as a bottle of Australian wine crashed against the port bow and the first H.M.S. Queen was named.

Samaria (II) – Unmarked
  Cunard Lines
  LA: 8/21
  P: Liverpool to Boston and world cruiser
  T: 1941 – Canadian troops, later families
  R: 9/48
  P: London to Quebec and Montreal
  6/14/51 – Liverpool to Quebec and Montreal
  R: 6/15/53 – represented the Cunard Line at the coronation review, Spithead, England
  SC: 1/56

Saturnia – Unmarked
  Cosulich Lines (Italian)
  LA: 12/29/25 (world's largest liner at launch)
  P: Trieste to New York then 1927 – Trieste to Rio
  T: 1935 – Italian troops to Africa
  R: 1943 – Commandeered by U.S. for Mediteranean Hospital Service as *Frances Y. Slanger*
  R: 11/46 – Returned to Italian Line
  P: 1/20/47 – Naples to New York and ports of call
  SC: 12/1/65

Soley – Zell Fifth Avenue
  U.S. Navy
  LA: 9/8/44 – Destroyer "Allen M. Summer Class" (James R. Soley, 1850 Ass't Sec. Navy Dept.)
  P: 9/7/45 – Tokyo Bay Peace Signing
  6/52 – TF77 w/*U.S.S. Missouri* – Korean Action One Battle Star
  Quantanamo Bay – Cuban Crisis
  SU: 9/1/70 – U.S. Navy target practice off Charleston, Virginia

Stefan Batory – Stratton
  Gdynia American Lines –(Polish)
  LA: 7/52 – *Maasdam* – Holland American Lines
  P: Rotterdam to New York – occasional call at Halifax
  4/63 – Bremerhaven to New York immigration service
  R: 2/15/63 – rammed sunken wrecks in Bremerhaven
  P: 1966 – St. Lawrence Seaway Trade
  SO: 12/68 – Polish Ocean Lines – renamed
  P: 12/19/70 – Gdynia to New York under flag "GAL"
  10/7/87 – last line voyage
  SO: 1987 – City Shipping Intl. (Swedish) renamed *Stefan*

Sussex – Unmarked
  Royal Navy Cruiser – "London Class"
  LA: 2/22/28
  P: part of "H" force out of Gibraltar; in Capetown during *Graf Spee* battle — no fatal war damage
  SC: 2/23/50

Warwick Castle – unmarked
  Union Castle Lines
  LA: 1931
  P: Southampton to Capetown
  R: 1938 – refitted: double to single funnel
  SU: 11/14/42 – Atlantic duty

York (IX) – Unmarked
  Royal Navy Cruiser – "Standard Class"
  LA: 1928
  SU: 5/29/41 – Luftwaffe damage at Suda Bay, Crete

American Export Lines – Unmarked
  LA: 1931 – passenger service
  Ships – *Exeter, Independence, Atlantic*, and *Constitution*
  LU: 1968 – service ceased

American President Lines – Wadsworth
  Dollar Lines successor – 1938
  P: Atlantic routes then freighter/passenger service
  LU: 1965 – discontinued service
Note: All ships had American presidential names — used extensively by U.S. Navy as troop and hospital ships during W.W. II, too many name changes to list, either sunk under action or scrapped by 1948.

Blue Star Lines – Stratton
  U.K. Passenger Liners – 1927 – 1972
  P: Liverpool/London and ports of call
  SU: total fleet (5) lost to U-boats
  LA: 1947 – 48 – *Brazil Star, Uruguay Star, Paraguay Star*
  SC: 1972
Note: All ships after 5/29 had Star in name. Now major world cargo carrier.

Delta Lines – unmarked
  Delta Steamship Lines
  LA: *Del Norte*, flagship (1946), *Del Mar* and *Del Sud* (1947)
  P: U.S. to Brazil via New Orleans – 18 day passage and 42 day cruise
  SC: 1972
Note: Largest passenger liners out of port of New Orleans.

United States Lines – unmarked pendant
  P: 1921 New York to Southampton
  Ships: commandeered W.W. I German liners:
  Vaterland to *Leviathan*
  Amerika to *America* (I)
  Prinzess Alice to *President Arthur*

Glossary

Abalone – Large flattened oval marine shell with bluish mother of pearl lining.

Acanthus – Plant leaf used as an architectural motif such as capitals on Corinthian columns.

Art Deco – Art movement with beginnings in the middle 1920s featuring linear flora, fauna and human forms.

Art Moderne – Art movement which broke with Art Nouveau traditions and was concurrent with Art Deco, emphasizing sharp cubistic and geometrical patterns.

Art Nouveau – Art movement begun in London with the "Liberty Style" in 1875, using sinuous interlacing lines. First modern break with historic art forms.

Bakelite – Protected tradename for synthetic resin and plastic material, usually opaque, can be molded or carved.

Baguette (Fr.) – Oblong shape or cut.

Baroque – Design with much ornamentation and curved lines.

Bas-Relief – Slight pattern projection on a flat surface.

Beauty Box – A vanity case containing cosmetic items other than powder and rouge, such as eye make-up.

Belais – Trademark white metal process, "The white gold that stays white." David Belais, Inc., N.Y.

Bevel – Sloping angle of a surface.

Bijou – A small and exquisite trinket.

Brevete (Fr.) – Patent or patented.

Burgee – "Swallowtail" flag.

Butterfly Wing – Amazonian Blue Morpho Butterfly with wing span of 9", used for costume jewelry and cases.

Cabochon – A rounded stone without facets.

Cabriole – Furniture legs shaped in a reflex curve.

Cameo – Gem carving usually through two or more layers.

Can Compact or Vanity Case – Early twentieth century box-shaped hinged cases containing mirror and puffs, with removable interior fittings for storage of buttons, pins, shirt studs, snuff, etc. usually with very tight closures.

Carryall – Cosmetic case which serves as a purse substitute.

Baton – Long oval carryall, with or without a carrier, resembling a staff of office, sliding band closure.

Clutch – All carryalls without carriers.

Cylinder – Round carryall, with or without carrier.

Demi – Early carryalls holding coins, combs, powder, or puff and an empty compartment usually too small for cigarettes.

Oversize – Evans term for larger carryall that usually contains a lighter.

Petite – Evans term for small box carryalls with lighter and cigarette compartments.

Portmanteau – Name given by Volupté for clutch carryalls that open like a briefcase and have no handles.

Purse – Carryalls with detachable cloth carriers, or carriers with exterior compacts or vanity cases.

Standard – Evans term for the classic carryall.

Super – Pseudo minaudiéres usually carried as a clutch.

Vanity – Carryalls with attached exterior items to handles, such as lipsticks or perfume bottles.

Celluloid – Trademark thermoplastic material used as substitute for ivory, horn, or tortoise-shell.

Chameleon Finish – Case light reflections created by interacting glossy and brushed case lacquer application.

Champlevé (Fr.) – Enamel fused into design cells which are sunk in the metal base plate.

Chasing – Ornamental metal work using engraving or embossing techniques.

Chatelaine – Ornamental chains, hung from a brooch or belt, from which are suspended small objects such as keys, note cases, boxes or mirrors, etc.

Chevron – "V" shaped bars or lines.

Chinoiserie – European interpretation of Oriental motifs.

Cloisonné – Fused powdered glass placed in separate case cells formed from thin strips of metal.

Clutch – Woman's purse with no wrist handle.

Cofferet – Small box for holding valuables.

Collet – Non-prong ring mounting for stones.

Compact – Small cosmetic case containing only face powder and a mirror.

Convertible Case – Interior adapted for either pressed or loose powder.

Cornucopia – Horn of plenty.

Czechoslovakia – European country noted for outstanding artisan work in glass, faux gemstones and metalwork. Established as a nation: 1918, divided: 1938, reformed in: 1945, and 1993: the Czech Republic.

Damascening – Several layers of different metals cut with a tool exposing their color characteristics.

Decal – The process of transferring designs printed on specially prepared paper to wood, glass etc. surfaces.

Depose (Fr.) – Register or registered.

Dhow – Arabian wooden ships which carry one or two lateen (triangular) sails.

Diamanté (Fr.) – Glittering ornamentation, i.e. rhinestones or other sparkling materials.

Ebonite – Black variety of vulcanized rubber capable of being cut and polished for combs, buttons, and cases.

Embossing – Carved or hammered design that is raised above a flat surface.

Engine-Turning – Ornamental engraving done by machinery.

Facet – Small polished plane surfaces.

Faux (Fr.) – Fake, false.

Femme (Fr.) – Female figure

Filigree – Lace-like ornamental metal work.

Flapjack – Round thin compact resembling a pancake. Term also used on international rectangular cases which have a spring action lid.

Cookie – to 2½" diameter.

Baby – 2½" to 3½" diameter.

Standard – 3½" to 5" diameter.

Super – 5" to 6" diameter.

Floret – Any of the individual flowers making up the head of a plant.

Gazelles – Usually leaping, small, swift antelope which became a favorite Art Deco motif. Early use by Raymond Loewy as a Neiman Marcus logo in 1923.

Glove Vanity or Compact – Small rectangular case which fits in the palm of a gloved hand.

Goldtone – Any gold colored metallic finish.

Granulate – Roughen surface by the addition of granules or tiny bulges.

Guilloche (Fr.) – Layers of transparent enamel over a prepared surface, generally engine-turned.

Gun-metal – Nearly neutral gray alloy of low brilliance.

Hallmark – An official stamp to guarantee and identify the standards of precious metals.

High-Relief – Sculptured figures which project by more than half from background.

Incising – Engraving or carving into a flat surface with a sharp tool.

Intaglio – Design incised or engraved into material below the surface — the opposite of cameo work.

Kamra – Case resembling early collapsible camera cases.

Limoges (Fr.) – A fine French porcelain from this city.

Logo – A word, letter, symbol, or character representing an entire phrase or name.

Lucite – Trademark name for acrylic or plastic material, high translucency.

Lunette – Crescent shaped.

Marabou Puff – Stork under feathers.

Marcasite – Mineral or polished steel cut in the form of brilliants.

Marquetry – Decorative inlay of wood.

Matte – Dull surface or finish — not shiny or glossy.

Monogram Cartouche – An ornamental outline which offers space for initials or name.

M.O.P. – Mother of pearl – Hard pearly interior layer of certain marine shells.

Nacre (Fr.) – Iridescent effect of mother of pearl.

Nickel Silver – Hard alloy of nickel, copper, and zinc.

Niello – Black compound of silver, copper, etc. used to fill engraved portions of metal for highlighting.

Objet d' Art (Fr.) – Art ornament.

Passementerie (Fr.) – Heavy fabric trimming usually of gold or silver gimp, cord, or braid.

Patch Box – Small round compact with a set-in lid, akin to eighteenth century box used for beauty patches or spots. May also be a unit on a chatelaine.

Pâté de Verre (Fr.) – Glass substance resembling jade or other carved gemstones.

Paten – Tin or glass tray on which pressed powder or rouge is based for insertion in cosmetic cases.

Pavé (Fr.) – Stones are placed close together so that very little case metal shows between the mountings.

Peking Beads – Hand blown drilled glass beads made in China, sometimes called "frivolous beads," used for decoration.

Pendant Cases – Compact or vanity case suspended from a chain or ring.

Perspex – U.K. term for Lucite or Plexiglas.

Petit Point – Small needlepoint stitch.

Pewter – Dull silvery-gray alloy of tin and lead.

Plexiglas – Trademark name for thermoplastic synthetic resins.

Portrait Case – Picture frame feature in compacts and vanity cases for snapshot insertion.

Porcelain – Hard white nonporous variety of ceramic ware.

Post Deco – A revival of Art Deco motifs after W.W. II, namely, the leaping gazelle. The design lines are rounder and the flora is more realistic.

Powder Disk Compact – Case has a small hole or slot in bottom allowing replacement of used pressed powder disk.

Purse Kit – A small fabric or leather case with a snap closure, usually containing compact, lipstick, perfume, and comb.

Quatrefoil – Flower or stylized design with four petals or florets.

Repoussé (Fr.) – Decoration achieved by pushing out the metal into relief by reverse tooling.

Reverse – The exterior back of an object.

Rhinestone – Artificial gem made of glass.

Rococo – Ornamental design of swirls, imitating shellwork and foliage.

Ruching – Ruffled strip of fine fabric or ribbon.

Shagreen (faux) – Rough granular surface resembling sharkskin.

Sheraton – English furniture style designed by Thomas Sheraton (1780 – 1806) with straight severe lines. Leg detail can be reeded or plain.

Sifter – Powder control screen usually made of fine mesh.

Silvertone – Any silver colored metallic finish.

Soutache (Fr.) – Narrow flat decorative braid used for trim.

Sterling – Standard pure silver with minute variable alloys.

Tambourine – Small drum-like instrument with loose brass jingles in the side rim.

Tortoise-shell – The back and underside shell platelets of the Hawksbill tortoise. Amber and brown streaked patterns are from the back plates, the underside yields the almost translucent honey blond.

Trifids – Three lobes or parts.

Triptych – Set of three panels often hinged so the two side panels may fold over the central one.

Vanity Case – Portable case with mirror, powder, and rouge, sometimes called a double compact.

Carrying Case – Fitted miniature travel case with mirror and make-up accessories attached to lidded bottom compartment. Case has lock and key for jewelry storage.

Combination Case – Contains additional features other than powder and rouge such as coin holders, combs, etc.

Kit – A small slipcase for a compact with a lipstick mounted in an exterior sleeve.

Kit Bag – Cloth pouch with drawstring closure, mirror, and puff accessories — no compartment for powder.

Pouch – Fabric or metal mesh bag with a vanity case serving as a lid.

Triple Case – Vanity case with lipstick.

Velour – Fabric or finish with a soft velvet-like nap.

Vermeil – Gilded silver or white metal.

Votary – A worshipping figure.

War
 World War I "The Great War" – 1914 – 1918
 European Declaration: August, 1914
 U.S.A.: April, 1917
 World Armistice: Nov. 11, 1918

 – World War II – 1938 – 1945
 European (Austria): March, 1938 – May 7, 1945
 France: Sept. 1939 – May 7, 1945
 U.K.: Sept. 9, 1939 – Sept. 12, 1945
 U.S.A.: Dec. 8, 1941 – Sept. 2, 1945

Wedgwood – Fine English pottery best known for a white cameo-like relief ware on a tinted matte background, featuring neoclassical figures and scenes.

White Metal – Generic term for any unidentified silver looking metal composition.

Bibliography

BOOKS:

American Naval Fighting Ships, Vol III and VI. Dept. of the Navy, 1959 – 1981.

Arwas, Victor. *Art Deco.* London: St. Martin's Press, 1976.

——. *Art Deco.* N.Y.: Henry N. Abrams, Inc., 1980.

Battersby, Martin. *The Decorative Twenties.* NY: Walker & Co., 1969.

——. *The Decorative Thirties,* NY: Walker & Co., 1971.

Becker, Stephen. *Comic Art In America.* NY: Simon & Schuster, 1959.

Blake, George. *R.M.S. Queen Mary.* UK: Batsford Ltd., 1936,

Bonsor, N.R.P. *South Atlantic Seaway.* Channel Islands, UK: Brookside Publ. Jersey, 1983.

Braynard, Frank O., *Classic Ocean Liners.* UK: Patrick Stephens, Ltd., 1990.

Cairis, Nicholas T. *Era of the Passenger Liner.* London: Pegasus Books Ltd., 1989.

Contini, Mila. *Fashion.* NY: The Odyssey Press, 1965.

Corbett, Ruth. *Daddy Danced the Charleston.* NJ: A.S. Barnes & Co., 1970.

Culme, John. *The Jewels of the Duchess Of Windsor.* London: Thames & Hudson, 1987.

Darton, Mike. *Art Deco.* London: Tiger Books Int'l., 1990.

Dear, Ian. *Great Ocean Liners.* London: B.T. Batsford, 1991.

Dolan, Maryanne. *Collecting Rhinestones & Colored Stone Jewelry,* 3rd Edition. AL: Books Americana, 1993.

Dorner, Jane. *Fashion In The Twenties & Thirties.* London: Ian Allan Ltd., 1973.

Drake, Nicholas. *The Fifties In Vogue.* NY: Henry Holt, 1987.

Dunn, Laurence. *Passenger Liners.* London: Adlard Coles Ltd., 1965.

Edwards, Juliette. *Compacts, A Collector's Manual.* Surrey, U.K.: Private Printing, 1994.

Emmons, Frederick. *The Atlantic Liners.* NY: Bonanza Books, 1972.

——. *The Pacific Liners.* NY: Bonanza Books, 1974.

Gibbs, Cmdr, and C.R. Vernon, R.N. *Western Ocean Passenger Lines & Liners 1934 – 1969.* Glasgow: Brown, Son & Ferguson, 1989.

Grattidge, Capt. Harry. *Captain of the Queens.* NY: E.P. Dutton & Co., 1956.

Hillier, Bevis. *Art Deco.* London: Studio Vista/Dutton, 1972.

Howarth, David and Stephen. *The Story of the P&O.* London: Weidenfeld and Nicholson, 1986.

Jane's Fighting Ships of W.W. II 1941 – 1945. NY: Macmillan Co.

Jones-North, Jacquelyne Y. *Commercial Perfume Bottles.* PA: Schiffer Ltd., 1987.

Keen, Brigid. *The Women We Wanted to Look Like.* NY: St. Martin's Press, 1977.

Klein, Dan. *All Color Book of Art Deco.* London: Octopus Books Ltd., 1974.

Lauder, Estee. *Estee – A Success Story.* NY: Random House, 1985.

Lefkowith, Christie Mayer. *The Art of Perfume.* NY: Thames and Hudson, 1994.

Le Gallienne, Richard. *The Romance of Perfume.* Paris, Richard Hudnut, 1928.

Lesieutre, Alain. *The Spirit & Splendor of Art Deco.* London: Paddington Press, 1974.

Lewis, Alfred Allan. *Miss Elizabeth Arden.* NY: Coward, McCann & Geoghegan, 1972.

Loewy, Raymond. *Industrial Design.* NY: Overlook Press, Woodstock, 1979.

McClinton, Katherine Morrison. *Art Deco.* NY: Clarkson N. Potter, 1972.

Maryon, Herbert. *Metalwork & Enamelling.* NY: Dover Publ., 1971.

Maxtone, John. *The Only Way to Cross.* NY: The Macmillan Co., 1972.

Mendes, Suzy. *The Windsor Style.* London: Grafton Books, 1987.

Miller, William H. *Transatlantic Liners.* NY: Arco Publ. Inc., 1981.

Nadelhoffer, Hans. *Cartier.* London: Thames & Hudson, 1984.

Neret, Gilles. *Boucheron.* NY: Rizzoli, 1988

Newell, Gordon. *Ocean Liners of the 20th Century,* NY: Bonanza, 1963.

O'Higgins, Patrick. *Madame* (Helena Rubinstein). NY: The Viking Press, 1971.

Prior, Rupert. *Ocean Liners.* UK: Tiger Books, 1992.

Proddow, Penny. *Hollywood Jewels*. NY: Henry N. Abrams, 1992.

Rainwater, Dorothy T. *American Silver Manufacturers,* Hanover, PA., Everybodys Press, 1966.

——. *American Jewelry Manufacturers*. West Chester, PA.: Schiffer Publ. 1988.

Raulet, Sylvie. *Art Deco Jewelry*. NY: Rizzoli, 1989.

——. *Van Cleef & Arpels*, NY: Rizzoli, 1987.

Ross, Mary Steele. *American Women in Uniform*, NY: Garden City Publishing, 1943.

Schiaparelli, Elsa. *Shocking Life*. NY: E.P. Dutton & Co., 1954.

Ships of the Royal Navy, Vol. I. NY: J.J. Colledge, 1969.

Smith, Eugene W.. *Passenger Ships of the World*. Boston: Geo. H. Dean Co., 1978.

Stevens, Leonard A. *The Elizabeth – Passage of a Queen*. NY: Alfred A. Knopf, 1968.

Time-Life Editors & Melvin Maddocks. *The Great Liners*. VA: Time-Life Books, 1978.

Vargas, Alberto. *Vargas*. NY: Bell Publ. Co., 1984.

Weber, Eva. *American Art Deco*. Greenwich, CT.: Dorset Press, 1985.

Winter, C.W.R. *The Queen Mary*. NY: W.W. Norton & Co., 1986.

PERIODICALS:
The American Perfumer, Jan. 1909 to Nov. 1950.

Drug Topics, Nov. 1928, June 1930

Harper's Bazaar, 1931 to 1963

Junior Bazaar, 1946

St. Louis Dispatch, November 30, 1941

St. Louis Globe, December 2, 1928

Theatre, 1909 to 1925

Vanity Fair, 1917

Vogue, 1938 to 1963

EXHIBITIONS AND THEATRICAL PLAYBILLS
Minneapolis Institute of Art: *World of Art Deco*, July – September 1971

Rothman's Gallery, Stratford, Ontario, *Deco – 1925 to 1935*, June – September 1975

Hartman Theatre – Columbus, OH, Playbills – 1911 to 1954

CATALOGS:
Auction:
Christie's, Jewelry, 1987 to 1992

Sotheby's, Jewelry, April 2/3, 1987

MAIL:
Bennett Bros Inc., Chicago, 1955

Carson, Pirie, Scott & Co., Chicago, 1928

Chicago Mail Order Co., Chicago, 1931 – 32

Ft. Dearborn Mercantile Co., Chicago, 1938, 1941

H.M. Manheim & Co., NY: 1940

Plymouth Jewelry Co., NY: 1942

Wallenstein/Mayer Co., Cincinnati, OH, 1932

BROCHURES:
Armour & Co., *Luxor, Beauty Making at Home,* Chicago, 1917.

Hudnut, Richard. *Beauty Is Yours.* Du Barry Beauty Salon, NY: 1941.

—— *Marvelous*. NY: 1936.

—— *The Golden Jubilee of a Merchant of Beauty, 1880 – 1930 Fifty Years of Richard Hudnut.*

Primrose House. *The New Beauty Book*, 1923

Princess Pat. *For You – Exquisite Beauty*, 1932.

Rubinstein, Helena *Beauty in the Making*, 1932, 1933.

ARTICLES:
"All in a Day's Shopping." *Ladies' Home Journal*, December 1930.

"Give Gifts For Beauty." *McCall's Magazine*, November 1928.

Farnsworth, Helen A. "A.A. Vantine's Perfumes." *Perfume Quarterly*, Vol III, #3.

Mueller, Laura M. "Flacons, Minis and Compacts." *Perfume Quarterly*, Vol III, #1.

Mueller, Laura M., "Collecting Compacts." *Baby Boomer Collectibles*, February 1995.

Mueller, Laura M., ed. "Reflection On The Fair Vanity." *Powder Puff*, Vol #3/ 2 & 4.

Plimpton, George. "Stalking the Great Spangled Fritillary." *The New York Times Magazine,* Sept. 3, 1995.

"New Winkles." *Woman's Home Companion*, March 1932.

"New Winkles." *Woman's Home Companion*, May 1932.

"Powder In The Hand." *Woman's Home Companion*, January 1936.

Index

COLLECTOR BOOKS

Informing Today's Collector

For over two decades we have been keeping collectors informed on trends and values in all fields of antiques and collectibles.

BOOKS ON GLASS AND POTTERY

1810	American Art Glass, Shuman	$29.95
1312	Blue & White Stoneware, McNerney	$9.95
1959	Blue Willow, 2nd Ed., Gaston	$14.95
4553	Coll. Glassware from the 40's, 50's, 60's, 3rd Ed., Florence	$19.95
3816	Collectible Vernon Kilns, Nelson	$24.95
3311	Collecting Yellow Ware – Id. & Value Gd., McAllister	$16.95
1373	Collector's Ency. of American Dinnerware, Cunningham	$24.95
3815	Coll. Ency. of Blue Ridge Dinnerware, Newbound	$19.95
2272	Collector's Ency. of California Pottery, Chipman	$24.95
3811	Collector's Ency. of Colorado Pottery, Carlton	$24.95
3312	Collector's Ency. of Children's Dishes, Whitmyer	$19.95
2133	Collector's Ency. of Cookie Jars, Roerig	$24.95
3723	Coll. Ency. of Cookie Jars-Volume II, Roerig	$24.95
4552	Collector's Ency. of Depression Glass, 12th Ed., Florence	$19.95
2209	Collector's Ency. of Fiesta, 7th Ed., Huxford	$19.95
1439	Collector's Ency. of Flow Blue China, Gaston	$19.95
3812	Coll. Ency. of Flow Blue China, 2nd Ed., Gaston	$24.95
3813	Collector's Ency. of Hall China, 2nd Ed., Whitmyer	$24.95
2334	Collector's Ency. of Majolica Pottery, Katz-Marks	$19.95
1358	Collector's Ency. of McCoy Pottery, Huxford	$19.95
3313	Collector's Ency. of Niloak, Gifford	$19.95
3837	Collector's Ency. of Nippon Porcelain I, Van Patten	$24.95
2089	Collector's Ency. of Nippon Porcelain II, Van Patten	$24.95
1665	Collector's Ency. of Nippon Porcelain III, Van Patten	$24.95
4712	Collector's Ency. of Nippon Porcelain IV, Van Patten	$24.95
1447	Collector's Ency. of Noritake, 1st Series, Van Patten	$19.95
1034	Collector's Ency. of Roseville Pottery, Huxford	$19.95
1035	Collector's Ency. of Roseville Pottery, 2nd Ed., Huxford	$19.95
3314	Collector's Ency. of Van Briggle Art Pottery, Sasicki	$24.95
2339	Collector's Guide to Shawnee Pottery, Vanderbilt	$19.95
1425	Cookie Jars, Westfall	$9.95
3440	Cookie Jars, Book II, Westfall	$19.95
2275	Czechoslovakian Glass & Collectibles, Barta	$16.95
4716	Elegant Glassware of the Depression Era, 7th Ed., Florence	$19.95
3725	Fostoria - Pressed, Blown & Hand Molded Shapes, Kerr	$24.95
3883	Fostoria Stemware - The Crystal for America, Long	$24.95
3886	Kitchen Glassware of the Depression Years, 5th Ed., Florence	$19.95
4772	McCoy Pottery, Coll. Reference & Value Guide, Hanson	$19.95
4725	Pocket Guide to Depression Glass, 10th Ed., Florence	$9.95
3825	Puritan Pottery, Morris	$24.95
1670	Red Wing Collectibles, DePasquale	$9.95
1440	Red Wing Stoneware, DePasquale	$9.95
1958	So. Potteries Blue Ridge Dinnerware, 3rd Ed., Newbound	$14.95
4634	Standard Carnival Glass, 5th Ed., Edwards	$24.95
3327	Watt Pottery – Identification & Value Guide, Morris	$19.95
2224	World of Salt Shakers, 2nd Ed., Lechner	$24.95

BOOKS ON DOLLS & TOYS

4707	A Decade of Barbie Dolls and Collectibles, 1981 - 1991, Summers	$19.95
2079	Barbie Fashion, Vol. 1, 1959-1967, Eames	$24.95
3310	Black Dolls – 1820 - 1991 – Id. & Value Guide, Perkins	$17.95
1529	Collector's Ency. of Barbie Dolls, DeWein	$19.95
2338	Collector's Ency. of Disneyana, Longest & Stern	$24.95
3727	Coll. Guide to Ideal Dolls, Izen	$18.95

4645	Madame Alexander Price Guide #21, Smith	$9.95
4723	Matchbox Toys, 1947 to 1996, Johnson	$18.95
4647	Modern Collector's Dolls, 8th series, Smith	$24.95
1540	Modern Toys, 1930 - 1980, Baker	$19.95
4640	Patricia Smith's Doll Values – Antique to Modern, 12th ed.	$12.95
4728	Schroeder's Coll. Toys, 3rd Edition	$17.95
3826	Story of Barbie, Westenhouser, No Values	$19.95
2028	Toys, Antique & Collectible, Longest	$14.95
1808	Wonder of Barbie, Manos	$9.95
1430	World of Barbie Dolls, Manos	$9.95

OTHER COLLECTIBLES

1457	American Oak Furniture, McNerney	$9.95
3716	American Oak Furniture, Book II, McNerney	$12.95
4704	Antique & Collectible Buttons, Wisniewski	$19.95
2333	Antique & Collectible Marbles, 3rd Ed., Grist	$9.95
1748	Antique Purses, Holiner	$19.95
1426	Arrowheads & Projectile Points, Hothem	$7.95
1278	Art Nouveau & Art Deco Jewelry, Baker	$9.95
1714	Black Collectibles, Gibbs	$19.95
4708	B.J. Summers' Guide to Coca-Cola, Summers	$19.95
1128	Bottle Pricing Guide, 3rd Ed., Cleveland	$7.95
3717	Christmas Collectibles, 2nd Ed., Whitmyer	$24.95
1752	Christmas Ornaments, Johnson	$19.95
3718	Collectible Aluminum, Grist	$16.95
2132	Collector's Ency. of American Furniture, Vol. I, Swedberg	$24.95
2271	Collector's Ency. of American Furniture, Vol. II, Swedberg	$24.95
3720	Coll. Ency. of American Furniture, Vol III, Swedberg	$24.95
3722	Coll. Ency. of Compacts, Carryalls & Face Powder Boxes, Mueller	$24.95
2018	Collector's Ency. of Granite Ware, Greguire	$24.95
3430	Coll. Ency. of Granite Ware, Book 2, Greguire	$24.95
1441	Collector's Guide to Post Cards, Wood	$9.95
2276	Decoys, Kangas	$24.95
1716	Fifty Years of Fashion Jewelry, Baker	$19.95
4568	Flea Market Trader, 10th Ed., Huxford	$12.95
3819	General Store Collectibles, Wilson	$24.95
3436	Grist's Big Book of Marbles, Everett Grist	$19.95
2278	Grist's Machine Made & Contemporary Marbles	$9.95
1424	Hatpins & Hatpin Holders, Baker	$9.95
4721	Huxford's Collectible Advertising – Id. & Value Gd., 3rd Ed	$24.95
4648	Huxford's Old Book Value Guide, 8th Ed.	$19.95
1181	100 Years of Collectible Jewelry, Baker	$9.95
2216	Kitchen Antiques – 1790 - 1940, McNerney	$14.95
4724	Modern Guns – Id. & Val. Gd., 11th Ed., Quertermous	$12.95
2026	Railroad Collectibles, 4th Ed., Baker	$14.95
1632	Salt & Pepper Shakers, Guarnaccia	$9.95
1888	Salt & Pepper Shakers II, Guarnaccia	$14.95
2220	Salt & Pepper Shakers III, Guarnaccia	$14.95
3443	Salt & Pepper Shakers IV, Guarnaccia	$18.95
4727	Schroeder's Antiques Price Guide, 15th Ed.	$14.95
4729	Sewing Tools & Trinkets, Thompson	$24.95
2096	Silverplated Flatware, 4th Ed., Hagan	$14.95
2348	20th Century Fashionable Plastic Jewelry, Baker	$19.95
3828	Value Guide to Advertising Memorabilia, Summers	$18.95
3830	Vintage Vanity Bags & Purses, Gerson	$24.95

This is only a partial listing of the books on antiques that are available from Collector Books. All books are well illustrated and contain current values. Most of these books are available from your local book seller, antique dealer, or public library. If you are unable to locate certain titles in your area, you may order by mail from COLLECTOR BOOKS P.O. Box 3009, Paducah, KY 42002-3009. Customers with Visa or MasterCard may phone in orders from 7:00–5:00 CST, Monday–Friday, Toll Free 1-800-626-5420. Add $2.00 for postage for the first book ordered and $0.30 for each additional book. Include item number, title, and price when ordering. Allow 14 to 21 days for delivery.

Schroeder's ANTIQUES Price Guide

... is the #1 best-selling antiques & collectibles value guide on the market today, and here's why . . .

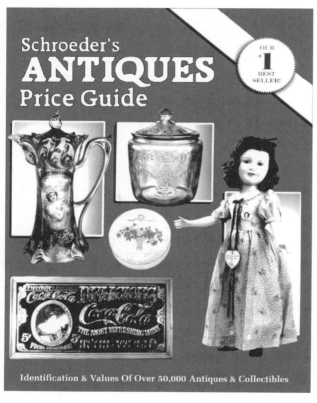

Identification & Values Of Over 50,000 Antiques & Collectibles

8½ x 11, 608 Pages, $12.95

• *More than 300 advisors, well-known dealers, and top-notch collectors work together with our editors to bring you accurate information regarding pricing and identification.*

• *More than 45,000 items in almost 500 categories are listed along with hundreds of sharp original photos that illustrate not only the rare and unusual, but the common, popular collectibles as well.*

• *Each large close-up shot shows important details clearly. Every subject is represented with histories and background information, a feature not found in any of our competitors' publications.*

• *Our editors keep abreast of newly developing trends, often adding several new categories a year as the need arises.*

If it merits the interest of today's collector, you'll find it in *Schroeder's*. And you can feel confident that the information we publish is up to date and accurate. Our advisors thoroughly check each category to spot inconsistencies, listings that may not be entirely reflective of market dealings, and lines too vague to be of merit. Only the best of the lot remains for publication.

Without doubt, you'll find
SCHROEDER'S ANTIQUES PRICE GUIDE
the only one to buy for
reliable information and values.

COLLECTOR BOOKS
A Division of Schroeder Publishing Co., Inc.